Let the Earth Rejoice

365 Devotions Celebrating God's Creation

WORTHY
Inspired

THANK YOU TO OUR CONTRIBUTORS

George Bowers
Lauren Craft
Penny Cooke
Michelle Cox
Victoria Duerstock
Barbara Farmer
Tama Fortner
Carlton Hughes
Penny Hunt
Pauline Hylton
Danetta Kellar
Sandy Kirby Quandt
Diane Nunley
Michelle Medlock Adams
Edie Melson
Trish Mugo
Dee Dee Parker
Leigh Powers
Ramona Richards
Bonnie Rickner Jensen
Lucinda Secrest McDowell
Julie Smith
Shelia Stovall
Kim B. Teague
Tammy Van Gils
Jeannie Waters
Evelyn Wells

A Joyful Sunrise

The whole earth is filled with awe at your wonders; where morning dawns, where evening fades, you call forth songs of joy.

PSALM 65:8 NIV

The stoplight turned green too quickly, for I was looking out my car window enjoying the most beautiful sunrise I had ever seen. Just as I was marveling over the brilliant pink, orange, and red colors in the eastern sky, it was time to resume driving to my workplace. I hoped, oh how I hoped, I would hit another red light.

The colors were changing rapidly but I was in luck; the next light was red. Now, in addition to the colors I had noticed at the last stoplight, I saw yellow, mauve, and an unusual shade of blue. The sunrise was incredible! It was almost more than I could comprehend and I whispered a prayer, thanking God for the magnificence of His creation. What a way to begin my day! Joy flooded my heart as I beheld the beauty of the incredible sunrise He had painted.

God fills the earth with His wonders. His power and glory are evident in all of His creation. Mountains, rivers, oceans, valleys, and all He has made attest to His power and glory, and expresses Who He is—the God of love.

* * * * * * * * * * *

Creator God, thank You for the incredible beauty You have placed in our world so we can know how very much You love us. Amen.

There All Along

The light shines in the darkness, and the darkness has not overcome it.

JOHN 1:5 ESV

One of my favorite summer evening activities is watching fireflies. As a child, I'd capture enough lightning bugs in a jar to create a lantern. Then I'd release them and flecks of fluorescent gold would float around me.

One evening, as the night swallowed the shadows, blinking orbs appeared, hovering over the fresh-cut lawn. The fireflies had been there all along, but in the sunlight, I hadn't noticed them. It took the blackness for me to see them.

Sometimes, perceiving the light of Jesus requires a dark period too. During my teen years, when the world seemed to be my friend, I took His presence for granted. Occasionally, I'd lift a prayer, but I had nothing close to a personal relationship with Him. Then a crisis came, and the threads of my life unraveled. In fear, I ran to Him, and I am thankful for His open arms.

Don't make the same mistake and wait until the darkness almost overtakes you before discovering the light of Jesus. You can bask in the warmth of His love and friendship every day. The firefly's glow reminds me that the darkness can never overcome me because I have the light of Jesus. May others be drawn to His spirit in me—whether there be light or darkness surrounding us.

. . . .

Father, help me be like the firefly and shine Your light in the darkness. Amen.

Swimming in the Shallows

Practice these things; be committed to them, so that your progress may be evident to all.

1 TIMOTHY 4:15 HCSB

I'm not a terribly good swimmer, so swimming in the lake has never been a favorite part of getting away. I used to prefer hanging about in the shallows, watching others venture into the deeper water. But one day I changed my mind.

It was a sultry day with big puffy clouds and calm water. The rest of my friends were splashing around the floating dock, while I wandered the shore skipping rocks. I bent to pick up a perfect rock and the shadow beside it slithered away. I jerked my hand away and squealed, turning to run. That's when I nearly tripped over a second snake. This time my screams brought reinforcements from off the floating dock.

Turns out that snakes love the cool shade close to the edge of the water. So if I wanted to avoid the snakes, I needed to be willing to move to deeper water.

Funny how that holds true spiritually. When we only hang out in the shallowest part of a relationship with God it seems like snakes are everywhere, slithering around to trip us up and keep us off balance. We can try to avoid them, but all we really need to do is dive in and go deep.

. . . .

Dear Lord, don't let me be content in the shallows, but always willing to get deeper. Amen.

God Is My Lamp

You, LORD, are my lamp; the LORD turns my darkness into light.

2 SAMUEL 22:29 NIV

Turtle hatchlings making their way to the ocean have been affected by nighttime artificial lighting on the coastline. Recently, there have been ordinances passed to prohibit the use of artificial lights on the beach during nesting season. God designed turtles to instinctively turn in the direction of the ocean because of the moon's reflection on the water. Artificial lighting can create a disruption in this natural process.

While this is helpful for the turtles, it is not always so convenient for humans. Have you ever taken a walk in the dark and *not* run into something? Me either! My instinct for running into things like table legs and walls is quite powerful!

The same way that I trip and stumble in the darkness physically, I stumble emotionally and spiritually over obstacles as well. Whether it is cancer, divorce, job loss, or parenting struggles, we have all faced the darkness of trials in this life.

All we can do in these circumstances is trust that God will walk us through the darkness back into light. He never promises us that He will remove our difficulties, but He promises to be our lamp and He will guide us through.

· · · · · · · · · · ·

I'm incredibly thankful, Lord, that You are my lamp when my circumstances are dark, and that You will lead me through. Amen.

Creatures Big and Small

*There is the sea, vast and spacious, teeming with creatures beyond
number—living things both large and small.*

PSALM 104:25 NIV

While drifting euphorically along the live reef in my
scuba gear, I noticed something from the corner of
my eye. A shark! It was lurking under the rock ledge ahead.
I back-paddled as quickly as I could. My husband saw my
bulging eyes through the dive mask and motioned to me with
hand signals. I pointed to the shark. It was big enough to star
in a Hollywood movie.

Turned out it was a nurse shark, which are usually pretty
harmless. So for a while we kept swimming. However, the
rest of the time we kept peering behind us to see if the shark
wanted another look at us. Finally, I couldn't stand it anymore. Poking my husband with my finger, I pointed to us and
then up. He nodded.

There is something about seeing a monster-sized fish
in its own domain that makes you want to stay away. After
all, God did give us a brain, and a sense of what we should
fear. His Word says to fear evil—run from it. It also says we
should fear Him. Hmm . . . what does that mean? Well,
God not only made the shark and us, He also made the sea
and the land. Both domains. What power and intelligence
and creativity! I can respect that.

. . . .

*Lord, thank You for Your marvelous creation, and thank You that
sharks don't live on land. Amen.*

The Grand Canyon

Do not forget this one thing, dear friends: With the Lord a day is like a thousand years, and a thousand years are like a day.

2 PETER 3:8 NIV

The Grand Canyon is evidence of God's handiwork throughout the ages. With origins going back thousands of years, it's proof that the best things in life really are worth waiting for. Over time, ancient rivers crafted the Grand Canyon, wearing down the rock into the wide ridges that attract visitors from all around the globe. Today, it plunges a mile deep and stretches eighteen miles across. The Colorado River is still forming the canyon, etching away pieces of rock little by little.

Sometimes faith journeys are like the slow forming of the Grand Canyon. One may grow near to God piecemeal, until finally inviting Him in. Others seem far from God for ages, until a wake-up call draws them suddenly close. No matter the path taken, God waits patiently, not wanting anyone to perish (2 Peter 3:9).

Just as the rivulets of the Colorado River still mold the Grand Canyon, God yearns to keep sculpting our faith. The work can seem slow and rough, yet He uses every moment as a chisel, shaping us more into His image. If we let Him, our lives will become a masterpiece—one He envisioned long before we were born.

. . . .

Father, thank You for standing with me as I improve, and please give me the same patience with others. Amen.

Love Notes from God

For God so loved the world that he gave his one and only Son,
that whoever believes in him shall not perish but have eternal life.

JOHN 3:16 NIV

From a casual stroll in the forest to a serious study of botany, it is difficult to miss God's obvious message. Scattered liberally throughout His magnificent creation, we encounter heart-shaped leaves at virtually every turn. From trees to shrubs to vines, there are hundreds, perhaps even thousands, of plant species with leaves in many variations of the basic heart shape.

While some might argue against their intentional design by a loving Creator, why not embrace His tender gestures available on almost every continent and in every climate? Even though it may be unclear how that particular shape came to be associated with love, is it not possible that the all-knowing Creator would have known in advance what universal meaning it would eventually possess? And knowing this, is it not also logical that He would sprinkle these abundantly throughout His world to remind His creatures of His primary attribute?

As we visit the woods or our gardens, let us notice God's love notes that He has planted all along our pathways and let us return His love in praise and service. Let us thank Him for these self-perpetuating reminders of His unmistakable love for us.

* * * * * * * * * * *

O, Creator of all, thank You for Your infinite love for me and for
planting reminders of it throughout Your creation. Amen.

The Chameleon

He performs wonders that cannot be fathomed, miracles that cannot be counted.

JOB 5:9 NIV

Beneath the broad leaves of the banana tree, the bright green chameleon posed like a warrior ready to strike. Stealthily, he measured each step nearer to a swarm of unsuspecting flies, one eye fixed on me, and the other focused on his prey. In a fraction of a second, his long, silvery blue tongue unfurled like a whip. Breakfast was served. My small son squealed in delight.

The chameleon's conical eyes have a 360-degree arc of vision and can look in two separate directions at once. His tongue stretches up to twice the length of his body, and his feet are divided into tong-like pincers, making it easy to grip tree branches. He is most famous for his ability to change skin color. Light, temperature, and mood can cause chameleons to change color within twenty seconds. The chameleon is surely one of the fathomless wonders of creation.

The Creator who fashioned the marvelous chameleon designed you and me. The God who gifted this tiny reptile with expression gifted us with the wonder of feeling His love. All God has made intricately displays His magnificent, creative intellect.

· · · · · · · · · ·

Lord, may I pause to notice around me the delight of Your creativity and intellect today, and give You praise for all You have made. Amen.

The Beautiful Gift of Life

You formed my inward parts; you knitted me together in my mother's womb.

PSALM 139:13 ESV

The personal touch of God overwhelms my understanding. Simply search online for some size comparison charts that line up the heavenly bodies next to us. You can find the entire universe, galaxy by galaxy, planet by planet, and beyond. The size of a human being by comparison is laughable. We are so incredibly insignificant in that big picture!

Despite our smallness, God designed and created our human body to be just what it is. He knows the very intricate and intimate details of our bodies from the moment of conception. Purposefully and intentionally He formed each part. There are approximately 7.5 billion people alive on earth today, and God knows each of us the same. Since the beginning of time, He has known everyone; and in the future, He will know all those who come after us. They will also be able to claim the same thing: that our creator God designed each of them personally and intricately.

Can you wrap your mind around that? Isn't it overwhelming and amazing? Fingers, toes, skin, heart—each part is God's precision work. The knowledge of this reality brings comfort in a world that seems unhinged. Our heavenly Father, the creator and sustainer of all, planned for us to be exactly who we are!

* * * * * * * * * * * *

Father, I praise You for lovingly crafting me in Your image and giving me just the right features You wanted me to have. Amen.

Crustacean Demonstration

If anyone is in Christ, he is a new creation. The old has passed away; behold, the new has come.

2 CORINTHIANS 5:17 ESV

Seafood aficionados are familiar with soft-shell crabs. These sautéed or deep-fried delicacies delight the palate and are user-friendly since the meat can be consumed without the work of cracking and picking. Soft-shell crabs are not a unique species or variant strain, however. They are ordinary blue crabs that are harvested immediately after molting and before their new exoskeletons harden. Since they molt twenty to thirty times throughout their short lives, the opportunity to end up on a dinner plate is considerable.

As a crab prepares to molt, it absorbs water, which causes its tissues to swell. Since its hard shell has been partially dissolved by enzymes, it splits apart across its back. The now-flexible crab backs out of its old confining shell and begins its next phase of growth. Within two to four days, its new, larger shell hardens again and will be its home until it too becomes outgrown.

Every time a crab molts it provides a vivid demonstration of a believer's rebirth. When we are born again, Jesus splits apart the old sin that holds us captive and it is left behind so our new life can begin. Unlike the crabs, we can continue to grow in the freedom that comes with following Jesus.

* * * * * * * * * * *

Lord, thank You for cracking open my hard shell of sin and for setting me free to truly live. Amen.

Crossroads

Your ears will hear a word behind you, "This is the way, walk in it," whenever you turn to the right or to the left.

ISAIAH 30:21 NASB

Through the years our family has gotten more daring with the hikes we choose, moving from easy-to-follow paths to those more advanced. One of our first advanced hikes led us to a fork in the road. We stopped, debating which way to go for so long that we almost ran out of daylight and had to turn around early. But with practice, we learned that even if we took the wrong path, it wasn't hard to get back on track.

I used to agonize over decisions in my life when I came to a spiritual fork in the road. I worried that I'd choose wrong and the consequences would be devastating or at least unpleasant. I'd spend so much time waiting to be certain about God's path, I missed opportunities. Then I realized my need for God's confirmation before I moved forward was actually a lack of faith. I figured out that my waiting to hear from God was dependent on me, not God. I lacked the belief that God could—and more importantly, *would*—correct my steps if needed.

Now, until I hear God's voice directing me differently, I choose a path and keep moving, confident He will make any needed corrections.

. . . .

Dear Lord, give me the confidence to move forward, certain You are guiding my steps. Amen.

Seasonal Changes

To everything there is a season, a time for every purpose under heaven.

ECCLESIASTES 3:1 NKJV

Gentle winds urge red and yellow sweet gum leaves to release their grip and float downward. Cooler nights and blooming pansies announce summer's transition to fall as part of God's creative plan. Hints of seasonal change signal preparation for the calendar's progression and prod us into action. As days grow shorter, our thoughts turn to raking leaves and checking heaters.

Just as Earth's seasons change, so do stages of life. Starting a family, a different job, a move to a larger city, retirement, and other milestones require adjustments in our attitudes and schedules. Mechanically following old patterns in a new season can feel like fitting the proverbial square peg into a round hole. It just doesn't work. Smooth transitions are thwarted by living in status quo mode. Life can be miserable when we clench past habits, refusing to alter our ways.

When change feels so peculiar, how can we align our attitudes and priorities to God's plan for us? Releasing our will and seeking His voice in Scripture and prayer help afford access to His peace and guidance as we make adaptations. Letting go of the familiar branch is much less frightening when we yield to the breeze of God's sovereign ways.

. . . .

Heavenly Father, remind me daily to release my own agenda and accept Your plan and purpose for this season of life that You may be glorified. Amen.

Mountains and Seas

The LORD upholds all who fall and lifts up all who are bowed down.

PSALM 145:14 NIV

It was a gorgeous morning for walking the beach. However, as I walked along the coast, my mind kept going to the mountains. Though there are places where mountains and seas meet, I do not live in such a place. This caused me to pray, "Why, Lord, do I keep thinking about mountains while on this beautiful beach?" I felt His answer in my heart; it was prompt and gracious. *I want you to know you can have a mountaintop experience with Me even when you feel you're at sea level in your life.*

It's not necessary to wait until a conference or retreat to gain a spiritual high. Have you ever had a mountaintop experience after a time of just prayer and worship? The Lord taught me that even when I feel life dragging, I can enjoy the heights of the mountaintop with Him.

Standing on a mountain allows us to see the world from a different perspective. Standing on a mountain with the Lord in fervent prayer and His Word enables our life to come into focus as we see it from His perspective. Then, if we will listen, we'll hear His still small voice as clear as waves on the sea shore.

* * * * * * * * * *

Lord, from the ends of the earth I call to You as my heart grows faint; lead me to the rock that is higher than I (Psalm 61:2 NIV). Amen.

Lord of All

Yours, O LORD, is the greatness, the power, the glory, the victory, and the majesty. Everything in the heavens and on earth is yours, O LORD, and this is your kingdom. We adore you as the one who is over all things.

I CHRONICLES 29:11 NLT

On a clear day, visitors to the top of Clingman's Dome can see for more than a hundred miles in all directions. The highest peak in the Great Smoky Mountains provides a vista that is breathtaking—and a bit overwhelming. The terrain of seven states is visible, but none of the borders. Lines of division drawn by human hands are invisible, made moot by the spectacular array of towering mountains, dense forests, and cloud-filled valleys.

A place such as this is a frank reminder that the majesty of our world is all due to God. He created it, as He did each of us, and proclaimed it good. His hands formed the mountain peaks as sure as they separated the oceans from the land. From the splendor of the mountains to the tiniest creature in the sea, they are all His.

As I looked out over the Great Smoky Mountains, I was reminded to cherish God's stunning handiwork as His gift to us.

* * * * * * * * * * *

Father, as David prayed in this passage, I adore You as one who is over all things. Thank You for sharing this glory, this grandeur with us. Amen.

Choose Love

Love never fails.

1 CORINTHIANS 13:8 NIV

Did you know that several animals in nature choose a mate and stick with that mate their entire lives? Wolves, barn owls, coyotes, French angelfish, swans, prairie voles, beavers, shingleback skinks, turtle doves, albatrosses, termites, bald eagles, gibbons, and Magellanic penguins all mate for life.

That's very romantic, isn't it? In fact, the shingleback skinks (lizards) do everything together, and when one of them dies, the other stays near its partner's body for days, nudging and licking it, trying to revive it. Prairie voles not only practice monogamy but they also build homes together, groom each other, defend one another from predators, and share in raising their babies.

Not all animals mate for life, and sadly not all humans do either. I am so grateful that my husband and I have stayed together for twenty-five years, through good times and bad. I can't imagine losing a mate, through whatever circumstances. But no matter who is in our life—a spouse, a sibling, a parent, a child—the choice to love is there. Some days, it's "butterflies and sunshine." Other times? Not so much. Maybe you can relate. On those days when we may not "feel" the love, we can still choose to love.

The celebrated "love chapter" of the Bible, 1 Corinthians 13, defines love as it truly is. Let the poetic words transform your life and relationships.

. . . .

Father, help me to love like You love every single day. Amen.

Lest We Tremble

Can you shout to the clouds and make it rain? Can you make lightning appear and cause it to strike as you direct? Who gives intuition to the heart and instinct to the mind?

JOB 38:34–36 NLT

I grew up terrified of tornadoes, having been rushed through the rain and lightning of many a harmless thunderstorm to the neighborhood storm shelter. This paralyzing fear continued into adulthood, and a weather radio only made it worse.

The fear didn't break until I was actually caught outside in a tornado. I was coming home from my father's funeral, too concerned with grief and leaving my mother alone to notice the weather. All of a sudden, my radio's music cut out, replaced by screeching reports of a tornado touchdown less than a mile from the river bridge I was crossing. With nowhere to go, I shook uncontrollably, my mind numb with fear. I finally prayed, "Please don't do this to my mother. Not now."

An indescribable sense of peace flooded me. A reassurance that "I will take care of you" soothed me, and for the first time I saw the beauty, the magnificence of the storm. I turned off the radio and turned to God. And that paralyzing fear has never returned.

God's glory is in all creation, even tumultuous weather. When we trust in Him for all our paths, He will see us safely through.

. . . .

Lord, help me remember Your strength and glory is in all things, and that You are with me always. Amen.

Glimpse of Wonder

As a deer longs for streams of water, so I long for You, God.

PSALM 42:1 HCSB

They walked out of the woods, the doe and her twins; the fawns were tiny with white spots covering their backs. Staying within close proximity to the shelter of nearby trees, their mom nuzzled them gently, urging them to quickly continue making their way across an open grassy area. She knew the vulnerability of traveling through open spaces, where danger often lurked. She was probably leading them to a nearby stream since they were walking in that direction. The twins seemed not to be in a hurry, stopping to watch two squirrels running up and down and around a large oak tree. Suddenly some noise or movement startled the deer family, and they swiftly bounded into the nearby brush and trees.

What a pleasure God allowed me, letting me watch those graceful deer walk across our yard. How like Him to share His work of art—the world—to give a glimpse of the wonders of His creation. God created so many things for us to enjoy. He placed such a variety of His handiwork in what we consider to be "everyday" things, such as sunsets and the change of seasons where we enjoy snow, blossoms, garden vegetables, and beautiful fall leaves. He draws our thirsty souls to Him by showing us the incredible splendor of His creation.

* * * * * * * * * * *

Thank You, gracious God, for showing me Your beautiful creation and Your love. Amen.

The Beauty
of Big Bend

They who dwell in the ends of the earth stand in awe of Your signs; You make the dawn and the sunset shout for joy.

PSALM 65:8 NASB

Standing at a fence in Big Bend National Park, I imagined myself as the only person in the world. The view was magnificent, and lonely. My friend was looking for unusual rocks while I marveled over the beauty and vastness of the landscape. This was my first trip to West Texas, and I had fallen in love with the desert flowers and the distant mountains and the cactus. Every direction I faced told of the glory of God's creation.

God shows us how very much He loves us by showing us the wonders of all He has made. The color of the desert flowers was varied, some brilliant and others muted; all were exquisite. The distant mountains were brushed with shades of purple, soft brown, and a scattering of green. The cactus stood like sentinels with their prickly arms outstretched as if they stood in a posture of praise and worship to the One who had created them. The beauty I witnessed was overwhelming and glorious.

How like our God to create such splendor! This place, and others like it, are evidence of His great love for us.

. . . .

Lord of creation and beauty, thank You for Your love for me, and through all that I behold in nature around me, may I be more aware of Your presence. Amen.

A Rainbow
of Reassurance

When I send clouds over the earth, the rainbow will appear in the clouds, and I will remember my covenant with you

GENESIS 9:14–15 NLT

I couldn't believe my daddy was gone. I thought we'd be packing him up and moving him from the rehabilitation center to his home later that week, but Dad chose to go to his eternal home instead. I was happy for him but so sad for all of us.

I think I was still in shock as we headed home that day after saying good-bye to my father. I stared blankly at the highway in front of us when all of a sudden a double rainbow stretched across the sky. It was as if God was saying, "I've got your daddy, and this is a promise that you'll see him again someday."

Just as I was processing the beautiful display of God's promise to me, one of our daughters, who was only eight at the time, said, "God put two rainbows in the sky just for us— one for me and one for Abby—because He knew how much we would miss Papaw."

Both girls had also grabbed onto that promise, giving them the same comfort I was experiencing. Since then, reassuring rainbows have appeared in life over and over again. God has some rainbows just for you too. All you have to do is trust Him and look up.

* * * * * * * * * *

Father, thank You for loving me the way You do and for comforting me when I need it most. Amen.

Solace in the Stars

Look up into the heavens. Who created all the stars? He brings them out like an army, one after another, calling each by its name. Because of his great power and incomparable strength, not a single one is missing.

ISAIAH 40:26 NLT

The night sky fills us with wonder and we can feel tiny, remote, and even abandoned. When we consider the power and creativity that put the stars, planets, and moons into the sky, we begin to doubt that God cares for the petty problems we put before Him. David, perhaps, said it best when he cried out, "What is man that You are mindful of him?" (Psalm 8:4 NKJV).

But there is solace in the night sky as well because just as He cares for each of the stars, He also cares for every sparrow (Psalm 84:3). Like the stars, each one of us is God's creation, intimately held close and considered precious.

When darkness cloaks the world, we can look upward in awe, and a peace can settle around us—if we let it. Let the night be a time when you place your problems before God, and even as you bask in the glory of His work in the heavens, know that God loves you, surrounds you, and cares what happens to you.

. . . .

Lord, Your glory surrounds us, encouraging us; and just as You care for the stars You scattered across the heavens, You love and care for each one of us. Amen.

Scarification

❧ ❀❀❀❀❀❀❀❀ ❧

Consider it pure joy, my brothers, whenever you face trials of many kinds, because you know that the testing of your faith develops perseverance. Let perseverance finish its work so that you may be mature and complete, not lacking anything.

JAMES 1:2–4 NIV

One of the most exciting miracles of nature is the transformation of tiny seeds into plants that grow to produce flowers, fruit, and eventually seeds of their own. A seed that has lain dormant beneath the snow all winter begins to swell, burst open, send down roots, and send up shoots.

It seems odd, but some seeds require exposure to hardship before they can grow. Scarification softens tough seed coats, enabling the seed within to germinate and develop. God arranged for this through freezing and thawing, microbial action, and even passing through the digestive tracts of animals. These processes must be traumatic and painful for the seeds, but such radical action is needed by some before they can ever begin to grow into their full potential.

We sometimes go through painful periods for which there are no explanations. When tempted to draw away from God, remember that trials can produce good results. Patient endurance beneath the soil of hard times is needed for growth that will result in a harvest later on. Such insight can help us to endure even the most difficult trials knowing that the Master Gardener has a purpose.

• • • • • • • • • • •

Heavenly Father, I submit to Your scarification process and trust You to prepare me for growth. Amen.

Larger Still

Who is able to build a house for Him, for the . . . highest heavens cannot contain Him?

2 CHRONICLES 2:6 NASB

I live at the base of the Cumberland Mountains. The sun rises and falls here in displays that rival those I've seen in the majestic Rockies or the mysterious Smokies. The mountains share the same thrill of open, endless skies.

The psalmist has said these expansive heavens display God's handiwork; the moon and the stars, evidence of His talented fingers. According to the ancient scribe, creative hands of this magnitude cannot be contained within the highest realms. I've been on some of the tallest peaks and observed: no matter how high I've climbed, the skies are higher still. The color wheel of His Spirit is painted on these hills behind my house, each season revealing His creative thought for the day. He coordinates a spectrum of azure to cerulean or magenta to gold as He drapes color over the ancient ridges.

I am blessed to appreciate the view each day in every season, and reminded that my source of help comes from the One larger than the eternal skies above. A sovereign, loving God who hangs the stars and paints the sunsets is eternal and always near. No matter how big my problems seem, He is larger still—His unfathomable grace is unbounded as the infinite skies.

* * * * * * * * * * *

Lord, help me to remember the conflicts in the valley are no match for the One who resides above the hills. Amen.

Blessings in the Valley

Rejoice in our confident hope. Be patient in trouble, and keep on praying.

ROMANS 12:12 NLT

I live in the foothills of the Blue Ridge Mountains. I never get tired of exploring this region, and am always amazed at the beauty found here, from the highest peak to the lowest valley.

But in life, I've always equated a mountaintop with something good or an easy time. A valley was a time of want or need, even a time of death. I'd unconsciously assumed my mountaintops were a sign of God's blessing and the valleys a place of testing or discipline.

In nature that doesn't hold true. We can find great beauty and perspective from standing on a high peak, but there is equal joy found in the hidden valleys nestled between the mountaintops. It made me wonder if spiritual mountaintops and valleys weren't quite so clear cut in their purposes.

Those mountaintop experiences with God are breathtaking. They fuel us for those times when we're struggling and His perspective isn't clear. But those valley experiences—those times of want—also reveal God's perspective if we just take time to stop and look.

When we see our struggles through His eyes, walk with His feet, and reach out with His arms, we can find a mountaintop experience even in the lowest valley.

* * * * * * * * * *

Dear Lord, don't let me miss the joy found in the valleys. Amen.

The Ocean Speaks

I placed the sand as the boundary for the sea, a perpetual barrier that it cannot pass; though the waves toss, they cannot prevail; though they roar, they cannot pass over it.

JEREMIAH 5:22 ESV

Have you ever prayed desperately for something but God answered no? It is easy to praise God when He answers with a yes. Hearing a negative response can be so much more difficult! Perhaps you can relate. Maybe it's the loss of a loved one that has been ill for a long time, or the loss of a home or business, or maybe the loss of health or no relief from constant pain.

The ocean, in its massive presence on our planet, has clear boundaries. God said the sand was the limit and that no matter how the waves toss and roar, the ocean cannot move beyond this barrier. Scripture does not record that God explains to the ocean why it has boundaries, because that would be foolish, right?

In the same way, we also may not know on this side of eternity why we received what we think is a negative answer to certain requests we have. But we can trust in the knowledge that God is good, and He only does good. Sometimes that answer that we don't want to hear is the one that keeps us safe and protected in His loving arms.

. . . .

Lord, thank You for the yes and for the no; and help me to rest in the truth that You respond only for my good. Amen.

Natural Light

Your word is a lamp to guide my feet and a light for my path.

PSALM 119:105 NLT

Mankind sometimes tries to replicate God's work, but our results fall short. Natural light is one of those unmatched creations. When sunlight peeks through the clouds after a dreary few days, it lifts people's spirits. After a long winter, the glow of the springtime sun has the same effect. Natural light also offers proven health benefits. Workplaces with sunlight streaming through the windows will leave employees more alert and happy at the day's end than work sites lit by electric bulbs. In schools, sunshine helps children concentrate better.

Sunlight also has a unique beauty. At dawn, the sunrise brings out the colors in the landscape after a dark night. Just before dusk, the sun is sometimes framed by pinks, oranges, and purples before disappearing from view. Photographers often take headshots of their subjects in natural light, knowing the result will be more flattering.

In a similar way, God's hand in our lives has no real substitutes. His gifts, including peace, far outweigh what the world gives (John 14:27). The world shows love like a nomad—here today and gone tomorrow—but God's love is constant. In reflecting on God's natural wonders and how they are beyond comparison, I find His many generous gifts deepen my desire to know Him better.

. . . .

Father, I give You praise for all that You've given me—even the everyday things I often take for granted. Amen.

My Neighbor's Backyard

The flowers appear on the earth, the time of singing has come, and the voice of the turtledove is heard in our land.

SONG OF SOLOMON 2:12 ESV

My next door neighbor is a florist and grows many of the flowers he uses in his own backyard. It is a wonderland of blooms and a favorite place for garden parties. A water fountain stands in the middle of all this beauty, the sound of its gently flowing water soothing to the ear and the spirit.

I especially like the many varieties of daffodils that grow there in the spring, and the lovely white hydrangeas that bloom in the summertime. Camellia bushes are everywhere, laden with pink, white, and red flowers; they bloom late fall through early spring in the region we live in. In wintertime, the Nandina bushes produce red berries that are beautiful in Christmas bouquets. Although these are my favorites, he grows many different kinds of flowers, shrubs, and trees.

No matter what time of year, caring for flowers or any growing plant is like God caring for His children. God feeds us with His Word, just as we feed plants with plant food. Pruning cuts out unhealthy growth, and similarly, God prunes our lives so we can be rid of unhealthy habits or sin. And as we pick flowers to place in a bouquet, He shapes our character to become a sweet witness for Him.

Father, thank You for bringing beauty into our lives by giving us Your beautiful flowers to enjoy. Amen.

Wash Me Clean

❦ ❋ ❋ ❋ ❋ ❋

Purge me with hyssop, and I shall be clean; wash me, and I shall be whiter than snow.

PSALM 51:7 ESV

Snowfall is quite an event in the mountains where I live. Even the slightest amount of snow will close schools, restrict businesses, and slow life in general to a crawl. Excited children take to the hills for some sledding, and adults enjoy extra time at home.

Last winter I was out and about after a snowfall and drove by the high school football stadium. It is a relatively new facility with artificial turf, and the snow had created a beautiful scene. The turf was covered, making it look like a clean, freshly pressed sheet on wash day. No wrinkles, no bumps, no disturbances. It was a perfect blanket of snow, pristine, even.

That sight got me thinking about how God sees us after we have accepted His Son, Jesus Christ. When we believe in the sacrifice Jesus made for us, we are forever clean in the Father's sight.

I'm not perfect by any means, but I have Christ on my side, continually washing me as white as that pristine snow on the turf—when I let Him. I guess that's why, even though it causes some inconveniences, I like a good snowfall. I need that reminder of the sacrifice that cleanses me.

• • • • • • • • • • •

Father, continue to wash me as white as snow and purge me of things that are unlike You. Amen.

Perfect Example

We all . . . are being transformed into his image with ever-increasing glory, which comes from the Lord, who is the Spirit.

2 CORINTHIANS 3:18 NIV

Some creatures are born with traits that stave off threats. One of the most well-known is the praying mantis whose shape and green color gives it the appearance of a plant stem. A particular type of butterfly scares off predators with large spots on its wings resembling owl eyes. Other creatures use the power of transformation, changing their color to match their surroundings, effectively camouflaging themselves. Chameleons change quite quickly into many amazing shades, including pinks, purples, yellows, oranges, browns, reds, blues—even a stunning turquoise. Certain fish and insect species can change their color even faster, matching the ocean floor, tree bark, or plant life.

Our transformation begins when we turn to Christ. It is not to hide or conform, but to stand out and make a difference. And the perfect example is Jesus Himself. He set the example for compassion when He brought healing and comfort. He taught us how to pray, often in private, making time for a one-on-one, genuine relationship with the Father. He modeled forgiveness and mercy, showing God's true character.

How reassuring to know that we have the perfect example of how to please God. We won't ever perfect it, but Jesus did. And letting Him live through us pleases the Father immensely.

* * * * * * * * * * *

Father God, show me how to become more like Your Son, Jesus, who modeled love flawlessly. Amen.

Eagle Eyes

Let us fix our eyes on Jesus, the author and perfecter of our faith.

HEBREWS 12:2 NIV[†]

Bald eagles are some of the most majestic of all birds. This characteristic, combined with their longevity, authority, and great strength, has earned them the right to symbolize the United States of America. These commanding predatory birds are some of the stateliest members of the raptor family, which also includes hawks, owls, falcons, and other eagles.

While most appreciate the grace, speed, and agility of all the birds in this distinguished grouping, many do not know of their visual acuity. The ability of raptors to distinguish objects is estimated to be eight times as effective as our own, and this enables them to detect tiny rodents at great heights. As they descend to seize them, they rapidly adjust their focus and keep their prey perfectly fixed in sight, even in high-speed pursuit. These noble birds also have the ability to inspire us in our journey with Christ.

In the midst of a million competing distractions, the author of Hebrews directs us to fix our eyes firmly on Jesus. When daily stresses and troubling news clamor for our attention, it is important to zero in on the author and perfecter of our faith. He is worthy of our singular focus for He alone can grant us peace in the midst of life's storms and lead us safely through them.

* * * * * * * * * * *

Maker of the eagle-eye raptors, may Your Spirit sharpen my focus and keep it fixed on Jesus. Amen.

Morning Birdsong

You are my hiding place; you will protect me from trouble and surround me with songs of deliverance.

PSALM 32:7 NIV

I usually wake to the sound of morning birdsong. Unless the weather is stormy, the air fills with music as the first sunlight penetrates the pre-dawn gray. Like grace, this symphony is a free gift from God—available to all. The twitters from God's warblers encourage me to rise before a precious minute of the day is wasted. It's a joyful way to greet the morning. Yesterday, during an early morning walk, chirps floated on the breeze. As I neared the end of the trail, all became quiet. Suddenly, the heavens opened and the rain came down. After the deluge, whistles abounded from the canopy with rejoicing.

I've learned many lessons by listening to songbirds. They've taught me to meet the day with a joy regardless of my circumstances. When I'm in the midst of a storm, it may seem that God is silent, but He is always with me and is my shelter.

I hope and pray my praise song fills Him with as much pleasure as His songbirds' melodies bless me. Whatever trials I face, I will sing songs of praise to the Lord, for He has delivered me from the clutches of Satan, and I can never be separated from Him again.

. . . .

Father, thank You for the beautiful birds' song that wakes me each morning, and for hiding me in the shadow of Your wings through each and every storm. Amen.

My Very Own Rainbow

Whenever the rainbow appears in the clouds, I will see it and remember the everlasting covenant between God and all living creatures.

GENESIS 9:16 NIV

During the last two years of my mother-in-law's life I helped care for her on a daily basis. She suffered from Parkinson's and her body was in a weakened state. Her mind, however, was as sharp as ever. I struggled to help her find a bright spot each day because my days were also dimming. Two active teenagers, a husband traveling for work, and caregiving duties nearly 24/7—I was exhausted.

The weather fit my mood one day when my heart felt particularly heavy. The clouds were rolling in as I went about my work. I barely noticed when the sky let loose. About midafternoon I went to the kitchen to wash a few things. After loading the dishwasher I happened to look out the window. I noticed a sharp contrast between the glistening foliage and the asphalt driveway. It dawned on me that the day had brightened even as the rain continued. My eyes then focused on more color than just green.

I caught my breath. A rainbow! In my yard! It curved down from the trees and touched the black pavement. It was close enough to touch. The significance of God's promise was right there in front of me—better than any pot of gold. Even in the storm He never forgets me.

* * * * * * * * * * *

Lord, thank You for showing me Your presence; showing me through Your creation that You care and I'm not alone. Amen.

Dead-headed

Do not conform any longer to the pattern of this world, but be transformed by the renewing of your mind.

ROMANS 12:2 NIV

The deep red begonia needed the dead blooms pinched off so that its beauty could be seen. Many flowering plants must be "dead-headed" like this so that the old dried parts make way for fresh new blossoms. All flower plots must be weeded as well. If we fail to pull out the weeds that inevitably appear in a garden, they greedily grow bigger and take over the soil, choking out the beauty we desire to see in our yards.

Some days I pray, "Please, Father, I need to be dead-headed today. The old dried up thoughts that keep me 'ugly' are taking over my being. The new creation blossoms are being outnumbered by old lies and voices. I need Your help!"

We have all experienced how the "weeds" of this world want to choke out our life in Christ. Much like a flower garden, we need God to dead-head us and pull out our weeds on a regular basis. Unlike a flower garden, we can ask our Gardener and He listens. He gently plucks out the old dead parts that distort the beauty He created us to be. He shows us our "weeds" and pulls them out, root and all, to help us blossom for another day.

. . . .

Father, please "dead-head" me today and pull out the weeds that choke out my life in You. Amen.

Springtime Renewal

Though outwardly we are wasting away, yet inwardly we are being renewed day by day.

2 CORINTHIANS 4:16 NIV

One morning I noticed the first springtime bud on our azalea bush. At first I wasn't sure what that reddish spot was. It seemed out of place among the barren trees of winter. Upon closer inspection, I discovered several more buds nearly opened. Every fall those azaleas go dormant and look rather pathetic. I've often considered uprooting them and planting something different, but thankfully I never do. I enjoy their beauty too much when they bloom in the spring.

In those seasons of life when I'm not so vibrant, when things become a bit dormant, I wonder why God doesn't just uproot me and plant something new. He must see some buds of promise ready to open. The Bible says even though our physical being is gradually decaying, a fact we can't reverse, our spiritual being is being renewed daily.

Each winter God works on the inside of the trees, plants, and shrubs. And each spring He presents what He has renewed. They burst forth at just the right time in glorious splendor. He does the same with us. He works on the inside to renew our spirits that burst forth at just the right time to display the work of our mighty Creator.

* * * * * * * * * * *

Father, even when my physical body shows the signs of wear and tear, renew my spirit daily to bloom for You. Amen.

Morning Glory

The grass withers and the flowers fall, but the word of our God endures forever.

ISAIAH 40:8 NIV

"Morning, Glory!" I shouted to the silky white flower that crept across our pasture. Don't worry, it didn't talk back. But talking to flowers made me smile. Some people would say that morning glories are weeds—I think they're wonderful. In fact, I'm amazed at the variety and beauty of the vegetation I see as I trek across our pasture each day to feed our chickens.

During the winter, even while I stepped lightly on ice and some snow, large patches of green still lived along the edges of the desolate woods. Once the days got longer, cheery daffodils popped up in surprising places. Next came the wild spray-roses. They flowed artfully from treetops just out of reach. They only bloom a few days, yet their bright pink flowers are unforgettable.

This last week, I've noticed morning glories. They open in the morning, show their colorful intricacies, and close up before noon. Many people spray them because they choke out other crops, but I enjoy them. They reveal the handiwork of God.

Have you taken time lately to see the beauty of a single flower? Even one that grows just for the day because God told it to? As the saying goes: Take time to smell the roses. You could even say good morning.

* * * * * * * * * * *

Lord, the variety of Your creation is astounding—thank You! Amen.

Becoming Beautiful

Break open your words, let the light shine out, let ordinary people see the meaning.

PSALM 119:130 MSG

Spring comes and things change. Every day brings something to life, initiating an ongoing renewal of things that were for a time dull and lifeless. I noticed a goldfinch on my bird feeder, his top feathers partially brownish gray but clearly giving way to vibrant yellow feathers beneath. The season of going "unnoticed" would soon be over for him. He's being prepared to put on a brightly animated show for us to enjoy and his female counterparts to observe.

You and I are on a never-ending journey of becoming beautiful—Christ-like beautiful. We go through seasons in our lives when our reflection of Him can be dulled by our attitude or our reaction to circumstances. But the truth is, the vibrant, life-giving, and breathtaking beauty of our Lord is always within us, ready to shine, to give life, to draw others to Him. We were made to become a home to His love and grace, a place from which His glory can shine for the world to see.

Even in the dark seasons, we have a choice. We can choose to become dull and lifeless, or we can let His brightness pierce through, perhaps in a more brilliant way than at any other time.

. . . .

Dear Father, let Your light shine out from within me—and let everyone who crosses my path see it. Amen.

Tangled Vines

What do people get for all the toil and anxious striving with which they labor under the sun?

ECCLESIASTES 2:22 NIV

In my haste to start a garden, I overlooked directions on the correct planting distance between seeds. Consequently, my cucumber vines were a tangled mess. It was hard to find the cucumbers. Worse, it was hard to spray organic pesticide underneath and on top of each leaf. The tiny cucumbers began to grow and then . . . they stopped. Next I noticed the leaves had holes and black specks on them. It was aphids—tiny pests that suck nutrients while injecting a virus. My only option was to dig them all up and throw them away. What did I get for all my anxious toil?

As I removed the tangled vines, I thought about my family's crowded schedule. We rush through life these days planning too many things too close together thinking we can do and have it all. What did we really get for all our anxious toil?

The Enemy's purpose is to destroy (John 10:10), just like the aphids. Our crowded schedules make it easy for him because we're too busy to cover each leaf of our life with God's organic pesticide—prayer.

Now the plan is to remove some things from our schedule and surround each item in prayer. I know we'll be more fruitful and able to guard against that pesky Devil.

* * * * * * * * * * *

Lord, lead me to how You would have me spend my time, and help me spend more time with You. Amen.

Queen Anne's Secret

I am afraid that just as Eve was deceived by the serpent's cunning, your minds may somehow be led astray from your sincere and pure devotion to Christ.

2 CORINTHIANS 11:3 NIV

Have you ever seen Queen Anne's lace? Shaped like a bouquet, the white blooms are simple and delicate. It grows abundant and wild in parts of the United States. But it has a secret. For most of the summer in central Virginia, these gorgeous flowers host an enemy to humans. Chiggers! These barely visible orange mites live in the beautiful flower. Count yourself blessed if you've never experienced an invasion of chiggers on your body. Even after they are eliminated, severe itching can last up to several weeks.

Chiggers lurk in the beauty of the flower, much like Satan sneaks around hoping to deceive with his cunning "good looks." His ultimate agenda is to separate us from our Creator by inflicting doubt and tempting us to sin—the same tactic he used on Eve with the apple. In the same way knowledge of chiggers in Queen Anne's lace may prevent suffering, being aware of the Devil's snares may prevent deception and hardship.

So how can we avoid being led astray? Staying grounded in sincere devotion to Christ—studying God's Word, prayer, and seeking guidance from the Holy Spirit—will help us stay focused and on the right path.

* * * * * * * * * * *

Father, when Satan tries to lead me astray, open my eyes to his devious ways and help me to keep my focus on You. Amen.

Fully Alive

You have been born again, but not to a life that will quickly end. Your new life will last forever because it comes from the eternal, living word of God.

1 PETER 1:23 NLT

Cicadas are the world's longest living insects. Although the males annoy us by buzzing in late spring, they do little damage, even to the trees in which the females deposit their eggs. What we see and hear is their short-lived adult life. For up to seventeen years, they dwell in the soil as larvae before emerging from the ground and crawling up the nearest tree trunk, at which time their exoskeletons split apart and the mature insects appear. Adults only live about three weeks, and once out of their shells, they fly from tree to tree searching for mates and egg sites.

Bound tightly within their shells for most of their lives deep in the ground, the larval cicadas can't fly, sing, or relate to others, and know nothing of the beautiful world above. Similarly, we are bound in our sins, unable to really sing, fly, relate, or enjoy life. We grovel in the dirt of worldly pursuits, finding them empty and unsatisfying. Then, through the miracle of Christ's atonement, we can be set free and begin to fully live! Thankfully, we don't have to wait till our existence is nearly over as do the cicadas, for we can do it any time by acknowledging our condition and receiving Christ's forgiveness.

Heavenly Father, thank You for freeing me from my sins to truly sing, really love, and fully live. Amen.

The Unseen Root

Blessed is the one who trusts in the LORD, whose confidence is in him. They will be like a tree planted by the water that sends out its roots by the stream. It does not fear when heat comes; its leaves are always green. It has no worries in a year of drought and never fails to bear fruit.

JEREMIAH 17:7–8 NIV

The little green tomato plants stood stubbornly upright, daring the rock-hard, thirsty soil to defeat them. Day by day I watched over my project, waiting eagerly for the first sign of fruit. To my dismay, the tomatoes did not appear to be growing taller. I examined the roots only to discover that the root ball was three times as large as the green plant. During my impatience, the root system had been quietly gaining strength, spreading its arms wide and anchoring the plant for future fruit.

Sometimes we get frustrated with the growing seasons in our lives. Time passes with no sign of increase. We search in vain for fruit and grow impatient tending our hearts. But it is precisely at such times that our roots are being strengthened, anchoring our souls for the fruit that will come.

As we trust the Lord, we can stand with confidence knowing we are growing exactly where we need to most.

. . . .

Lord, help me be patient when I am growing in the unseen places, and increase my trust and confidence in You. Amen.

Words Like Dew

Let my teaching fall like rain and my word settle like dew, like gentle rain on new grass and showers on tender plants.

DEUTERONOMY 32:2 HCSB

On my early morning walk in the Blue Ridge Mountains, blooming rhododendron and cobwebs glistening with sparkled dew filled me with gratitude for the Creator of such natural beauty. Dew forms when certain conditions come together at just the right time. What a great example of how nature is both simple and complicated. I was reminded that each new day is a fresh opportunity for nourishment and filling.

Having arrived at a writing conference facility jet-lagged and weary, I needed to be refreshed like dew. On the first night, I enjoyed sitting at a table with young authors eager to soak up wisdom. These women were both excited and concerned about how they could responsibly incorporate publishing into their busy family life. It reminded me of my younger self attending this very conference thirty years ago. As a teacher, I wanted my words to be full of grace and encouragement—droplets of hope and tender mercy for those who would carry God's Word forward.

This conference was just the right place for me to "let my teaching fall like rain," trusting God for the outcome. Perhaps some "tender plants" would be nourished by the wisdom I had accumulated through the years. And in refreshing others I found myself refreshed.

* * * * * * * * * * *

Lord, help me to always have a gentle spirit so that all I say honors You and encourages others. Amen.

Call Upon the Lord

∘○∘○∘○∘○∘○∘○

Don't worry about anything; instead, pray about everything. Tell God what you need, and thank him for all he has done. Then you will experience God's peace.

PHILIPPIANS 4:6–7 NLT

It had been over fifteen hours and I still hadn't heard from my husband. He had gone fishing with his friend early that morning and should've been back by five o'clock. Since this was before the days of cell phones, I couldn't text him and find out what was going on. I worried he might've been caught in the thunderstorms earlier that day. I called all of my friends and family to see if they had heard from Jeff. No one had. When I got ahold of my sister, I confessed, "I'm really worried . . . what if something terrible has happened?"

"Worrying never changed anything. Stop worrying and start praying." It was just the tough love I needed. As it neared 11:00 p.m., I stood outside, looked up into the night sky, and prayed, "God, I am trusting You to bring Jeff home safe and sound. Surround him with Your angels and protect him from any harm."

Shortly after, Jeff came home, dragging himself up the driveway. The boat's motor had died and they'd had to swim the boat back to the dock, in the dark, in cold water! But, they'd made it. I hugged his neck and praised the Lord.

Prayer works. God takes your worries and guards your heart with His peace.

. . . .

Father, help me to make prayer my first instinct. Amen.

The Walking Trail

Oh, taste and see that the LORD is good! Blessed is the one who takes refuge in him.

PSALM 34:8 NIV

Most days, I walk on a trail through our farm. Above all months, June is my favorite as it offers a feast for the senses. The ancient mulberry tree provides a sampling of its fruit while floating clouds of Queen Anne's lace wave across the breeze. I pass a field of sunflowers with anticipation, but the tight buds are still clutching their golden treasure. The scent of honeysuckle wafts on the breeze while hummingbirds sip sweet nectar from its blooms. Wild blackberries line the fence row, and I taste the first of the dark fruits while eyeing a hedge filled with red orbs and anticipate a future banquet. As I round the curve, the purple blooms of alfalfa carpet the hillside, and to my left a patch of common milkweed host a kaleidoscope of butterflies. Even the odd thistle with its purple bloom is a thing of beauty—its seeds, a favorite food for the goldfinches.

How can I ever doubt God's goodness when He presents such splendid gifts. Every step I take reveals a glimpse of what heaven must be like. But the most wonderful pleasure I experience here is His presence by my side. It's the greatest gift of all as I meander the walking trail.

* * * * * * * * * *

Father, thank You for Your beautiful world, for walking with me and guiding my every step. Amen.

The Violets

You, O LORD, have made me glad by what You have done, I will sing for joy at the works of Your hands.

PSALM 92:4 NASB

"Come with me." My brother had something he wanted to show me. We crossed what had once been my grand-father's cotton field and went into the woods. We stepped over briars and brambles, and it seemed we walked forever but eventually we arrived at a meadow. Spread out before me in brilliant display was a meadow of purple violets. In all of my short life I had never seen so many violets in one place, and I stood and stared in amazement at this evidence of God's loving creation. I was delighted with the beauty of the flowers, and I knelt down to touch their velvety softness. My brother had given me a special gift that day, one I will always remember and cherish.

As I look back on that day long ago, I am reminded again of how God speaks through the beauty of His creation. It speaks to me of His great love and His tender care. It tells me how special I am to Him, how He plants precious things like violets just for my pleasure.

If we open our eyes and look about every day, we are sure to see beauty in some form around us, pointing to God's love.

* * * * * * * * * * *

Father, thank You for the beauty of the earth and the skies and all of Your incredible creation. Amen.

Peaceful Paths

Every word of God proves true. He is a shield to all who come to him for protection.

PROVERBS 30:5 NLT

I love being outside, but I'm not a big fan of flying insects. Particularly irritating are those swarms of gnats that sometimes come out of nowhere and surround me. It invariably happens when I'm in the middle of something, and it's not convenient to move away. But convenient or not, that's the only way I've found to get rid of them. I've tried batting at them, waving my arms around like I'm trying to take off. I only end up looking foolish. The only way I've found to get rid of them is to take action, to move down a different path.

My thoughts are like that. Sometimes they get stuck in the most ridiculous rut, swarming around lies or topics that have no relationship to truth and no business being in my mind. They circle around my best intentions, overpowering my puny efforts to bat them away. As with the gnats, the only way I've found to battle these errant thoughts is to move down a different path.

The path that leads to peace is the one that winds through Scripture. As I focus on God and His Word, I'm able to move past my troubling thoughts and into more peaceful paths.

* * * * * * * * * * *

Dear Lord, remind me that the path of peace is as close as Your Word. Amen.

Camp Stove Breakfasts
at the Lake

*Only fear the LORD, and serve Him in truth with all your heart;
for consider what great things He has done for you.*

I SAMUEL 12:24 NKJV

I don't think there are many finer moments than waking up at the lake and catching a whiff of biscuits baking and the aroma of bacon frying on the camp stove. As a little girl, I spent many wonderful moments at Lake James with my aunt, uncle, and cousin. It still makes me smile when I remember those delicious breakfasts that Uncle Ellis cooked for us, those special times laughing with family, and lazy summer days of fishing, boat rides, and swimming.

They were the best of times and memories that I cherish. I have other memories, though, that I cherish even more, moments with the One who also cooked breakfast beside the water. I have memories of mornings when I woke to moments of sweet grace, of times when I felt God's arms wrap around me, giving comfort during difficult days.

There've been times of sweet fellowship when I felt like I could almost reach out and touch Him because His presence was so close. And just as my uncle provided breakfast for us each morning, God has provided ongoing moments that have fed my soul with just what I needed.

* * * * * * * * * * *

Father, help me live my life in a manner where I make sweet memories with You. Amen.

Peppers in My Yard

He makes grass grow for the cattle, and plants for people to cultivate—bringing forth food from the earth.

PSALM 104:14 NIV

'll get a pepper from the kitchen garden," I told my friend. I meandered down to our kitchen garden and walked under the trellis teeming with blackberries. Swiss chard and kale, outlined with chives, filled the raised bed in front of me. I snipped some chives and clipped some peppers. I pulled a few beets to add to our feast. Smiling, I viewed the cheery herbs and stubborn mint. Green tomatoes flowed out of one bed—my mouth watered when I thought of tasting them in a few short days.

Lastly, I cut a few artichokes from the large pokey plants. We had planted them two years ago, and it was our first harvest. "How do you fix these?" I asked my friend and neighbor, pointing to the thorny choke.

"Turn them upside down and boil them until the leaves are soft," she said.

Dinner consisted of vegetables from our garden stir-fried in a peanut sauce. We mixed our onions with an heirloom zucchini we'd grown, which we served over rice. Great food, excellent company, al fresco—surrounded by trees and birds. How wonderful!

Can you imagine what the first vegetables and fruits tasted like? Me either. But one day we will taste them.

. . . .

Lord, thank You for the opportunity to taste and see that You are good. Amen.

Storm Warning

Be alert and always keep on praying.

EPHESIANS 6:18 NIV

We were having so much fun swimming at the sand-bar that we weren't paying much attention to my husband's warning of dark clouds in the distance. Suddenly he shouted for us to hurry. We quickly gathered our things, tossed them in the boat, and left. But it was too late. Despite the warning, it seemed the storm came out of nowhere. It was like those buckets of water spilling on you at a water park—with wind, thunder, and lightning added for extra thrill!

My husband tried to navigate the boat, but it was use-less. The wind and rain took control. We couldn't see a foot in front of us. It was terrifying. Miraculously, we came upon a low-lying area with trees and shrubs and hovered by it until the storm passed.

God has given us warnings too. Are we paying attention? The Bible tells us to be alert and prayerful. We are also warned that the Devil roams around like a lion seeking us as prey (1 Peter 5:8). The Enemy's tactics can sneak up like a storm we think is too far off to affect us, but it's unnecessary to be caught unaware or unprepared. The Bible can be our spiri-tual barometer, compass, and weather map; and prayer is our spiritual weather satellite.

* * * * * * * * * * *

Lord Jesus, help me to be attentive and alert. Give me the disci-pline to be in Your Word and prayer daily. Amen.

Grace Under Fire

The testing of your faith produces perseverance.

JAMES 1:3 NIV

Lodgepole pines are some of the most common trees in western forests. This conifer has two types of pinecones. There are the regular cones that open after ripening to disperse seeds. And there are the serotinous cones that remain on the tree many years, tightly locked by resin that seals its seeds inside until high temperatures melt the resin away. Normally, these trees reproduce from regular cones, but God designed serotinous cones to reseed after wildfires.

Like the common cones, some aspects of our character develop naturally. Other traits, however, remain dormant until exposed to severe conditions that require us to muster the spiritual strength to endure something every bit as devastating to us as fire is to the forest.

We may possess the potential for generosity but never share until we experience the heat of financial hardship ourselves. We may hold great possibilities for love and forgiveness, but our hearts remain closed and cold until faced with a crisis requiring them. We each hold unlimited strength through prayer, but we seldom use it until some trying circumstance forces us to our knees. God can use the heat of trials to produce good results in us if we allow Him to do so.

• • • • • • • • • • •

Heavenly Father, use the testing of my faith to release Your likeness in me. Amen.

Finding the Fun

This is what I have observed to be good: that it is appropriate for a person . . . to find satisfaction in their toilsome labor.

ECCLESIASTES 5:18 NIV

You've probably heard of them—the fishmongers of Seattle's Pike Place Market who toss fish back and forth, entertaining customers and tourists. Much like river otters teaching their water-shy young to swim, these fish market workers have discovered how to find the fun in an otherwise cold, wet, stinky job.

Otter pups, though instinctively playful, want nothing to do with cold water. Their clever parents have devised a way to introduce them to the life-giving river with playful piggy-back rides along its banks that include sudden dips and splashes. Soon the pups are drawn to the water, belly flopping and somersaulting beneath the surface, and catching fish on their own.

Perhaps the idea of getting up early to spend time with God, pray, and read the Bible is about as appealing as cold water is to an otter pup. Try finding the fun! Wake up to music. Buy a silly pair of slippers just for padding over to the place where you'll spend time with God. Pick a podcast you'd enjoy listening to and download it daily.

Finding the fun has helped draw me into the life-giving Word of God. I'm taking notes, marking my Bible with colored pencils, and sometimes even laughing out loud at what God shares with me.

. . . .

Lord, show me the way to have fun getting to know You. Amen.

The Loon

When you pass through the waters, I will be with you. And when you pass through the rivers, they will not sweep over you.

ISAIAH 43:2 NIV

A loon mysteriously appeared in the choppy waters. We were sitting on the shore of a large lake in northern Michigan. To see a loon on this lake was unusual. To see a loon with five tiny chicks riding on her back was truly amazing; loons commonly hatch only two eggs. The hatchlings ride on their parent's back to rest and avoid predators. We considered ourselves blessed to see this sight.

The unruffled mother loon doggedly paddled her way through choppy waves out into deep water. She appeared undaunted by nearby noisy boats and the huge waves. We lost sight of them as she swam farther and farther out into deep water. It was a mystery why the loon would risk taking her small offspring out into what appeared to be great danger, but the little chicks bobbed along on her back trusting completely in her wisdom.

On that day our family was passing through emotional deep waters. Choices and consequences, fear and temptation were threatening to sweep over us. I realized that even while passing through this trial, God was with us. Like the chicks riding confidently astride their mother, we could rest on our Father's back. We could trust that He would safely bring all His "chicks" through dangerous waters.

. . . .

Father, help me to rest in You and trust that You will carry us through. Amen.

Change that Tune

░ ○░○░○░ ○░○░○

I lie awake, I have become like a lonely bird on a housetop.

PSALM 102:7 NASB

A common complaint I hear about mockingbirds is that they sing through the night. A single bird can mimic a choir of songbirds at a time when sleep is needed most.

It's not always a nocturnal songbird that drives away the sleep. This psalm is actually a prayer "of one overwhelmed with trouble, pouring out problems before the Lord" (intro to Psalm 102 NLT). It is believed that this was written during the time when Israel was in Babylonian captivity. Talk about stress. The writer laments for a few more verses, but then remembers who the Lord is. "But you, O Lord, will sit on your throne forever" (vs. 12 NLT).

The night bird at my window challenges me to change my attitude and receive God's blessings. I can complain about my circumstances or I can follow the psalm writer's example and seek the Lord, choosing to change my concerns into prayers and praises. So instead of allowing my mind to wander over the stockpile of tribulations that steal my slumber, I meditate on the repertoire of songs given to one tiny creature by its Creator. As my focus changes from hearing irritation to listening to God, I gain rest instead of lose sleep. I simply listen to His comfort and assurance through the melody of a bird sent to my window.

. . . .

Lord, lead me into Your rest as I choose to pray and listen for Your song in the night. Amen.

Nonstop Fluttering

Consider the ravens: They do not sow or reap, they have no store-room or barn; yet God feeds them. And how much more valuable you are than birds!

LUKE 12:24 NIV

A ruby-throated hummingbird darts from a bright pink flower to a deep yellow bloom and over to a purple butterfly bush. At each stop, its pointy beak disappears in the fragrant blossom seeking nourishment, and yet its wings never stop fluttering. It will retrieve nectar up to eight times its body weight from approximately one thousand flowers daily.

There are days I feel like the hummingbird. Flitting around trying to cross items off a thousand things on my list. Work, post office, bank, grocery store, clean house, cook dinner. Like the busy hummingbird seeking food, my activities are crucial aspects of domestic life. Dwelling on the never-ending list, I feel overwhelmed and frustrated. No peace. No joy. Instead, grumble-grumble.

But wait, if God provides for the birds, I can trust He will do the same for me. He upholds me when I remain focused on Him and not on the list. "Because you are my help, I sing in the shadow of your wings. My soul clings to you; your right hand upholds me" (Psalm 63:7–8 NIV).

* * * * * * * * * * *

Father, today I need Your help to sing in the shadow of Your wings as I accomplish my daily tasks with a peaceful and grateful heart. Amen.

Treasures from
Secret Places

I will give you hidden treasures, riches stored in secret places, so that you may know that I am the LORD, the God of Israel, who summons you by name.

ISAIAH 45:3 NIV

It was a perfect day as my husband and I celebrated my birthday at the beach. Sunshine. Cool breeze. Blue skies. I should have been happy. But I wasn't. The reason was simple: I missed my dad just as I had every day since his death.

While I walked along the beach searching for shells, I prayed. I poured out my heart and my tears to God. I asked Him to heal the pain I felt from losing my dad—missing his birthday call first thing in the morning; hearing his voice; sharing my life with him. The more I prayed the more upset I became.

That's when it happened. A wave rolled to shore in front of me and placed a perfectly formed, three-inch conch shell at my feet. From the smoothness of the shell I knew it had been in the ocean for a very long time. Because conchs were not common to our area, I felt as if God sent me an exceptional treasure to let me know He hadn't forgotten my birthday.

During our times of sadness and distress when we feel forgotten, God often sends treasures from the dark, secret places to remind us of His love.

* * * * * * * * * *

Father, thank You for the treasures You send to remind me You are near. Amen.

Get a Grip

Let the beloved of the LORD rest secure in him.

DEUTERONOMY 33:12 NIV

On creation's fifth day, God fashioned our feathered friends, the birds. These incredible creatures are some of the fastest, oddest, and most beautiful in all the wild. Their ability to fly has long intrigued humans, and countless attempts to mimic this trait have resulted in many disasters. Indeed, the original Engineer designed the fowl with impeccable aerodynamics. Another trait shared by most birds is their unique ability to sleep perched on a limb. This minimizes their risk of being ambushed and consumed by nocturnal earthbound predators with a taste for poultry.

But how do they remain in the tree all night without relaxing their grip, especially as they fall off to sleep? The answer is a unique pulley system installed by their Maker. As the bird bends its ankles, two tendons in each leg automatically close the toes, causing them to grasp whatever is in their clutch. The grip remains secure until the leg is straightened again. As long as their ankles are bent, even twenty-pound turkeys can remain securely attached until sunrise.

This simple yet compelling feature encourages our own two-legged species. As we relax in Jesus, our hold on Him grows tighter. Conversely, whenever we worry, our grip on His peace becomes loose. As you ponder this engineering genius, relax in the One who designed it.

. . . .

Gracious God, I release my stress to You today and I will rest in You. Amen.

Perfectly Formed

The LORD has been mindful of us; He will bless us.

PSALM 115:12 NKJV

It's cliché, but I love long walks on the beach. The sound of the waves and the feel of the sand on my feet are relaxing to me. However, the main thing I love about it is finding seashells. I can't help it. I have to pick them up. After doing this for some time, I have noticed the best shells—the ones that are intact—are closest to the water or the "source."

On a recent vacation, I was strolling along the beach early in the morning and the shells were plentiful. I spotted a tiny one near the water and stooped to pick it up.

The shell was about the size of a dime or smaller. Beautiful shades of purple and ivory ran through it, and the design was intricate despite the size. It was perfectly formed, down to the tiniest detail. I was awed at the wonder of God's creation.

Sometimes I can feel insignificant, like a tiny shell in the midst of a vast ocean. But, on this day, God showed me He has perfectly formed me down to the last detail as well, and if I stay close to the "Source," I can add beauty to my little corner of the world, just as that shell brightened my day.

* * * * * * * * * *

Father, I am awed at Your creation, including me. Help me to add beauty to the world around me. Amen.

Water and Sunshine

Crave pure spiritual milk, so that by it you may grow up in your salvation.

1 PETER 2:2 NIV

My mother has the greenest thumb of anyone I know. She can make anything grow and thrive. Since her name is Alice, my father had a sign made for her garden years ago that read "Alice's Wonderland." It truly was. But not so with me. My plants are usually withering and dying. Since I didn't pay attention to her efforts and only reaped the fruit of my mother's gardening labor, I am just now learning how to garden. Basic gardening lesson number one: water and sunshine are wonderful things. Who knew?

Our spiritual lives work the same way. God's Word is like water, and the Holy Spirit like sunshine. We become dry and wilted if we don't water ourselves with the Word regularly. But water without sunshine isn't good either. Just as water and sunshine work together, the Holy Spirit "sheds light" on the Word, helping us to understand it (1 Corinthians 2:14). This is the basis of spiritual growth.

And we're told to crave spiritual milk, God's Word. How do we crave something? It begins with a taste. Once we've tasted it, we will crave more until it becomes a steady diet. Then, God's Word will keep our spiritual life thriving and healthy.

· · · · · · · · · · ·

O Lord, thank You for Your Word that refreshes and nourishes as it waters my inner garden, and for Your Holy Spirit who lights my understanding. Amen.

Certain as the Dawn

My soul waits for the Lord more than the watchmen for the morning.

PSALM 130:6 NASB

We clambered out of the tent onto the damp sand, filling our lungs with the cool, salty air. Seabirds scrabbled for shellfish exposed by the retreating tide. The sky went from gray to brilliant pink and then orange as the sun slowly rose above the horizon. It was morning.

The writer who composed Psalm 130 wrote out of a deep need and longing to see the Lord move. He waited with his whole being, putting his hope in the word of the Lord and waiting "more than the watchmen for the morning." In biblical times, cities were surrounded by walls with gated entrances. They closed their gates at night and watchmen took stations along the walls, guarding the city when it was most vulnerable. Watchmen looked for the morning, but it was not an empty waiting. They waited expectantly, knowing the dawn would surely come.

We can wait on the Lord with similar expectancy. When we experience the seasons of spiritual crisis and doubt that some call "the dark night of the soul," we may wonder if God will ever move in our lives again. But just as we can wait expectantly for the morning, we can wait in confidence for God to move on our behalf, for our God is as certain as the dawn.

· · · · · · · · · ·

Lord, in times of crisis and doubt I will wait expectantly for You, certain of Your unfailing love. Amen.

Weighing the Clouds

Test everything that is said. Hold on to what is good. Stay away from every kind of evil.

I THESSALONIANS 5:21–22 NLT

How much do you think a cloud weighs? One of those nice, fat, fluffy ones that float along on a summer's breeze? You may be surprised to learn that the average cumulus cloud—that white, fluffy one—weighs over one million pounds. Looks can certainly be deceiving, can't they?

Looks can indeed be deceiving in so many areas of life. What appears to be truth may in fact be a lie. What appears to be safe may instead be deadly. And what appears to be good may be the very essence of evil. That's the way of temptation. Satan doesn't say "Tell that lie," "Steal that money," or "Cheat on your spouse." No, he cloaks the weight of his evil in nice, fat, fluffy clouds of whispered thoughts. *No one will ever know. Everyone does it. No one will get hurt.*

So how do we know what is truth and what is a lie? By testing everything against the pure and perfect Word of God. For unlike the Devil, the father of lies (John 8:44), it is impossible for God to lie (Titus 1:2). And the truth of His Word will free us from the tempter's snare—even when it appears as harmless as fluffy, white, summer clouds.

. . . .

Lord, teach me to seek Your truth always, and to see the Devil's snares for the lies they really are. Amen.

What's Your Flower Persona?

Thank you for making me so wonderfully complex! Your workmanship is marvelous—how well I know it.

PSALM 139:14 NLT

I always read the comics section of the newspaper, and recently *The Born Loser* comic strip featured the wife saying, "If I could be a flower, I would be a sunflower—tall, majestic, and reaching for the sun!" Then her husband Brutus says, "With my luck, I'd probably be a dandelion—short, plain, and unwanted!"

It was funny, yes, but it made me wonder how many people actually feel like Brutus on a daily basis, and that made me sad. Be honest: If someone asked you what kind of flower you would be, how would you answer? Would you say, "I'd be a rose because I am lovely and elegant but a bit prickly at times"? Or would you say, "I'd probably be a wildflower you find next to the highway because I feel pretty ordinary and like life is passing me by most of the time"?

I've had seasons of my life when I would've given "the Brutus answer," but that's not true about me and it's not true about you. The Bible tells us that we are fearfully and wonderfully made. That means we are magnificent magnolias in God's eyes. So cheer up, buttercup. You are worthy, valuable, and fabulous!

. . . .

I praise You, God, that I am fearfully and wonderfully made. Father, help me to see myself through Your eyes. Amen.

Nature in Manhattan

Let's go off by ourselves to a quiet place and rest awhile.

MARK 6:31 NLT

After one day of navigating New York City I am exhausted. A cacophony of sounds—horns, shouting, loud music. A mass of humanity—crushing crowds, gawking tourists, street vendors. A tangle of transportation—first the train, then the subway, a boat, and a bus. By the time I reach my kid's apartment in upper Manhattan I'm ready for a respite. A strong cup of hot tea, feet propped on a stool, and the air conditioner's cool breeze revive me. Then, it's time to go across the street with my daughter and grand-dog to the park.

The hundred-year-old Fort Tryon Park boasts an unspoiled view of the Hudson River as well as eight miles of walking paths. That day we ended up at the Cloisters, a branch of the Metropolitan Museum of Art made up of French monastery courtyards. Here we could be quiet "and rest awhile."

Truly the park was an oasis among the high-rise buildings. Greenery against the gray. Upon entering, I felt transformed into a calmer, gentler person, one who ambles slowly down the paths and even finds delight when the dog stops at every bush. Why not stop? We are not in a hurry here.

God longs to meet us daily in such a place. He enjoys sharing quiet interludes with us.

. . . .

Lord, I'm grateful that despite our incredibly busy lives, we can always find a quiet corner to rest awhile with You. Amen.

Heaven's Breath

We don't yet see things clearly. We're squinting in a fog, peering through a mist. But it won't be long before the weather clears and the sun shines bright! We'll see it all then, see it all as clearly as God sees us, knowing him directly just as he knows us!

I CORINTHIANS 13:12 MSG

Mornings in the mountains are special, especially when heather-gray fog fills the hollow. I have named this mist heaven's breath. I walk quietly among the balsam pines, sentinels along my path. Their outstretched limbs welcome me in a place I love dearly. I am not afraid of stumbling because I know the path well.

Sometimes in life, though, I feel as if I am trapped in a harmful fog and cannot find my way out. Too often, I allow fear and doubt to settle in.

We all experience times when a thick curtain of uncertainty descends on us. Job choices, relocation decisions, and financial reversals steal our peace, our sense of well-being. We may wonder where God is when we walk through the dense gloom of sadness or shame. We may fear this fog will never lift. *But it will.* The God we serve is the same on the clear days as He is on the foggiest days of our lives.

. . . .

Thank You, Father, that through You we not only can see a clear path for ourselves, but also light the way for others when the fog of uncertainty is dense and scary. Amen.

The Impact
of the Ordinary

Let all that you do be done with love.

1 CORINTHIANS 16:14 NKJV

I have the privilege of living along one of the Great Lakes, and every chance I get I hop on my bicycle and ride to a lakeshore park to watch the sunset. I'm never there alone. Sunsets draw attention. They're a spectacular color show and a powerful reminder of our faithful, breathtaking Creator.

But I've found that it's often the ordinary things in life, not the spectacular, that shed light on the extraordinary God we serve. Our days aren't typically made up of remarkable events. We can walk through them mechanically at times, following schedules and deadlines, until we find ourselves at the end of a workday thinking only about what we have to do the next. And so on.

If we pay attention, there's a good chance we'll notice our days are filled with moments that *seem* ordinary: a smile given; a kind word spoken; a few minutes to stop and talk with a person in line at the store whose eyes let you know it's nice to feel cared for. These are the countless and endless ways God's love is expressed through us—and these are the ones building the Kingdom.

We might be called upon to do great things in our lifetime, but the small things done on a daily basis will likely leave the most spectacular impression of the God we serve.

. . . .

Dear Father, let me be a vessel of love in the little things I do today. Amen.

Vines and Branches

I am the vine; you are the branches. If you remain in me and I in you, you will bear much fruit; apart from me you can do nothing.

JOHN 15:5 NIV

Something about seeing a field of grapevines stills the heart. Maybe it's the bright purple or golden fruit next to the greenness of the vines, or the elegant shape the leaves take. Perhaps it's the intrepid way the vines grow, stretching and curling around nearby structures.

We toss out the stems when we eat grapes, but those stems were once part of the vine. Without it, the fruit wouldn't have grown in the first place. Nutrients move through the vine, working their way out to the grape. Water travels from the soil through the vine, giving grapes their moisture. As grapes develop, the vines continue to anchor them in place.

God is our sturdy, loving vine. He gives us the breath of life—we wouldn't exist without Him. Like the soil, He is a sturdy foundation, providing love and wisdom whenever we call on Him. His Spirit allows us to produce fruit far sweeter than the grape, including joy, peace, gentleness, kindness, and love. Through it all, He sustains us with the living water of eternal life, the source of our greatest hope.

* * * * * * * * * * * *

Father, help me to thirst for Your nurturing guidance so that I may produce fruit that pleases You. Amen.

Creature Comforts

The righteous care for the needs of their animals.

PROVERBS 12:10 NIV

My friend believes the cleanliness of an oven reflects the integrity of its owner. Maybe she's right, but I prefer to evaluate character by how well a person cares for their animals.

In the Old Testament, Balaam struck his donkey three times before the Lord gave it speech to appeal for mercy. The perturbed angel who came to take out the prophet defended the little equine and reminded Balaam that the beast had saved his life. Further on, Jesus tells a story about a substitute shepherd who flees in the face of danger, adding that any real shepherd would violate the Sabbath to rescue his sheep from a pit. And since no sparrow's demise goes unnoticed by its Creator, any effort to comfort and care for His creatures is valued by the same watchful eyes.

I'm humbled to partner with the Lord in this endeavor. Caring for an animal's well-being reflects my character as well as reveals the depth of appreciation I have for its presence in my life. The heartbeats lying at my feet are God's gift to me. I may be more virtuous to some with a clean oven, but the loving care I give my animals catches His attention. Perhaps my friend can appreciate me for my attentive heart-keeping and ignore my worthless housekeeping.

. . . .

Lord, help me to be an good example as I responsibly care for pets in my home and other living things that cross my path. Amen.

Whale Songs

%。○。°。°○% ○。°。°○

Now the LORD had appointed a huge fish to swallow Jonah.

JONAH 1:17 HCSB

Barging into my father's office at the Salvation Army church was not unusual, but what I heard playing on his record player was. Dad's eyes were closed as he leaned back in his office chair.

"What's that?" My face contorted like I'd swallowed a lemon. He straightened. "*That* is the beautiful mating sounds of the humpback whale."

My teenage mind couldn't fathom such a thing, and I had to ask him why he wanted to listen to them. "Because God made these huge creatures so unique and complex. Did you know the male sings this song nonstop for over twenty-four hours? Some think it is a mating call, other scientists think it could be the male challenging the other males. It is very much like the music we humans structure."

I checked out the albums (yes, there were two). Both showed pictures of the whales. Who knew? I couldn't help but smile. Dad loved God's creation so much and he loved to talk about it.

Maybe it was a humpback whale God sent to swallow Jonah. The Bible doesn't say. Only that he stayed there three days and nights. If I were Jonah, I'd rather be swallowed by a singing whale than, say, a killer whale. I'm just saying. Either way, my dad was right. It is amazing.

. . . .

Lord, thank You for those people around me who love Your creatures and worship You, the Creator. Amen.

Broken Shells

He heals the brokenhearted and binds up their wounds.

PSALM 147:3 NASB

The day at the beach had been perfect—a calm surf with rippling waves, salty breezes cooling the sun's heat, the peaceful call of seagulls gliding overhead. As I pushed my toes into the warm sand, I emptied the bag of shells gathered on an earlier walk. I picked through my collection, tossing the broken shells to one side and saving the whole ones.

As I looked at my little pile of discarded shells, God reminded me of the wonderful truth of His love. He found us in the brokenness of our sin, but He didn't leave us there. He sent His Son. Jesus came to bind up the brokenhearted and to set captives free. To the woman caught in adultery, He showed mercy and forgiveness. To a dying thief on a cross, He gave life. To our world today, He continues to offer forgiveness through His death and resurrection.

God doesn't despise our fractured hearts. He longs to mend them. He is near to us when our hearts are broken, and He saves us when our spirits are crushed. When the waves of this world threaten to batter and break us, we can take courage. God won't leave us in our brokenness. He redeems and restores us. He takes our worn-out hearts and revives them. His healing love can make us whole again.

. . . .

Lord, thank You for rescuing me in my brokenness and redeeming me with Your love. Amen.

Share and Share Alike

&&&&&&&&&&&&

Those who drink the water I give will never be thirsty again. It becomes a fresh, bubbling spring within them, giving them eternal life.

JOHN 4:14 NLT

The hummingbird migration through these parts got me thinking about something I ponder each year. Why can't these birds get along and share?

At first only one bird showed up. We called him Rufous for his reddish-brown color. Then Jade arrived; and with the addition of Ruby the aggression began. I've been other places where hummingbirds coexist; however, that does not seem to be the case in our backyard. I thought three feeders would satisfy everyone and they'd be content. But Ruby and Jade proved me wrong. Those two birds were vicious. They would dive-bomb any bird who even thought about approaching one of the feeders. Poor Rufous. If he wasn't at the feeders early in the morning or late in the afternoon he had no peace.

These birds didn't seem to realize that while they spent their energy chasing others away, they missed out on enjoying the sugar water they tried so hard to defend. They did not understand: you can't chase and drink at the same time.

As I watched the hummers defend their water, I thought about Jesus, our living water. He invites all to come to Him— even those like Rufous who are chased away. All are welcome, and there's plenty to go around.

· · · · · · · · · · ·

Jesus, help me share the good news of Your living water with anyone and everyone. Amen.

Rising Above the Gnats

For our present troubles are small and won't last very long. Yet they produce for us a glory that vastly outweighs them and will last forever!

2 CORINTHIANS 4:17 NLT

The trail calls out to me. It's the hum of crickets and whir of solitude that invites me to lace up my hiking shoes. I've hiked some easy trails, the flat kind through woods and prairies. But something in me yearned for a more rugged terrain—to leave behind the paved path and explore wild country. When the opportunity arose to hike in the mountains, I jumped at it.

Aren't we all mountain climbers in a sense, navigating sometimes rocky spiritual terrain? Following God requires endurance, but it also requires focus. The day I hiked the mountain, gnats swarmed me. I swatted the air but the gnats kept coming back. The more gnats that buzzed near me, the more irritated I became. In my angst, I failed to see the beauty all around me.

The routine troubles of life are like those gnats. They never go away. If we focus on them, we allow life's nuisances to rob us of the view. We'll lose the ability to enjoy God's handiwork all around us. Knowing trouble, like gnats, may come, I've learned to prepare with prayer . . . and mosquito netting.

* * * * * * * * * *

Lord Jesus, I'm often tempted to fix my eyes on the little troubles and not on You; show me how to rise above them and open my eyes to Your beauty. Amen.

Fruit Trees
That Flourish

They are like trees planted along the riverbank, bearing fruit each season. Their leaves never wither, and they prosper in all they do.

PSALM 1:3 NLT

I did battle with Japanese beetles today. They are all over my apple trees and already snacked on the few cherries that grew on my three-year-old sapling. When I moved to North Carolina from a suburb in Florida, I had romantic notions of flourishing fruit trees. Beautiful, ripe sweets would be available at my every whim. Right now if I ate an unripe apple, I'd also choke on a few beetles.

Fruit trees take a lot of work. First, they have to be carefully planted and watered. You have to protect them from harsh weather while they are young. As they grow, they must be staked upright to secure the sapling in order for it to grow strong and straight. You must also ward off pests and deer that love the tender leaves.

King David opened Psalms with a call for righteous living—a person who takes delight in the Word of God and meditates on it. He describes such a person like a tree, firmly planted by water, bearing fruit—not bugs. I want to be that kind of tree. Like the kinds that surround my house—tall and green and flourishing. Birds nest in them. They shade my house and provide beautiful scenery. They are trees nurtured by the Creator.

* * * * * * * * * * *

Lord, help me to be firmly planted in Your Word. Amen.

A Walk in the Woods

The earth brought forth vegetation, plants yielding seed according to their own kinds, and trees bearing fruit in which is their seed, each according to its kind. And God saw that it was good.

GENESIS 1:12 ESV

I was overwhelmed! The trees were showing off brand-new leaves, and the honeysuckle and redbuds smelled heavenly. The dogwood trees wore an abundance of blossoms. The rich green grass was scattered with wild violets, dandelions, and stray daffodils. The young squirrels chased each other up trees, scolding us as we walked through their paradise. God's creation was bursting at the seams with springtime.

Daddy was leading us through our woods and fields, identifying the various plants and trees that grew there. This was a springtime ritual; no matter what we had learned on walks in previous years, we never minded him telling us again. Invariably, we learned new things and relearned things we had forgotten. All in all, these were special times with Daddy and we looked forward to exploring with him. Our earthly father was showing us the good things our heavenly Father had created for our enjoyment.

We don't have to look far to see the beauty of God's creation. We find it beside paths leading to a patch of woods, a mountainside, a seashore; we even find it in suburban back yards or window boxes along city boulevards. We find His love for us everywhere we look.

* * * * * * * * * * *

Creator God, we are so thankful for the love You show us through the beauty of Your creation. Amen.

Relying on
His Coordinates

Commit your way to the LORD, trust also in Him, and He will do it.

PSALM 37:5 NASB

We had decided to try a different type of a hike, one that used a map and GPS coordinates. We'd be venturing off-trail and relying completely on those tools.

The specific route we chose had been used by others before us, so we knew that if we paid close attention we'd arrive safely. I was careful to keep my eye on the GPS, as well as the map, staying alert to any signs that indicated a change in direction.

While I groused about not knowing exactly where I was going, it hit me that my life with God was like that hike. As a believer, I know that my ultimate destination is heaven, but I have no idea what path my journey between here and there is going to take. When I follow God closely I can stay on the right path. I have to remain alert, looking for His guidance, and be ready to change direction.

Not easy for a girl with control issues.

But just like following that GPS, I've learned to relinquish control to God. He's taken me down paths I hadn't dared dream about. I'm not the one in control, God is; and I've learned to trust that He knows the best way to get to where we're going.

. . . .

Dear Lord, remind me that following You is the journey I always want to choose. Amen.

Morning Melodies

Each morning I will sing with joy about your unfailing love.

PSALM 59:16 NLT

I've never been much of a morning person. This was especially true when I was a child. I'd wait until the absolute last possible moment to get out of bed. But my morning "wake-up call" began at six o'clock every weekday, courtesy of my mother. She didn't just knock on the door and say, "Time to get up." Oh no—she was far too joyful for that. My mother had an entire musical extravaganza worked out. She'd begin with her rendition of "This is the day that the Lord has made. We will rejoice and be glad in it!" accompanied by very loud clapping.

So a few months ago when a mama bird and her very vocal babies made their home right outside my bedroom window, I had flashbacks of my mother's melodic morning wake-up call. At the break of dawn, those little birdies started chirping at the top of their lungs, as if to say: "Hey, wake up! Praise the Lord!"

I actually got used to the little songbirds, and when they flew away and made their homes elsewhere, I even missed them a little. Now, don't get me wrong. I'm still more of a night owl than an early bird, but I have learned from those birdies. Getting up with a song of praise is a good thing. It's even scriptural! Who knew?

. . . .

Father, I will praise You in the morning and all day long! Amen.

Remain Alert

Put on the full armor of God, so that you can take your stand against the devil's schemes.

EPHESIANS 6:11 NIV

During a visit to the Blue Ridge Mountains, my husband and I decided to walk to a nearby lake. I made a last-minute decision not to pack my hiking boots and was ill-prepared to hike through the woods. So, we walked on the road instead. A small stream on the right captured my attention as we rounded a bend. I leaned over the edge of the road and stared down to the water below while I kept walking.

"Stop! Snake!" my husband yelled. Just two steps in front of me lay a healthy-sized copperhead stretched halfway across the road. Head erect, he lay motionless, unperturbed by our presence. My husband suggested we walk around it and continue up the mountain to the lake. NO! I was not about to expose my ill-shod feet to venomous fangs.

Suffice it to say, I underestimated the possibility of a threat while walking on the road. I didn't pay attention to where I was going, nor was I dressed appropriately for the environment. If my husband hadn't warned me, I could have been in serious trouble.

The Bible tells us to stay alert because we face an enemy far more dangerous than a copperhead. What's more, God provides protection—a full suit of armor, including the shoes of peace.

• • • • • • • • • •

Father, thank You for providing protection against the Enemy. Help me put on Your armor daily. Amen.

Sunrise on a School Day

Arise, shine, for your light has come, and the glory of the LORD rises upon you.

ISAIAH 60:1 NIV

As the saying goes, I would be a morning person if morning happened around noon. But my kids' school insisted on starting just after sunup so to avoid a visit from the truancy officer, I complied. Begrudgingly. Now and then I would feel it was worth my while to get up that early when the sunrise was particularly noticeable. But I always thought sunsets were more spectacular. I will never forget the day when I was proved wrong.

Driving out of our neighborhood we faced west but soon we turned onto the main road and rumbled toward the east and out of the woods. The kids chattered about everything and nothing all at the same time while I rolled my eyes at their silliness. Then suddenly it was silent. We all saw it at once. I pulled over to really take it in.

The colors were spectacular. The clouds enhanced the colors, or did the colors enhance the clouds? I quickly took a picture on my phone. And I'm glad I did. The scene before us was not a painting, but a flowing collection of color and form. We got back on the road and I couldn't help but think, We didn't do anything to deserve that. That was a sheer gift from God. Wow!

. . . .

Thank You, Lord, for blessing us just because. Amen.

Six Bluebirds

Be sure of this: I am with you always.

MATTHEW 28:20 NLT

I love the eastern bluebird. This vibrant bird became my personal glimpse of God's presence—a sweet reminder that our extraordinary God breathes life into the ordinary, sometimes difficult, days. In those tough times, I can feel devoid of God's presence, becoming forgetful of the glimpses He's given me of His love.

Bluebirds are an elusive sight in the urban setting I now call home. They don't settle here and rarely visit. It was a cold day with winter on the ground when I found myself with a broken heart, forgetting the many times I'd seen a bluebird. But God, in His beautiful and overwhelming grace, decided to send a reminder. Outside my office window on the branch of a barren tree, I saw blue. I stood up in disbelief. A bluebird! And another in the brush behind the tree—and then, nearby, four more!

This is our God. Not one bluebird, but six—an improbable gift from a personal God. Through tears of joy, I knew what God was saying: "This is the measure of things to come. I am with you, close to your broken heart."

You are never alone. You are never ignored. God is paying close attention to everything that concerns you. Today there will be glimpses of His love meant *just for you.* I hope you see every one of them.

. . . .

Father, help me see the things You do to reveal Your love and presence to me. Amen.

All Him

❀ ⦾ ⦾ ⦿ ⦾ ⦾ ⦿ ❀ ⦾ ⦾ ⦾ ⦾ ⦾

*You shall love the Lord your God with all your heart and with
all your soul and with all your strength and with all your mind.*

LUKE 10:27 ESV

Seasons. They're a reminder of constant change around us
. . . and in us. I've called this season of growth in my life
"distraction extraction." I have a Spurgeon quote on my desk
that reads, "So long as we are occupied with any other object
than God Himself, there will be neither rest for the heart, nor
peace for the mind."

Extractions are painful. What do you spend most of your
mental energy thinking about? Worrying about? For many of
us it's simply the task at hand or the next item on our to-do
list. But a quiet time eventually comes. And when it does, the
landscape of our minds can be cluttered. Let God clear it out.
Give Him full rein. Let Him have the thing you don't think
you can let go of. Let yourself be occupied with nothing other
than Him.

And then the peace will come like spring in full bloom.
The joy will surface, the hope will emerge, the heart will rest.
These are the gifts of letting God have control. These are the
blessings of focusing on Him. These are the reasons to be
thankful He'll extract every distraction from our lives if we
let Him.

. . . .

*Dear Father, take all but You from my heart and mind, so Your
will becomes my all. Amen.*

A Tap at the Window

The LORD is near to all who call on him, to all who call on him in truth.

PSALM 145:18 NIV

Beside our back deck is a large tree that offers bountiful shade in the summer, jewel-toned leaves in the fall, and the beauty of snow-tufted branches in winter. Spring brings birds nesting among the tree limbs.

A family of finches did not seem to mind when my husband and I sat at a table under their nursery. We heard the baby birds' noisy welcome for their mother each time she flew to the nest after gathering food.

We assumed that once the young birds could fly on their own we would not see them again. Not so.

As the birds grew older, we hung bird feeders on a pipe that ran the length of the house. One morning, while I washed dishes, one of the birds tapped on the window above the sink. The feeder we had hung right in front of that window was empty, and the bird seemed to be scolding me for forgetting to refill it. I responded with fresh seed because I cared about the bird family.

So it is with the Lord. In times of despair, He will lift our heads; He will dry our tears in times of grief; He will even keep fear that may cripple us at bay. He answers our call for help because He loves us.

. . . .

Father, thank You for remaining near and reminding me that You care. Amen.

Spiders

You're blessed when you're at the end of your rope. With less of you there is more of God and his rule.

MATTHEW 5:3 MSG

I was irritated as I sat on our deck trying to listen to the birds. Small spiders were falling down on me from the tree above. The tiny creatures drifted down on wisps of silk thread. When I impatiently tried to whisk them away, they tenaciously clung to the threads and were unwilling to let go of their lifelines. It seemed they were purposefully aiming for me.

Then it hit me. Here's a message from my Maker in the form of a tiny spider: When I am at the end of my rope of endurance, hang on in trust. Hang on to my lifeline— Jesus Christ. If I let go of my striving, God can really take over. Finding myself at the end of my effort can be a blessing. It forces me to hang onto Jesus. It allows Him to take over where I have failed.

I had puzzled over the meaning of the first Beatitude, "Blessed are the poor in spirit," until I read it in the Message translation. It became clear to me that, like the tiny spiders, if I let go of my efforts and hang on in trust, God will gently but surely glide me into His place of rest.

* * * * * * * * * * *

Father, thank You so much for teaching me to trust through the tiny creations of the earth. Amen.

Waves Wash Over Me

☸☸☸☸☸

Wash away my guilt and cleanse me from my sin.

PSALM 51:2 HCSB

Far out to sea the waves began to roll, eventually making it to the sandy beach where I lingered alone. The ocean is never still. As the wind blows across the waters, energy surges and causes waves. I dug my barefoot heel into the wet sand, writing my thoughts in big letters on the shore. WORRY. WORDS. ME.

My concerns of the day . . . WORRY: I was churning inside over unresolved issues and relationships, refusing to trust that God could help me. WORDS: There were far too many of them I wished I had never said, hurled like grenades in a defensive manner. ME: Ah, now that was my core problem—an unending focus on myself and my own needs, too concerned with myself to help others.

I sat on the beach and confessed all three to God, asking desperately to be free of such tendencies. As I opened my eyes, a wave gently poured over all my words and they disappeared. The beach became smooth. As though mercy and grace had simply washed it all away. A clean slate. A place to rewrite my life. I asked God to give me *new* words. Words of release and renewal, hope and purpose. Brushing off the sand, I walked down the beach into a new day.

• • • • • • • • • •

Lord, thank You that I can confess my sins, receive forgiveness, and live each new day in trust and obedience. Amen.

Different
Yet Equal Parts

I planted, Apollos watered, but God gave the growth.

1 CORINTHIANS 3:6 ESV

Don't you just love the word pictures in the Bible? This passage reminds me of the many gardens I've planted. A good garden depends on soil, seed, and water. No one element is more important than the other, but each is necessary. The seeds must be sown for the plant to grow. Preparing the dirt for planting is crucial. Water is vital. Both under watering and overwatering are a disaster for a crop. There must be a proper balance.

As I read this passage, I am reminded that this problem—of how we tend to give prominence to certain teachers of God's Word—is not new. God was very clear that it takes a combination of people to do the work. Anytime we feel like we are not good enough to work in God's ministry, we must recognize that this sentiment does not originate with God. We each play a particular role, and just because someone else is doing something similar, it does not mean that the job God gave us is unimportant. Rather, as we carry out what He calls us to do, He produces a harvest through us because of the special talents He has given us. We all play a part.

* * * * * * * * * *

Lord, please remind me to be faithful to the task I've been called to, knowing that obedience is my responsibility and the harvest is wholly up to You. Amen.

Let Your Light Shine

You are the light of the world. A city set on a hill cannot be hidden. . . . In the same way, let your light shine before others.

MATTHEW 5:14, 16 ESV

I have discovered the best time to witness fireflies is while walking through our wooded neighborhood in the evening just as dusk is approaching. I see them first among the trees where it is darker. As soon as I see one I perk up and look for others.

Have you ever seen a firefly not lit up? It just looks like a bug. Something I'd swat off my arm. The fascination is in the light. Even more intriguing is how this tiny light overcomes the darkness. Darkness cannot overtake this quarter-inch of light, or any light for that matter. When a firefly allows air into its abdomen, a chemical reaction occurs with an organic compound found in there. The glow, small as it may be, lights up the darkest of nights.

When we allow the light of Christ to fill our hearts, His loving grace creates a reaction within our lives that ignites a flame within us. The darkness we once knew is shattered by His light. This is amazing! How can we keep it to ourselves? We can't, and God doesn't want us to. He wants us to shine!

. . . .

Lord, help me open up my life to others so that they may see Your light and be drawn to You. Amen.

The True Vine

I am the true grapevine, and my Father is the gardener. He cuts off every branch of mine that doesn't produce fruit, and he prunes the branches that do bear fruit so they will produce even more.

JOHN 15:1–2 NLT

Experts tell us how grapevines are not allowed to produce fruit the first year because the vines are not yet sturdy enough to support the grapes. They are pruned so they can grow in a controlled manner and be strong enough to bear fruit. As the vines mature, they become robust and able to produce abundant fruit.

As we mature in our walk with the Lord, we are to produce abundant fruit. Living by the guidance of the Holy Spirit, He cuts off the branches in our lives that are not bearing fruit, such as the desire to return to our former ways, neglecting to study God's Word, or anything that causes us to distance ourselves from Him. He prunes and cultivates the areas that are fruit-bearing, such as being a testimony to His love and grace, or loving and serving others who are lonely or in despair. This empowers us to live the life intended for us—a life that pleases God, a life worth living for us, and a life lived for others who will see His love through us. We were created to bear fruit.

. . . .

Dear Lord, prune those areas of my life so that I can live in a way that produces fruit for You. Amen.

Perfect Protection

You have been my help, and in the shadow of Your wings I sing for joy.

PSALM 63:7 NASB

I relaxed on the deck while our brown lab, Gibbs, wandered around the trees bordering our fenced yard. Suddenly, squawks sounded and feathers flew. A female cardinal dove toward Gibbs, circled around him, then dove again. This maneuver continued for several rounds. Gibbs looked at me with doleful eyes and trotted away. I cautiously walked over as the cardinal flew to a tree branch and settled on a nest. Her babies were safe!

As I watched her, I thought about the strong, tender, perfect protection of our God. His Word assures us He fights for His people. The Israelites witnessed this over and over as God brought them out of Egypt and into the land He had promised.

God still fights for His people today. His power to protect hasn't changed. When we face the battles of life, we can have confidence. God is our help. He calls us to seek refuge under His wings. He shields us with His faithfulness. When we stumble and fall, He spreads His wings and catches us. We can rest in His healing care and depend on His unfailing love.

So listen to the birds sing! And be reminded of the joyful songs to be sung in the shadow of God's wings.

. . . .

Lord, thank You for Your perfect protection. Help me rest in the shelter of Your wings. Amen.

No Green Thumb Here

God has given each of you a gift from his great variety of spiritual gifts. Use them well to serve one another.

I PETER 4:10 NLT

My great-grandfather owned a nursery, providing beauty for yards and gardens throughout his community. I seem to have missed that green-thumb gene. Yes, I kill every plant I touch. Whenever I take a fern home from the store, they might as well just give me a death certificate for it as they hand me the receipt. I think I must take after my dad. His idea of landscaping was using a can of green blackboard paint to spray the dead bushes around the house.

I love beautiful flowers and potted trees, but if we're going to have colorful blooms on our deck or plants in our home, my husband has to care for them. And that's okay. Gardening isn't my gift, but God's given me other talents and life experiences. And He's done the same for you.

And therein lies the question: Are we using our unique God-given talents, or are we trying to be like somebody else? Because if we don't do what God has called us to do, then the task goes undone or someone else will get the blessing of doing it. Let's bloom where He plants us—because the Master Gardener excels at making something beautiful out of our lives.

· · · · · · · · · · ·

Lord, help me use the talents You gave me. I want to be a blessing to You and to others. Amen.

Restored Beauty

Even though the destroyer has destroyed Judah, the LORD will restore its honor. Israel's vine has been stripped of branches, but he will restore its splendor.

NAHUM 2:2 NLT

An area in our yard is filled with tropical plants. Recently, I noticed shredded leaves had destroyed their beauty. While puzzling over what caused the damage, I realized the leaves were fine before I placed the bird feeder in that area. It seems the pesky squirrels would shred the leaves with their sharp claws as they tumbled from the feeder. Easy fix. I moved the feeder.

As I relocated the feeder I thought about the harmful situations that could shred and destroy our inner beauty. Sometimes we don't notice the damage until it's done. The problem of restoring beauty to my plants was simply a matter of moving the bird feeder. To restore inner beauty takes courage and strength to remove ourselves from the destructive elements of this life. While that process is a bit more complicated and may even be painful, preserving our inner beauty is well worth the effort.

The good news is, when we separate ourselves from things that shred our souls, God is there to help and promises to renew and restore. As we draw close to Him, He repairs our brokenness and gives us a crown of beauty.

. . . .

Father, repair the broken places in my life, and crown me with Your beauty. Amen.

The Emerging Butterfly

Not only that, but we rejoice in our sufferings, knowing that suffering produces endurance, and endurance produces character, and character produces hope, and hope does not put us to shame, because God's love has been poured into our hearts.

ROMANS 5:3–5 ESV

A friend of mine runs a butterfly farm, providing food for them by growing the flowers they like. When the caterpillars appear, then the cocoons, she guards them from their natural enemies with nets and other protection. Most importantly, she leaves them alone.

Watching a newly formed butterfly writhe and shove at its encasement provides an overwhelming temptation to almost anyone. Helping it out is the natural inclination—but a serious mistake. A butterfly needs the struggle to strengthen its new body. If freed from confinement too soon, the weak wings cannot function well, leaving the small creature to wither and die. And, as any parent knows, letting children make their own mistakes can be heartbreaking but necessary if they are to learn how to survive and function in the world.

God understands that struggles have to be lived through in order for us to develop endurance and character. And from our well-rounded character comes a hope that recognizes God's love has been poured into each of us. Through our struggles, we can emerge strong and ready to face the world.

* * * * * * * * * * *

Lord, when I become discouraged in my struggles, help me remember that You are there, and I will emerge, strong and sure in Your love. Amen.

God's Got You

∘⚬ ⚬₀∘₀∘∘○⚬ ₀∘₀∘∘○

God is our refuge and strength, a very present help in trouble.

PSALM 46:1 NKJV

I recently read a story about a mama duck that simply wouldn't be quiet. She frantically quacked at every passerby until she finally got the attention of Bill Cobun. Leading him over to a nearby storm drain, the mama duck looked down through the storm drain and then back up at Cobun as if to say, "Hey, look in here. I need your help!"

Cobun knelt down and discovered seven little ducklings. He solicited the help of Lt. Dan Werner of the Columbus State Police Department and together they assembled a team to save the ducklings. Meanwhile, the whole beautiful rescue was captured on video—from the mama duck's frantic quacks for help to the joyful reunion with her ducklings. All seven followed her into a nearby body of water and swam off huddled together behind her. Mama duck was finally at peace. All was well in her world because her babies were safe.

As I watched the accompanying video, I thought, *Isn't that just like a parent?* Human or animal, we parents are protective of our young and would risk our own lives for our babies. You know where we get that protective instinct? From our heavenly Father. The Word tells us that He will never leave us nor forsake us. It also says that He protects us and hides us in the shadow of His wings. So, don't worry. God's got you.

• • • • • • • • • • •

Father, thank You for being my protector. Amen.

Cardinal Moments

Look at the birds of the air. . . . Are you not much more valuable than they?

MATTHEW 6:26 NIV

When my father succumbed to his battle with cancer, his passing was complicated by an epic storm and historic flooding that washed away the bridge leading to our subdivision. Unable to reach us themselves, our hospice team made alternate arrangements for our immediate evacuation and assistance in the removal of my father's body.

A trickle of fear crawled up my spine as lightning flashed, thunder roared, and water began to lap across the car port floor. My mother and I were stranded and alone. I stretched to look out the kitchen window, straining for a glimpse of the evacuation team, when a flash of conspicuously red movement caught my eye. I turned my gaze toward it and was amazed by what I saw. There, in the midst of a truly horrific storm, was a crimson cardinal, serenely seated at the bird feeder.

Words of God's love and promised care came to mind as I watched him pluck saturated sunflower seeds, one-by-one, from those afloat in the feeder. *See how I care for the birds? You are far more precious to Me.* I was not alone and God was going to take care of us.

Although I lost sight of the bird when the rescue team arrived, I will always remember those precious cardinal moments with God.

. . . .

Help me, Lord, to always remember how important I am to You, and thank You for that. Amen.

The Seed Potential

You have given me your shield of victory. Your right hand supports me; your help has made me great. You have made a wide path for my feet to keep them from slipping.

PSALM 18:35–36 NLT

Potential. That's all a seed has going for it. The possibility to develop and grow into its true calling—a plant or a tree. Seeds come in various sizes, from the tiny Swiss chard seed to the larger almond. And different shapes, from the flat cucumber seed to the bumpy beet seed. Nature automatically provides seeds for the renewal of life. For example, the oak drops its acorns and the watermelon grows next year's crop tucked inside its juicy red fruit.

Did you know a seed has needs? Proper sunlight or shade, correct soil balance, water, and maybe fertilizer also. But a seed is mostly worthless except for its extraordinary potential. So where does the potential originate? What makes the tiny seed grow exponentially into a fruitful crop?

Only the Creator of life could possibly take a seed's mundane existence and transform it into a majestic tree or a tasty tomato. He performs the miracle of growth so nature can perpetuate. I've come to realize that He performs that same miracle of growth for me—He shields me, supports me, and guides me along life's path. God sees potential in me.

* * * * * * * * * * *

Heavenly Father, thank You for the reminder of Your continual faithfulness as witnessed in the seed's potential, and for Your provision in my own life. Amen.

The Shelter
of His Wings

How precious is your unfailing love, O God! People take refuge in the shelter of your wings.

PSALM 36:7 NIV

This spring a mother robin built her nest in the lower branches of our plum tree. We got to watch as the sky-blue eggs hatched and the baby birds grew from scrawny, naked things into squabbling chicks clamoring to be fed. But a thunderstorm blew up one afternoon before the babies were fully fledged. We watched from inside as the slender tree swayed in the strong winds and hail battered the branches. When the storm passed, we ran out to check the nest, hail crunching beneath our feet. The babies were safe. The mother robin had sheltered them through the storm, hiding them beneath the protection of her wings.

God also protects us, but following Christ does not ensure that life's storms will pass us by. In Scripture, God's people faced trials such as sickness, barrenness, famine, prison, persecution, and exile. Yet God was always with them, offering the protection of His presence and peace. Through their trials they came to understand the treasure of God's unfailing love.

God does not abandon us to face the storms of life alone. He is with us, working in all circumstances for our good and His glory. The storms will come, but God protects us beneath the shelter of His wings.

• • • • • • • • • •

Lord, remind me that even in the storms You are there, protecting me beneath the wings of Your unfailing love. Amen.

Message from the Stars

The heavens declare the glory of God, and the sky above proclaims his handiwork.

PSALM 19:1 ESV

We sat on benches under the night sky and pulled our jackets closer around us as darkness fell. A cool breeze blew across the desert. The astronomer gave us time for our eyes to adjust to the darkness, then used his laser pointer to highlight different objects of interest in the night sky— Mars, Jupiter, the Milky Way. As he pointed out constellations, he told us the stories of the mythological heroes the Greeks named them after. The stories make it easier to remember the constellations and the names of the stars.

The stars also tell us a deeper and more powerful story. The skies testify to the glory of God, creator of heaven and earth. They remind us of God's power. He spoke them into existence, stretching out the heavens like a weaver stretches out cloth on a frame. God spangled the heavens with light so even at night we could be reminded of the beauty and glory of the Lord. The stars are a silent invitation to respond to the power and wonder of our God.

As you look at the stars tonight, listen to their wordless message: *There is a creator. He is powerful. He is glorious.* Feel free to respond to their proclamation with your own.

* * * * * * * * * * *

Lord, thank You for giving us the skies as a reminder of Your greatness, power, and love. Amen.

Fallen Birds and Dancing Bees

⁙ ⚬₀°₀°⚬ ⁙ ⚬₀°₀°⚬

Are not two sparrows sold for a penny? Yet not one of them will fall to the ground outside your Father's care.

MATTHEW 10:29 NIV

Look at the intricacies of the feathers," Dad explained to my ten-year-old self. A small bird lay nestled in Dad's hand after falling to the ground. "See how the colors are so vibrant and varied." I bent down to get a closer view. Patterns of black and brown merged together to weave a complex display of beauty. My daddy always took time to point out God's creation and the care of His creatures. "He could have made all birds alike, but instead He created thousands of species from the magnificent eagle to the tiny hummingbird." I pictured the birds in my mind as my father continued.

"See that bee?" A purple flower hosted the hungry bee. "Did you know the bees send out a scout to look for food? When she finds it, she flies back to the hive and performs a dance that shows the other bees the location of the food." He smiled as I soaked up the information while watching the bee.

I've never forgotten the lessons I learned from my father that he received from his Father. They warm my soul to this day. I know that just as my heavenly Father cares for His creatures, He cares for me and you.

. . . .

Lord, help me to know that just as You care for the sparrow, You care for me. Amen.

Soul Food

How sweet are your words to my taste, sweeter than honey to my mouth!

PSALM 119:103 NIV

What is sweeter than honey?" Samson's cheating enemies ask him in answer to his riddle. Indeed, that is still a very challenging question for us today, for honey's delicious sweetness continues to enhance everything from simple buttered bread to complicated casseroles.

The incredible ability of bees to manufacture this perfect food of nature is truly miraculous, but it doesn't come without work. Thousands of flights and individual flower visits are necessary to produce each spoonful of this substance that is chockfull of energy and can endure for decades without mechanical canning.

The Psalmist, however, does tell us of something even sweeter than this wonderful natural substance, and it's not saccharine or stevia. It's the holy words of God Himself. The author of Psalm 119 had discovered that like the bees' product, God's Word also endures forever and delights not man's tongue, but his soul. It is crammed with vital truths capable of sustaining us in times of spiritual hunger and need.

As we consider the similarities between honey and Scripture, let us, like the bees, make many trips to all of its various passages that we might be enriched by its abundant sweetness.

* * * * * * * * * * *

O God, thank You for Your sweet Holy Word. May it nourish my hungry soul today. Amen.

The Fabulous
Firefly Parade

*To give light to those who sit in darkness and the shadow of death,
to guide our feet into the way of peace.*

LUKE 1:79 NKJV

One charm of the Southern Appalachian Mountains is the summer spectacle of fireflies. At dusk one evening, thousands of the mesmerizing insects gave our daughter, Brooke, her first view of their enchanting show. Their appearance seemed instantaneous, magical. "The fireflies are having a parade—a fabulous firefly parade!" she exclaimed, her face wrapped in wonder as the fireflies blinked off and on.

"Do you want to gently touch one of the fireflies?" I asked. "Oh yes," Brooke answered. She squealed with joy as we walked into the midst of the parade, but as quickly as the fireflies appeared, they vanished into the trees and grass. Darkness enveloped us. "I'm scared," Brooke cried, grabbing my hand. "Where did the light go?"

Darkness does that—catches us by surprise. Jobs that seemed secure are snatched from us, long-standing marriages crumble, a doctor delivers an unexpected diagnosis, and loved ones pass away regardless of their age. Fear may overwhelm us in the sudden darkness of such circumstances.

When these times of life come, when we see no way out, Jesus's hand is always outstretched to help us. The light of His love can dispel any darkness.

. . . .

Jesus, thank You for being the light that guides our paths and calms our fears. Amen.

God's Peace in the Storm

A fierce windstorm arose, and the waves were breaking over the boat, so that the boat was already being swamped.

MARK 4:37 HCSB

As we drove—four women on the way to a Christian conference—our phones began wailing in unison. The urgent weather alert warned us to seek shelter. A tornado was nearby. As we strained to see through the downpour, we discussed our options. Inside, though, I thought about the unfairness of it all.

We were in the middle of God's will, and we'd done everything we should—prayed before we left, checked the weather—and now this. I'd always known the storms of life would come. But somehow I hadn't clued into the fact that sometimes being in the middle of God's perfect will would propel me into the path of a tornado.

I'd clung to the mistaken idea that God's will was a safe haven. When I was there, I'd be sheltered and safe. That day I realized these storms have a God-driven purpose. He sends me into difficult situations to strengthen me and to give me a foundation for my faith. Every time my own boat seems swamped and danger surrounds me, He's there. He calms the waves of chaos when I turn to Him, each time making my faith stronger and more unshakable.

. . . .

Dear Lord, don't let the storms of life annoy me and diminish my faith, but instead make me stronger. Amen.

Napping Fawns

In peace I will lie down and sleep, for you alone, LORD, make me dwell in safety.

PSALM 4:8 NIV

We live in a wooded, rural neighborhood with a grand view of unfiltered nature right next to our paved driveway and a patch of mowed lawn. No matter the season there is always something interesting to watch in our yard. A hawk preening his feathers. A red-headed woodpecker drilling a hole in the plastic bird feeder. A lizard curiously watching me wash the dishes through the kitchen window.

One of my favorite memories is the day I looked out back and saw two napping fawns. Their mother must have been nearby, keeping watch. I couldn't see her but it was clear that her children knew she was there, protecting them.

How peacefully they slept. I was a bit jealous. As a grown-up I struggle to recall the carefree days when someone else was responsible for all my needs. But then I remember, I do still have that. The memory of those baby deer reminds me of God's presence. He watches, guides, protects, and provides even when I cannot see Him.

The fawns stirred and started to rise. I saw the mother moving in, rousing them to follow her. Who knows why she felt it was time to go, but her children obeyed and trusted her lead. I pray that I am always that trusting with my Father.

• • • • • • • • • • •

Lord, thank You for Your presence and the quiet stirrings in my heart when You lead, guide, and protect me. Amen.

A Perfect English Garden

You will be like a well-watered garden.

ISAIAH 58:11 NIV

Inside the wisteria-covered London home lives a young family with small children. It's not surprising that their living room is filled with a playhouse, books, and building blocks. Sounds of life and learning. The clang of dishes as supper is made and the table is set. It all happens against a backdrop of floor-to-ceiling glass. A wall of windows reveals the world beyond: a backyard that takes your breath away. Order. Beauty. Symmetry. A perfect English garden. Quite a juxtaposition between the outside serenity and the inside chaos.

Our lives include both kinds of places. Are you living more in the chaos than the calm? Do you wish you had time to replenish your soul and body in a serene place? Nature has a rhythm—night and day, winter and summer, activity and rest. The verse today reminds us that God will fill us with His own kind of divine refreshment.

One day as I was playing inside that house with a toddler, a trio of gardeners arrived in the backyard and set about trimming and watering and mowing. They were preparing the perfect English garden so that we could enjoy it. When they left, we delightedly ran outside. Today God invites us to enjoy the nourishment of nature He has prepared. See, it's just outside your window. Run and enjoy!

* * * * * * * * * * *

Lord, deliver me from cloistered chaos, and help me walk freely in Your refreshing creation every day. Amen.

Kitten Boot Camp

The young lions roar after their prey, and seek their food from God.

PSALM 104:21 NASB

My breakfast room overlooks a bush that shelters a new batch of feral kittens. The summer rains have raged every day since their birth while I sit safely inside accompanied by the lazy house cats unable to survive outdoors. The kittens' destiny to defend the barn demands they develop skills to become proficient hunters.

I'm tempted to place them in a dry, warm box in my garage, snuggled in safety. However, the kittens must depend on their mother and acquire skills to hunt through her example. My interference would turn them into weak stalkers with no reserve for the brutal outdoors. If she releases them ill-prepared, my compassion would prove to be cruel.

My heavenly Father watches me in my storm and may choose to hold back for my good. He allows the rain to strengthen me for the trials ahead. He guides my steps through the tempest so I may grow strong. I depend on Him for my provisions, yielding to the drills that strengthen during the squall.

I decide to stay out of nature's way and let the kittens remain damp under the thundering skies. They must learn not to fear the storms and develop strength to persevere till the next hunt. Life in the bushes and not in the garage teaches even the smallest of lions to roar.

* * * * * * * * * * * *

Lord, I'm strengthened by You during life's raging storms. Amen.

Butterfly Landing

Jesus answered, "I am the way and the truth and the life. No one comes to the Father except through me."

JOHN 14:6 NIV

My neighbor's lantana bush, a colorful warm-weather perennial with tiny tubular florets that look like miniature bouquets, resembles a busy airport with numerous take-offs and landings. One morning I watched a beautiful monarch plunge its straw-like proboscis into a lantana floret. This particular butterfly knew what it wanted and immediately dived in, avoiding all other options.

In contrast to monarchs, we often try multiple methods for meeting our needs. Have you ever attempted a regimen for self-improvement? I certainly have. Many efforts to better myself failed and left me exhausted and frustrated.

One Sunday, a speaker explained that knowing about Jesus differs from actually knowing Him. She compared recognizing a national leader from his photograph to knowing the leader as a friend. Her analogy revealed the void in my life—a personal relationship with Christ. Although I believed Jesus to be God's Son, I did not know Him personally. That night, I confessed my sin and invited Jesus to be Savior and Lord of my life. Abandoning self-improvement plans, I began to enjoy a relationship with Jesus, the only Source I'll ever need.

. . . .

Lord Jesus, thank You for Your sacrifice on the cross, giving me freedom from sin and self-effort, and for offering me a relationship with You now and for all eternity. Amen.

A Sweet Aroma

Now thanks be to God who always leads us in triumph in Christ, and through us diffuses the fragrance of His knowledge in every place.

2 CORINTHIANS 2:14 NKJV

The summer my husband and I visited the Bay of Fundy in Nova Scotia, Canada, we walked onto the floor of the Bay whenever the tide receded and gathered lovely green rocks that we packed in the trunk of our car. Our trip took us from one corner of Nova Scotia to the other, and by the time we neared its conclusion, the rocks we had gathered at the Bay began to smell rather fishy. In fact, they stank.

At the cabin where we stayed our final night I boiled the stinky rocks in dish detergent water. Once I felt the rocks boiled long enough, I removed them and threw the used water out the door. I repeated the process until all the rocks were cleaned.

After I tossed the second pan outside, I heard seagulls calling. When I tossed out the next pan of water, I saw the largest seagulls I've ever seen. To me the fishy smell bordered on a nasty stench. To these seagulls it was a pleasant aroma that attracted them to our cabin.

Because Christ has washed away our sins, our stench has been removed and we have become a sweet fragrance that is pleasing to God.

. . . .

Father, because of Your Son I now am a pleasing aroma to You; help me to also be a sweet fragrance that attracts others to You. Amen.

God in a Window Box

The wasteland will rejoice and blossom. . . . Yes, there will be an abundance of flowers and singing and joy!

ISAIAH 35:1–2 NLT

My friend's window box had been barren for more than two years. Its location—in full sun all day, with any hope of rain blocked by the roof—meant most plants withered and died before spring ended . . . until the day the first petunia leaf poked through the dirt. No one knew where it came from. No petunia had ever been planted in the box. In fact, they stopped planting anything there because everything previously had died. My friend had simply given up hope of the box ever showing signs of life.

Those first tips of green, however, produced some unexpected hope. As before, she watered the tiny plants, weeded the dirt around them gently, and waited. She debated where the plants had come from, finally deciding that birds must have dropped some seeds from neighboring gardens. What human hands could not cultivate, God provided. Seemingly overnight, the box was flush with pink petunias that flourished all summer.

God's glory is in every detail of our lives, large or small. He cares for every sparrow, every hair on our heads. He provides us with not only the things we need but also the beauty that nourishes our souls, sometimes in the smallest of window boxes.

. . . .

Lord, You plant and nourish beauty all around me. Help me see Your hand in every seed sown. Amen.

After the Storm

We know that God causes everything to work together for the good of those who love God.

ROMANS 8:28 NLT

"A re you sure we shouldn't go in?" I asked my husband. "Those black clouds are getting closer." Just then, lightning darted across the sky followed by loud, cracking thunder.

"Yeah, we better head in," he said as the rain started coming down in sheets. We pulled the boat up near the ramp, tied it down, and headed for cover. Thankfully, the storm passed quickly and within thirty minutes we were back to boating on Dogwood Lake.

We fished the lily pads for a bit and as I let my fluke drop, I felt a pull. "I've got one!" I hollered. "And I think it's a big one!" For the next several minutes, I fought that largemouth bass before finally getting him into the boat. He was twenty-four inches long and weighed four pounds—the biggest bass I'd ever caught. We took pictures before releasing him back into the lake, and Jeff said, "You know, sometimes the best fishing comes after a storm."

That's true in life, too, I thought. If we will just wait out the storm and trust God, often "the best" is waiting for us. Many fishermen packed up and left during the storm that afternoon, but we chose to wait it out and get back on the lake. Our diligence paid off. Yours will, too.

· · · · · · · · · · ·

Father, help me to trust You through the storms so I can see what You have for me on the other side. Amen.

Pour into Me

Whoever believes in me, as Scripture has said, rivers of living water will flow from within them.

JOHN 7:38 NIV

Driving early one morning to a temporary job I had accepted, I began to doubt myself. This job was not exactly in a Christian environment, yet I felt God calling me to be a light to the people there. *How do I do that, Lord?* I wondered.

It started raining. Not just a sprinkle or two, but a hard, driving rain. I had a hard time seeing the road. Then it hit me—I needed God's Spirit to rain on me, to pour into me so I could represent Him to the people I would encounter that day. I needed the living water to flow through me just as the rain was flowing from the sky. I prayed that way and felt peace.

The rain continued off and on all day long, but it served as a reminder of the Living Water. I tried my best to represent Christ: I offered kind words to those I encountered, smiled often, and thanked my coworkers before I headed home that night.

Most of the people there responded cordially to my actions. It was not easy, but I felt God's presence even in that unlikely place. It was only a one-day assignment, but I hoped His light shone through me to those I connected with that day.

* * * * * * * * * * *

Father, continually fill me with living water so I can overflow to others. Amen.

Shout It Out!

Let everything that has breath praise the LORD. Praise the LORD!

PSALM 150:6 NKJV

Spring is not only beautiful to the eye, but also to the ear with melodic songbirds, chirping crickets, and peeping peepers. While most are familiar with the first two, we might be a little unfamiliar with the last. Spring peepers are small frogs that inhabit ponds, marshes, and damp areas. One inch in length, they are also known as pinkletinks, tinkletoes, pink-winks, and gritters.

As the weather warms in early spring, the males call loudly to attract mates. The exchange of air between their abdomens and throat pouches creates a sound that when singing all together can be heard over two miles away. For their size—one fifth of an ounce—they have to be one of the loudest critters on the planet.

Even though they are singing for dates, their combined nightly choruses around Easter seem to celebrate Jesus's resurrection. On the darkest night, their praises ring out, shouting victory over death and the grave. Perhaps it is more than a coincidence that their Latin name is *crucifer,* meaning cross carrier, referring to the cross-like pattern found on their backs. Romans 8:19–21 tells us that all creation eagerly waits for God's kingdom to be revealed, and these tiny amphibious musicians just may be getting a head start.

* * * * * * * * * * *

God of the springtime, I lift my voice, along with that of the peepers, in praise to the resurrected King of Kings. Amen.

Loyal Parents

See what great love the Father has lavished on us, that we should be called children of God! And that is what we are! The reason the world does not know us is that it did not know him.

I JOHN 3:1 NIV

For emperor penguins, good parenting comes naturally. After the female lays an egg, the father steps in right away to keep it off the icy ground. He places the egg on his feet and holds it against a fold of skin. Often, the parents take turns doing this so the other can hunt. When the egg hatches, the baby is covered in down that is not waterproof so it cannot hunt or swim on its own. The young penguin relies on its parents for about a year until it grows adult feathers.

God is even more nurturing. When Jesus gave His followers a prayer model, He began by saying, "Our Father in Heaven" (Matthew 6:9–13). Calling God a name like "father" was surprising to many in that day, but Jesus made it clear that God desires an intimate relationship with us, like father and child.

Unlike animal parents, God's role as a father lasts forever. As we grow older, we learn to rely less on other people, yet we need never stop turning to God. He's here for us at every age, always ready to teach, love, and protect.

· · · · · · · · · ·

Father, help me to come to You as a child does, running into Your open arms. Amen.

Conform or Transform?

*Do not conform to the pattern of this world, but be transformed
by the renewing of your mind. Then you will be able to test and
approve what God's will is—his good, pleasing and perfect will.*

ROMANS 12:2 NIV

Every spring the pink flamingos at our local zoo start building their nests in preparation for egg laying. The pairs
construct their tall nests out of mud, then take turns incubat-
ing the eggs. Interestingly, when the eggs hatch, the flamingo
chicks aren't pink—they're gray. So where does the pink come
from? The shrimp and krill the flamingos eat are high in
carotenoid pigments, similar to what we find in carrots. Over
time these pigments accumulate in their bodies and turn their
feathers from gray to pink. The flamingos are transformed by
what they consume.

We also experience transformation. God is at work to
transform us into Christ's image, and one of the primary areas
that takes place is in our minds. What we think and believe
determines our attitudes and actions. That's why it's so important for us to be conscious of what we put into our lives.
When we feed on the Scriptures, God uses it to change us
from the inside out. Just as flamingos consume their source of
pink, when we regularly consume God's Word and apply it to
our lives, it results in visible transformation.

• • • • • • • • • • •

*Lord, transform me from the inside out as I apply Your Word to
my life. Amen.*

Ducks in a Row

The LORD is my shepherd, I lack nothing. He makes me lie down in green pastures, he leads me beside quiet waters.

PSALM 23:1–2 NIV

My husband and I live in a town situated along two wide, beautiful rivers. We love to walk along the waterfront and feed the seagulls and ducks. One day, we were downtown doing errands. Traffic along the street had come to a halt, and we had a front row seat to all the commotion. A mother duck waddled from the sidewalk, stepped onto the street, and headed across in the direction of the nearby river. Behind her, in a perfectly straight line, marched eleven baby ducklings. Everything stopped as people watched the impromptu parade.

As I thought about the family of ducks, I marveled at God's wisdom and care. He instilled in those little ducklings the instinct to follow their mother. They didn't question. They didn't complain. They followed. God promises in His Word that He will go before us. He will lead. All we have to do is follow. His path is truth and love. His plan for us is always good. In the cacophony of voices around us, He calls us to follow Him. He knows the way home.

A lost world needs the Savior. And when we follow Jesus, people notice. Just as everyone stopped that day to watch the mother duck and her ducklings, the world watches us. May we point them to the One who goes before us.

. . . .

Lord, help us follow You each day. Amen.

Artesian Well

The water I give will be an artesian spring within, gushing fountains of endless life.

JOHN 4:14 MSG

Several artesian wells dot the base of the Blue Ridge Mountains. These unique water sources require no pump; instead, they need a mechanical device to contain the pressurized water. Artesian wells are formed when the majority of a naturally formed reservoir is captured high within a nearby mountainside, trapped beneath impermeable rock or soil. When a well is drilled, all that hydraulic pressure finds an escape and creates the challenge of capping the opening. The weighty burden from up above often causes water to ooze out of the wellhead and saturate everything nearby.

This is what Jesus implied when He told the Samaritan woman, "The water I give them will become in them a spring of water welling up to eternal life" (NIV). We cannot generate such overflowing conditions by ourselves; it comes only from Christ living within us.

We are meant to be artesian wells in the lonely and painful deserts of this world. Jesus's joy and love are designed to bubble up naturally from each fiber of our being and positively impact everyone nearby. We sometimes try to cap off Christ's Spirit by closing ourselves off and hindering His influence. May we resist this temptation and instead be open channels and willing vessels for His love and grace to flow freely to a dry and thirsty world.

. . . .

God of the waters, make me an artesian well that will bless all those near me today. Amen.

Removing Weeds

I—yes, I alone—will blot out your sins for my own sake and will never think of them again.

ISAIAH 43:25 NLT

When we first moved into our house I enjoyed looking out at our back wooded lot. There was a small clearing surrounded by a variety of trees that grew down a gentle slope into a shady ravine. Being a busy young family, we didn't often explore out there; we spent more time in the cultivated part—the easily accessible front yard. As the years went by, the back yard became overgrown. We kept saying we ought to clear some bushes and vines, but the days were never long enough. Pretty soon it was a jungle. After six years of procrastinating we had to hire a custom grading contractor to plow over and push under the tangled mess. Nearly three thousand dollars later we had our back yard back.

Removing weeds is a lot like removing sin. It's easier to remove both of them when they are small. If we allow them to grow and take root, it takes significantly more effort to eliminate them. Sometimes we need help to get the job done. Fortunately, we don't have to do it alone. Jesus paid the price so our sins could be rooted out and removed forever. Admitting our sins and bringing them to Jesus, the Master Gardener, is the first step to transforming the tangled mess into a cultivated garden of peace.

• • • • • • • • • • •

Jesus, thank You for removing my sins and remembering them no more. Amen.

Waves of Doubt

If any of you lacks wisdom, you should ask God, who gives generously to all without finding fault, and it will be given to you. But when you ask, you must believe and not doubt, because the one who doubts is like a wave of the sea, blown and tossed by the wind.

JAMES 1:5–6 NIV

Having lived in Florida for years, I get the drift of the waves and the strength of the ocean. The consequences of underestimating the ocean are evident by the number of drownings that occur each year. The waves will push and pull you to locations you never intended. As a matter of fact, the way to avoid drowning in the riptide is to let the water take you in the direction it's going—don't fight it. Eventually, it pulls you to a place where it's calm, and you can swim back to shore. This instruction goes against our natural inclinations to fight back against the waves.

Just as the verses tell us today, we are to ask with faith for wisdom in our circumstances and not to waver and not be driven by the waves of our doubt. The amazing thing is that He tells us to ask, and He will answer! He wants us to want wisdom, and He wants to generously give it to us.

. . . .

May my prayers for wisdom, dear Lord, be filled with faith today as I seek Your face. Amen.

Forming Imagination

Sing to the LORD with thanksgiving; sing praises on the harp to our God, who covers the heavens with clouds, who prepares rain for the earth, who makes grass to grow on the mountains.

PSALM 147:7–8 NKJV

I am an only child, but, growing up, I spent a lot of time with my cousin Adam. One of our favorite things to do was to sit in the front yard, lean back, and look up at the clouds.

"That one looks like Snoopy on his house!"

"The cloud beside it looks like a bunny."

"Over there is a dinosaur!"

The clouds in their varied shapes and sizes remind me that we serve a creative God. He could have made the clouds to be formless orbs in the sky, but instead He chose to give them character, feeding our imaginations.

As a child, I was also different from the boys who liked to hunt and fish; I spent a lot of time drawing, writing, and daydreaming. This gave me a great appreciation for the shapes represented in the clouds. Even though I'm not the outdoorsy type, things in nature still feed my creativity. And I figure, if God can take the time to form clouds into intricate shapes, it only makes sense that I can be creative for Him as well.

. . . .

Father, thank You for Your creativity. Help me to use mine for Your glory. Amen.

Sunflower Showers

I shall give you rains in their season, so that the land will yield its produce and the trees of the field will bear their fruit.

LEVITICUS 26:4 NASB

To my father, they were just sunflowers, but to me they were tall, skinny ladies with suntanned faces encircled by golden bonnets. Their skirt-like leaves provided a shady spot to escape the summer's heat and dream of rain. Dad set up a sprinkler and I'd run through the oscillating spray, sharing the refreshment with my lanky floral girlfriends. When cloudy skies grumbled with thunder I'd run inside for shelter and watch the ladies dance in the downpour, their bonnets exchanged for shower caps. After the rain the girls stood tall, their faces turned upward toward the sun. Nature's rain brought greater nourishment than the paltry spray from the hose.

Even as a child I saw the difference between what I could offer and what God could do. Now I'm tall enough to look a sunflower straight in the eye. I may set out a sprinkler but I still pray for the rain only God can provide. I've not forgotten the lessons learned in Dad's garden, knowing the presence of clouds leads to refreshing, nourishing showers. As a gardener and a pilgrim of life, I still enjoy a dance with the sunflowers in the rain. I've learned not to fear the clouds but anticipate the blessings in them.

* * * * * * * * * * *

Lord, thank You for Your showers of blessings when my seasons have run dry. Amen.

Good Soil

Other seeds fell on good soil and produced grain, some a hundred-fold, some sixty, some thirty.

MATTHEW 13:8 ESV

"Nothing is going to grow in this rocky soil!" I moaned. I wiped tears off my face with a dirty T-shirt. We stuck squash seeds in clay soil as we moved along the row. My husband and I had moved from an overpopulated city to a big piece of land to farm, and we had never grown anything before. Each day we trounced out to our clay fields, hoping to view our seedlings. Then we'd mope back to the farmhouse in despair.

One day, we spotted green. Tiny leaves poked up through the soil. Our squash seeds grew! Tom and I were giddy with delight. You'd have thought we'd given birth. In reality, God made it grow. We just sowed the seed.

He is the One who gives growth in our spiritual lives too. In Matthew 13, Jesus tells the story of the sower. The sower only scattered the seed. Some seeds were eaten by birds, some grew in rocky soil but dried up, while others grew in thorny soil but were choked out. Some also grew in good soil, and they flourished—just like our squash seeds.

God wants us to scatter seeds of love. We can also water and nurture them, but God makes them grow. And His love always produces fruit. And it's good.

Lord, cultivate my desire to grow and sow. Amen.

Warm Welcome

They built a fire on the shore to welcome us.

ACTS 28:2 NLT

It's my favorite summer tradition—building a campfire, moving chairs whenever the smoke becomes too strong, slipping marshmallows onto straightened coat hangers, and trying hard to not burn them. Sliding the gooey concoction between the chocolate and the graham, I lick my lips and ask for "S'more, please!"

Everyone stares into the fire, almost mesmerized by the flames reflected on the lake's surface. Our family. Usually someone in our extended family of ten is missing. It has become harder to gather the clan from around the world. But when our number was only six, we did this often. It was noisier then, and I was so busy gathering materials and kids that I occasionally failed to miss the moment. Not tonight. Now I know how utterly precious the time around the fire can be.

I know that togetherness is a blessing not experienced by everyone. For those who aren't able to welcome loved ones at a campfire, remember: when all *seems* burned out, often a tiny hidden ember remains, the vestiges of what once was. And if it was once there, it *can* be rekindled. With a breath of hope and the Spirit, that flicker can flame. Hope burns bright to welcome loved ones home.

. . . .

Lord, help me trust You when releasing my children into a harsh world and to expectantly wait full of hope for the day they return. Amen.

Firmly Rooted

‰ ⊙‰•⊙‰•⊙‰ ⊙‰•⊙‰•⊙

Let your roots grow down into him, and let your lives be built on him. Then your faith will grow strong in the truth you were taught, and you will overflow with thankfulness.

COLOSSIANS 2:7 NLT

The oak towered above us, and we took respite in its shade. But this was no ordinary tree. It sprouted around the same time John Hancock scrawled his name across the Declaration of Independence. I stared at its massive trunk and wondered what it had seen. Did it witness pioneers pushing westward? Had Native Americans taken shelter in its shade? From all angles the branches jutted out like arms worshipping their Creator. Squirrels danced across branches, swallows sang out praises to God.

If this tree could survive the Texas heat, it meant only one thing. It had deep roots—roots designed to delve deep into the earth in search of water during droughts. Roots strong enough to anchor the tree throughout the centuries.

The shade we enjoyed that day wouldn't have been possible without a firmly established root system. Our lives are much the same. God wants us to establish a deep connection with Him where He supplies our every need. Without deep roots in God, we wilt and fail. They allow us to thrive in droughts and withstand the winds and storms of life.

* * * * * * * * * * *

Lord, help me grow roots deeper into You and anchor my faith in Your truth so You can produce in me a well of thankfulness. Amen.

Scorching Heat

In this world you will have trouble. But take heart! I have overcome the world.

JOHN 16:33 NIV

Unexpectedly, our weather spiked to triple digits without a trace of rain right after I planted a new gardenia bush. Day after day I watered my struggling gardenia and watched the buds die and the blooms turn brown. Once the temperatures returned to a more normal range there was hope. Tucked close to the branches of the gardenia, spots of green shone through the brown.

Struggling to save my gardenia bush reminded me of the times we struggle in this life. We start out strong, confident that we are doing what God wants us to do. Then Satan applies pressure. He sends scorching heat, dries up refreshing rain, and we wither. Satan does his best to kill the blooms God has planted in our hearts and shrivel the buds that are waiting to flourish. He is known for stealing dreams, hopes, and the desires of our hearts.

It is understandable then why Jesus didn't say "in this world you *might* have trouble." He said "you *will* have trouble." But wait! He also told us to be brave because He already defeated the world. A spot of hope remained on my gardenia bush despite the scorching heat. When we hold onto Jesus's hand a spot of hope remains in us.

* * * * * * * * * * *

Jesus, because You have overcome the world, I can have peace even through trying times, and I know You will lead me safely home. Amen.

Just an Off Day

Though the righteous fall seven times, they rise again, but the wicked stumble when calamity strikes.

PROVERBS 24:16 NIV

My oldest daughter had the opportunity to visit Europe on an educational tour between her junior and senior years of high school. As they toured Greece one afternoon, the tour guide pointed out the mountain goats in the distance and explained how their cloven hooves and keen sense of balance enabled them to live on the mountains. "They have powerful legs and can jump nearly twelve feet if needed," she went on.

"Do they ever fall?" a student in the group asked.

"No," the tour guide continued. "They may not look graceful with their woolly fur and horns, but they truly are . . ." but before she could finish her sentence, a mountain goat in the distance did a total face plant. It got up, shook itself off, and walked away like nothing had happened. Knowing the goat was okay, the entire group burst into laughter. "I guess that particular goat was having an off day," the tour guide added, never missing a beat.

We all have off days. Sometimes we fall down, spiritually speaking, but isn't it comforting to know that God is there to pick us up? The next time you have an "off day," don't beat yourself up about it; learn from the mountain goat. Get up, shake yourself off, and continue in your walk of faith.

. . . .

Father, thank You for loving me even on my "off days." Amen.

Sun or Shade

I have learned to be content, whatever the circumstances may be.

PHILIPPIANS 4:12 PHILLIPS

Walking through the eastern woodlands, we see quite a variety of plant life. We marvel at mature oaks towering overhead and shorter, though more colorful, dogwoods in the understory. Lower yet, we find ferns and young seedlings carpeting the forest floor. The diversity of a hardwood forest is beautiful to behold. These various layers, however, remind us that while some plants flourish in full sun, others need filtered sunlight, while still others require dense shade. Some plants will even grow most anywhere.

Which environment do we need? Do we require the sunshine of people's attention, or can we serve quietly in the shadows? One mark of Christian maturity is the ability to serve faithfully without being recognized or noticed, laboring day after day with no awards or glory, and no fame. Even though Christ had all the sunlight of heaven, He came to our earth to live in the dense shade to serve and to save us, adapting for our benefit.

Some of the most decorated saints in heaven will be folks we've never heard of on earth who labored faithfully in the shadows for Jesus. What a blessing it is to see individuals who can thrive in either full sun or dense shade and who have learned, like the apostle Paul, to be content no matter where they are planted.

. . . .

God of sunshine and shadows, help me to bloom wherever You plant me. Amen.

A Tree From Barren Rock

The rain and snow come down from the heavens and stay on the ground to water the earth. They cause the grain to grow, producing seed for the farmer and bread for the hungry. It is the same with my word. I send it out, and it always produces fruit. It will accomplish all I want it to, and it will prosper everywhere I send it.

ISAIAH 55:10–11 NLT

It stood on the very edge of a limestone cliff, alone, its roots clinging to the slight creases of dirt that had settled into the cracks of the rock. Nothing else grew around it. Nothing else could find a toehold in that barren place. But that tree did— its trunk sturdy, its leaves lush and green even in the heat of summer.

How like God's Word is this tree? We often give up hope in our world, in our relationships, only to have God act in His own time. How many of us have shared His message with others, only to have them finally accept it years later?

God speaks to the human heart in a variety of ways. Through the words of Scripture, the hope of a child, the love of friends . . . or the growth of a tree where no plant should survive. He is all around us, waiting for us to see and hear Him.

• • • • • • • • • •

Father, help me to not take Your work around me for granted. You are always present, showing me hope and guiding me through Your creation. Amen.

Summer Thunderstorm

God blesses those who patiently endure. . . . Afterward they will receive the crown of life that God has promised to those who love him.

JAMES 1:12 NLT

The stooped and weary flowers struggled to lift their heavy heads. An overnight summer thunderstorm had pounded the petunias toward the ground and forced the delicate blossoms to droop. The rain-laden pink flowers faced downward in the early morning hours, too fatigued from fighting the night winds to lift their faces.

The morning sunlight coaxed the petunias from their earth-bound bent as the storm's watery leftovers began to evaporate. The benefit of the rainfall was apparent in the vertical stance and beauty of the healthy plants later that afternoon. The nocturnal squall, first appearing as an adversarial foe, delivered sustenance and strength.

We may face thunderstorms—in life circumstances, in relationships, and even in our own hearts. These challenges threaten to burden us with fear, fatigue, and disillusionment. When we tilt our heads upward, like plants after heavy rains, God infuses us with strength. In His magnificent plan, nothing is wasted. He uses trials to nourish our souls and to transform us to the likeness of Christ. Thriving flowers after a summer storm are a beautiful reminder to look up!

Father God, whether my challenges are like thunderstorms or small dark clouds, remind me to trust You with a joyful outlook as You strengthen me. Amen.

You Can Do It!

*Now what I am commanding you today is not too difficult for you
or beyond your reach.*

DEUTERONOMY 30:11 NIV

Like soccer fans at a finals match, we stood before an underground viewing gallery and cheered as, one-by-one,
large adult salmon successfully traversed the fish ladder of
Chittenden Locks in Seattle, Washington.

The salmon's long, upstream migration back to the water
where they were hatched is one of nature's most awe-inspiring
events. The image of those fish, undeterred by the challenge of
jumping twenty-one steps through a man-made lock to reach
their goal, has spurred me on during times when the challenges before me have seemed too great.

God, who hard-wired those salmon with an unstoppable
desire to successfully complete their life cycle, has hard-wired
us with the desire and ability to successfully fulfill the unique
purpose for which we were created. It may be challenging at
times, but expending the energy necessary to reach our God-
given goals will be worth the effort on the day we hear the
Lord say, "Well done, good and faithful servant!" (Matthew
25:21 NIV).

What God has called you to He will equip you to do and
will help you see it through to the end. Just keep swimming
and don't give up. You can do it!

* * * * * * * * * * *

*Lord, help me stay the course, centered on You, with my eyes on
the prize of a life well lived. Amen.*

Hands in Prayer

Pray continually, give thanks in all circumstances, for this is God's will for you in Christ Jesus.

1 THESSALONIANS 5:17–18 NIV

Many gardeners welcome praying mantises to their plantings to assist with insect control. These large, imposing creatures appear otherworldly with their triangular heads and enormous eyes. Sinister antennae complete their ensemble to provoke horror in the hearts of unsuspecting flower- or vegetable-devouring pests.

Although they could be called either praying or preying, they certainly help to remind us of our ability to communicate with our heavenly Father. These wiry insects nearly always have their front legs folded as if offering prayers to their Maker. As such, they inspire us to do the same as we go about our daily activities. We may not have the time or opportunity to always fold our hands, but we can certainly bow our hearts in prayerful submission.

In 1 Thessalonians 5, Paul tells us that it is God's will for us to pray without ceasing, and throughout Scripture we see the importance of this most basic act of faith. Notice he does not say we should pray to discover God's will, which we do, but that praying itself is God's will. When we fail to pray, we forego God's benefits and attempt life in our own strength. Through prayer, however, we stay connected to our source of love, power, and life.

* * * * * * * * * * *

Heavenly Father, may the mantis remind me that the most important work I can do today is to spend time with You. Amen.

Peacock Roll Call

Even the very hairs of your head are all numbered.

MATTHEW 10:30 NIV

My aunt Grace was an intriguing woman. Her husband, who had died years before, left her a small farm. It had several gardens, and it provided a home for numerous animals she considered pets.

In the summer when I visited Aunt Grace, I pretended to be a farmer. I even wore a straw hat and bandanna. I helped with many chores, but my least favorite task was the feeding of the peacocks. They frightened me, so I held on tight to Aunt Grace's apron for protection.

Each morning, she stood in the yard and called her stately peacocks to breakfast. When the animals drew near, she put up her hand and called, "Stop! Let me count."

To my amazement, all the peacocks stopped and stood still while Aunt Grace did a head count. Assured they were all present, she scattered their food. She knew each of her beloved animals, recognizing the differences in their sizes and personalities.

Our heavenly Father loves us, knows each of us by name, and cares about every aspect of our lives. If He numbers the hairs on our heads, which seems such an insignificant thing, we should never worry about bringing even the least of our concerns to Him. If we ever feel worthless, lonely, or unloved, we must remember our great worth to Him.

* * * * * * * * * *

Father, knowing that You keep account of each hair on my head assures me of Your love. Amen.

View from
the Mountaintop

All the surrounding area on top of the mountain will be most holy.

EZEKIEL 43:12 NIV

I just wanted to stop climbing. Winded from the mountain's high altitude and burdened with a very heavy backpack, I begin to wonder why I chose this steep path anyway. I said to my hiking companions, "I think I'll just stop here and pretend I'm at the peak. After all, the view is already stupendous." But my friends wouldn't let me. They teased me. They encouraged me. If necessary, perhaps they might have even carried me.

Do you ever feel that life is one steep climb? Around each corner, there's another obstacle. You're breathless. You're tired. You're tempted to settle for what you already see, already have.

Friend, don't do it. Keep climbing. When I finally pulled my weary body to the summit of that mountain, I gasped in delight. Before me was a magnificent 360-degree panorama of beauty, color, and texture. A masterpiece by the Creator of all.

Perhaps it's time for you also to look up. If I had stopped climbing, I would have missed so much. God has a vista for each of us—one that not only encourages us on the journey, but also casts vision for potential. With help, we *will* make it to the mountaintop. And it will be worth it.

. . . .

Lord, when I'm weary and feel like giving up, remind me of all You provide as I endure the struggle to the peaks. Amen.

Fragile Seedlings

✿ ❍ ○ ○ ○ ❍ ✿ ❍ ○ ○ ❍

*Praise be to . . . the Father of compassion and the God of all comfort,
who comforts us in all our troubles, so that we can comfort those
in any trouble with the comfort we ourselves receive from God.*

2 CORINTHIANS 1:3–4 NIV

My friend tucked forget-me-not seeds into my birthday card. As I followed instructions to form a miniature greenhouse from plastic wrap and a small pot, I marveled at God's creative genius that packs the promise of blue blossoms into tiny seeds. After sitting on the windowsill for three days, determined sprouts muscled their way through the soil. The delicate seedlings required gentle handling throughout the transplanting procedure. Even gentle sprinklings of water flattened the slender stems to the soil. Forget-me-nots are hardy plants, but at this stage they were fragile and required tender care.

Have you ever felt as weak as a seedling from physical pain or illness? Or, like most of us, perhaps you've experienced emotional pain from broken relationships or heartbreaking news? We sometimes hide these issues under a shell of self-sufficiency or behind a verbal mask that says "Thanks, but I'm fine."

God beckons us to entrust our burdens to Him. Into heartfelt prayer, He plants comfort and hope. When we're as weak as tiny sprouts, God assures and strengthens us. Afterward, we can share the comfort we received with someone else.

. . . .

*Father, remind me to bring my heartaches to You and then share
Your comfort with other hurting people. Amen.*

Mountain-moving Faith

If anyone says to this mountain, "Go, throw yourself into the sea," and does not doubt in their heart but believes that what they say will happen, it will be done for them.

MARK 11:23 NIV

I arrived at the conference center in the Blue Ridge Mountains a day before the writers' conference was scheduled to begin. After unpacking and going over my notes for my upcoming sessions, I opened the curtains and the view of the mountains almost overwhelmed me. As I stared at their beauty and majesty, I felt God's presence so strongly. You see, I was facing some pretty big mountains in my own life at that very moment, and though I was putting on a brave face for everyone, I was hurting on the inside. I was discouraged and troubled, wondering if everything would really be okay.

As I stared at those mountains, tears streaming down my face, it was as if He was saying to me, "Stop focusing on the mountains in your life and focus on Me. I got this!"

I was reminded that the longer we stare at our problems, the bigger they become. What starts out as a miniature molehill suddenly looks like a massive mountain. So, rather than dwelling on how big our problems are today, meditate on how big our God is. He's got this.

. . . .

Lord, there are mountains in my life, but You got this, and I got You. Thank You! Amen.

Hanging Out with Daddy

I keep my eyes always on the LORD. With him at my right hand, I will not be shaken.

PSALM 16:8 NIV

While I was growing up, my dad's hobby was nature photography. We traveled the US in a VW bus, visiting amazing sites and camping in incredible places. Almost as soon as I could walk, I insisted on accompanying him as he hunted for just the right angle to take pictures. Sometimes that meant trips out in the freezing cold before dawn to catch the sun as it rose or scrambling up steep inclines to frame the shadows just right.

I remember one particular morning when Daddy took me to the top of a mountain. He made me sit down while he set up his tripod and got everything in place for when the sun appeared. I thought he wanted me out of the way so I pouted and kept begging to come to him. But looking back as an adult, I realize he was keeping me safe. Those were the days before fences kept wandering tourists away from danger, and the drop-off from that vantage point would have meant certain death.

As a child, I didn't care about dangers. I knew that as long as I was with my daddy, I was perfectly safe no matter what else surrounded us.

* * * * * * * * * *

Dear Lord, help me remember that with You I'm always in a safe place. Amen.

The Persistence
of a Spider

We can rejoice, too, when we run into problems and trials, for we know that they help us develop endurance.

ROMANS 5:3 NLT

As I thought about persistence and pushing past the odds, I thought of Robert the Bruce, king of Scotland in the thirteen hundreds, and a tenacious spider. It is said that in the early days of Robert's reign he was defeated by the English and driven into exile. While he sought refuge in a small, dark cave, he watched a spider attempt to spin a web. Time and time again the spider fell and then climbed slowly back up to try again. Finally, as Robert looked on, the spider managed to stick a strand of silk to the damp cave wall and weave a web. Inspired by the spider and determined not to give up, Robert the Bruce went on to defeat the English at the Battle of Bannockburn.

When we face the trials of this life and feel like giving up, we can remember a persistent arachnid in a Scottish cave. No matter how the odds are stacked against us, we must keep fighting until the very end. More importantly, we should remember we belong to the Creator who designed spiders that persist and weave amazing webs onto the sides of damp caves—the very same Creator who weaves amazing things out of our lives when we don't give up.

. . . .

Father, when I get discouraged and want to give up, remind me of who I am in You. Amen.

Redwoods

Be still, and know that I am God; I will be exalted among the nations. I will be exalted in the earth.

PSALM 46:10 NIV

We stood in the forest of towering two-thousand-year-old trees, struck by their awesome beauty and strength. One could not deny the presence of God that permeated the forest of redwoods. The ancient trees created a living cathedral where one could not help but "be still and know." The experience was powerful and reassuring to my heart.

Ordinarily, busyness crowds our days. Social media cries for our attention. Traffic roars around us. To-do lists grow longer. The ring tone on our smart phones alerts us to message after message. Yet God remains constant. He is always present. His messages are waiting to be read.

I've been known to walk through my days ignoring the messages God sends me. That lovely flower was placed there to call attention to God's beauty. The marvelous sunset that filled the sky was meant to show me His glory. That colorful butterfly crossed my path to remind me of His amazing creativity. That smile from another was to show me His love.

Time to stop and be still. He wants to refresh my heart. He wants to share life with me and have me know Him as my constant companion, always there, no matter what. How refreshing!

. . . .

Father, help me to hear Your messages and seek You each day. Amen.

The Voice of God

God's voice thunders in marvelous ways; he does great things beyond our understanding.

JOB 37:5 NIV

Where do you hear the voice of God? Is it in the snow-flake's whisper as it settles on the ground? Is it in the petal-soft patter of raindrops on a flower's face? Or perhaps it's in the roaring thunder of a storm? For God *does* speak to us, every day and in so many different ways. Through His Word, through His people, and, yes, even through the ever-changing faces of the weather.

Oh, we can certainly track the weather with its highs and lows. We can analyze its patterns and even attempt to predict storms. But as every meteorologist knows, there are "great things" happening "beyond our understanding." For with all our technology, all our sophisticated scientific insight, there are no perfect weather predictions. The weather is one thing that is undeniably under God's control; only He could be the master of such might and majesty.

From the roar of the thunderstorm to the small whisper of snowflakes falling, God speaks. He alone is supreme over all, riding upon the chariots of the wind, summoning the sun to rise and set. And while we may never fully comprehend the storms of nature or the storms of life, we can hear the thunder—the very voice of God—and know that He who speaks in the storm also speaks to us.

* * * * * * * * * * *

Lord, teach me to hear Your voice in the many different ways You speak to me. Amen.

God's Hidden Light

Even in darkness I cannot hide from you. To you the night shines as bright as day. Darkness and light are the same to you.

PSALM 139:12 NLT

God hung the moon to light the darkness, and He commanded the night to shroud the earth after each day. Day goes together with night—darkness on the heels of light, always keeping close company. Even in the depths of space God has hidden light. The Hubble telescope shows fantastic nebulae and constellations out where no one, until recently, ever saw them except God. God hides light in the ocean depths too, past where the sun's rays can reach. Creatures like jellyfish make their own light and plants glow to the glory of their Creator.

When darkness invades your soul and you wonder when you'll see another scrap of light, rest in knowing that the One who created both day and night knows your name. Even darkness is not dark to God. God does not keep anyone in total blackness. Condition your eyes to see the candle of God's presence flickering within. God's Word shines bright when we meditate on it, and the steady reassurance of His presence will conquer any insecurities and anxieties.

God allows darkness so He can be our light. When we choose to believe, not only will we see a light in the darkness, we will actually glow in the dark.

* * * * * * * * * * *

Precious Father, when the darkness will not lift, please help me to see by the light of Your presence and Your Word. Amen.

Climbing Life's Mountains

The Sovereign LORD is my strength. He makes my feet like the feet of a deer, he enables me to tread on the heights.

HABAKKUK 3:19 NIV

I can't believe you actually climbed this mountain!" I exclaimed to my son under the shadow of the Grand Teton in Wyoming. It was huge. I remembered receiving a photo from Tim fifteen years ago. He was literally hanging off that mountain. Back then, photos were not texted in real time so, although horrified, I at least knew he had survived to mail it to me.

I'm glad my son has the courage to climb mountains. It's something he's been doing his whole life, one way or another. What's more, he has wisely chosen the steep upward climb of obedience and discipline in his spiritual life as well. Such things strain every muscle and demand full attention, but the experiences along the way are priceless.

How do we pass along courage and perseverance to our children? By reminding them daily that only God can provide the kind of spiritual, moral, and physical strength needed for the mountains of life. And also by warning them that life is often an uphill climb that requires great endurance—a long obedience in the same direction.

Life is indeed a climb, but one day, we all shall stand on the heights with God.

. . . .

Lord, though it's hard to teach our children about the hard things of life, I'm thankful we can point them to the Source of all strength. Amen.

Divine Design

You saw me before I was born. Every day of my life was recorded in your book. Every moment was laid out before a single day had passed.

PSALM 139:16 NLT

Have you ever questioned the purpose of fire ants, house-flies, and that dreaded mosquito? One insect, however, dazzles onlookers for its pure beauty. Dressed like a king in metallic emerald green, even this beetle's name rings of beauty, *Chrysochus auratus.* Does the dogbane beetle know it's gorgeous among bugs? By scurrying from leaf to leaf, this beetle glorifies God and lives out God's purpose for it.

If God formed even the insects with design and purpose, know He designed us for far more. We bear His image and reflect His glory. In fact, He took His time to handcraft each of us: "You watched me as I was being formed in utter seclusion, as I was woven together in the dark of the womb" (Psalm 139:15 NLT).

Just as God clothed the lowly beetle in radiant green, He breathed your life into existence from His divine imagination. He handpicked everything, from the shape of your nose to your quirky sense of humor. He made no mistakes with you. So the next time you're tempted to try and be someone else or want a different life, remember the emerald-green beetle. Be who God made you to be because His design is flawless.

* * * * * * * * * * *

Father, help me to see Your image in me, and may I shine forth the beauty of Your presence and Your love. Amen.

Collecting Tears

You keep track of all my sorrows. You have collected all my tears in your bottle. You have recorded each one in your book.

PSALM 56:8 NLT

We stood outside one February morning and tried to catch the snowflakes as they fell. They were the big fluffy ones that we don't see very often in Mississippi. Mississippi snow tends to be more like ice than anything. We caught several flakes in our gloves to compare. Not one was like the others.

As magnificent as all of creation is, the idea that each snowflake, fingerprint, and even our tears are all unique is indeed stunning. Just as fingerprints are personal and different, so also is each snowflake distinctive and unique. Scientists agree, there are no two the same in the universe. Even our tears are unique! Photographs of tears under a microscope show the individuality of the chemical makeup.

How extraordinary to think that God keeps our tears in a bottle and notes them in His book. What a beautiful picture, that our creator God cares so deeply for us. He sees and knows and feels our pain. Jesus lived as a man on earth and felt our grief and emotions, and so we trust that our God can empathize with our suffering. How blessed we are to know and trust that God has heard our cry.

. . . .

Loving Father, I give You glory for caring about me, intimately and personally, and feeling my deepest sorrow and joy. Amen.

The Shepherd's Voice

I am the good shepherd; I know my sheep and my sheep know me.

JOHN 10:14 NIV

Sheep are smarter than you might think. With sharp eyes, sheep can recognize the faces of human caregivers and notice when they are absent. Sheep also know their shepherd's unique voice. If flocks of sheep intermingle, they can fall back into place later by following the call of their human masters.

Like a shepherd walking with sheep in the pastures, Jesus wants us to know Him well. His voice is distinct—filled with compassion, caring, and grace. Jesus not only laid down His life for His flock, He also longs for more sheep to join His herd. When one sheep goes missing, He sets off in pursuit of His lost little one (Luke 15:4).

We are these sheep—worth fighting for, priceless in His eyes. It is worth our while to know Christ's voice and to be ready to listen for His cues. We can hear Him more clearly by reading His Word, obeying His commands, and speaking to Him through prayer. In order to hear Him better, it helps to tune out the voices of this world that often lead us down disappointing dead ends. As we tune our ears to Christ, we won't be let down by what we hear. He will chase after us, defend us, love us, and never leave us.

• • • • • • • • • • •

Father, please dim the voices of this world so I can listen more to Your voice. Amen.

Mourning Dove

Blessed are those who mourn, for they will be comforted.

MATTHEW 5:4 NIV

I awoke early feeling very sad. Circumstances in my family were causing us much pain. As I lay there, I heard the soft calls of the mourning doves outside our window. Their mournful coos echoed the sadness in my heart. They communicated to one another, sending out their soft, plaintive coo. One calls, another answers.

Life is tough. Each of us have our own wounds. Some are obvious to others. Some are only experienced by the individual. The struggle is overwhelming when it's hard to see an answer. We hesitate to express our sorrow.

In times of trouble, I often puzzle and struggle on my own. I try to rely on my own wisdom and experience, stubbornly thinking I must handle this on my own. However, in times of trial I have a choice to make. Am I really going to trust in God? This is where my faith becomes real. This is where God becomes my true Father.

We all need to call out to our heavenly Father. We also need to call out to others. Just as the gentle mourning dove calls out to its own kind, we need to seek trusted followers who will help us turn to God for answers. We need to ask for help and strength. God will respond and call out with His wisdom.

* * * * * * * * * * *

Father, help me call out to You in my troubles and trust that You hear and care. Amen.

Free to Be

If the Son sets you free, you will be free indeed.

JOHN 8:36 NIV

I work at a beautiful greenhouse, one of the largest in the country. One day, a particularly sad day for me, I prayed for God to give me encouragement that I could see, not just feel. I was sifting through the emotions of being separated from someone I love.

Shortly after my prayer, I saw a black swallowtail butterfly on the wall having trouble with a bit of web on her wing. I gently pulled the web off and freed her for flight. She landed on my arm to rest, opening and closing her beautifully painted wings as if to say thank you. It wasn't long before she was off to her happy place among the hundreds of flowering plants surrounding her. There was nothing coincidental about this butterfly rescue; there was a clear message in it.

I knew, as you can know, God is here right now. He hears your heart before you speak and counts your tears before they come. He's ready to rescue you and lift you higher. He's set on setting you free to be and do every amazing thing He has planned for your life. Let Him have it all—the questions, the sadness, the fear—and in time, all you will see is the beautiful outcome.

* * * * * * * * * *

Dear Father, I trust You and look forward to the beauty of what's ahead. Amen.

Like a Lion

Look, the Lamb of God, who takes away the sin of the world!

JOHN 1:29 NIV

March is the windy month and the old saying is that if it comes in like a lamb, it will go out like a lion and vice versa. Although research may not have verified this, most of us are likely to forget what the weather was like thirty-one days earlier anyway.

This is true, however, pertaining to Jesus. When He came two thousand years ago, He came as a lamb, *The* Lamb of God that took away the sins of the world. In the Gospels we see a Savior who was fairly docile and even-tempered. His strong words for the Pharisees, however, and His cleansing of the temple were certainly that of a lion. But as we see Him standing before His accusers prior to His crucifixion, He was, in the prophet Isaiah's words, as a sheep before its shearers is silent.

Later, however, when He appears to John in Revelation 19, we see Jesus returning not as a sacrificial lamb, but as a victorious king! He is the Lion of Judah in all His glorious strength and power!

As we toss around the old lion and lamb witticism, may the wind of the Holy Spirit remind us of the spiritual truths hidden within it. And may we take an opportunity today to share this with others.

. . . .

Lamb of God, I trust in Your shed blood and I look forward to Your return as a conquering Lion! Amen.

Crocus Crowning

*Look, the winter is past, and the rains are over and gone. The
flowers are springing up, the season of singing birds has come, and
the cooing of turtledoves fills the air.*

SONG OF SONGS 2:11–12 NLT

Spring's arrival in the Southern Appalachian Mountains is
often ushered in on swirls of snow. Our harbinger of this
lovely season is the crocus. Pushing its way through ice, snow,
and frozen ground, the crocus shouts the message that spring
indeed will come.

Starting in March, I go on crocus patrol. I watch for what
my grandmother called crocus crowning—her name for the
time the plant thrusts its beautiful blossoms of purple, yellow,
and white above the frost line and onto the garden's surface.

Like the crocus, many of us struggle to push our heads
above the frost line of our hardships. Unfortunately, no one
else is present to rejoice when we crown. Or is there? Yes,
our heavenly Father knows when we have stayed the course—
when we have fought for our marriages, prayed for the prodi-
gals, and cried over ailing loved ones. He sees our crowning.

Are you waiting for winter's end? Do you feel trapped
under frozen ground and wonder if you will ever blossom
again? Wonderful, glorious news awaits you! You will burst
forth in bloom again, and God will celebrate your victory over
adversity.

* * * * * * * * * * *

*Thank You, Father, for the persistent crocus, which reminds me to
push upward where rebirth awaits me as I put my trust in You.
Amen.*

Scent-sational!

Thanks be to God, who always leads us in triumph in Christ, and manifests through us the sweet aroma of the knowledge of Him in every place.

2 CORINTHIANS 2:14 NASB

I love to take photographs. Flowers are some of my favorite subjects. Through this hobby I have observed that the beauty of a flower may not correlate to the sweetness of its scent. In the eastern part of the United States there's one particular flowering tree, a Bradford pear, that is absolutely gorgeous in the spring. It's not only the tree as a whole with its profusion of white flowers, it's also the individual blossoms that are a sight to behold—if you can stand to get close enough to take in their details. You see, the scent of this particular flower is horrible beyond belief.

Similarly, one can take on the appearance of Christ when viewed from afar. But when others get close, what do they sense? The odor of cruel words, worldly attitudes, and selfishness can push people away in spite of surface appearances.

Before coming to Christ, we carry the stench of death. When He conquered the grave, Jesus replaced the odor of death with the aroma of life. When we believe in Him, we are given new life; and when we allow Him to influence our lives, that sweet aroma leads others to Christ.

* * * * * * * * * * *

Dear Lord, help me always share the aroma of life. Amen.

Peacocks of Happiness

*Many, LORD my God, are the wonders you have done, the things
you planned for us.*

PSALM 40:5 NIV

Totally focused on the morning meeting, I hurried from
my car toward the office when all of a sudden I looked
up to see the most beautiful sight. Next to the front door of
the office building stood a brilliant blue peacock. No, I hadn't
been sniffing my pink highlighter. There really was a peacock!
I found out later that he belonged to a nearby rancher, but
this beautiful bird liked to roam, and on this particular day
he had roamed right into my life. What's more, I was able to
see him in his full glory. He showed off, fanning his lovely tail
feathers for me, and I stood there grinning from ear to ear.

Later as I thought about my surprise peacock visitation, I
realized that God drops "peacocks of happiness" into my life
all the time, but I'm often too busy to notice.

Now, you may never actually have a fantastically feathered friend show up outside of your home or office, but be
on the lookout for God's loving-kindness toward you every
single day. Drink in those moments of pure joy. God loves to
surprise us—especially when we appreciate the gifts He sends
our way.

. . . .

*Father, help me to recognize the "peacocks of happiness" that You
send into my life every day. Amen.*

The Smallest of Details

Sing, O heavens, for the LORD has done this wondrous thing. Shout for joy, O depths of the earth! Break into song, O mountains and forests and every tree!

ISAIAH 44:23 NLT

At the age of ten I had started to flounder in school. At my teacher's suggestion, Mother took me for an eye exam where we discovered that I had become nearsighted. No one realized how bad my vision had become until I walked out in the sun with my new glasses and exclaimed, "Oh, I can see the leaves on those trees!" I spent the rest of the day rejoicing in the details of the woods where we lived—the bark on the trees, the very blades of grass. The clarity so excited me that I felt as if I'd rediscovered the world.

Sometimes in the busyness of my grown-up life, the tiny details of God's handiwork escape me—the wonder in a leaf, a blossom's tight fist, the whisper of the wind. It is good to be reminded that God created all this not just for His own pleasure but for mine as well. No detail was overlooked. And the God who makes the blossom unfold also takes care with each moment, each detail of my life. I should indeed "sing and shout for joy!"

Lord, may I not overlook the tiny details of Your glorious creation. Let them remind me of the intimacy of Your care and love. Amen.

Cottontail Escape Artist

When you are tempted, he will show you a way out so that you can endure.

1 CORINTHIANS 10:13 NLT

From our deck I spied a cottontail rabbit. Two long ears jutted up above the grassy horizon as I walked closer for a better view. The bunny froze, prompting me to return to my chair. Once the alert little mammal noticed my retreat, it continued to nibble the tender clover leaves. Each time she relocated, she extended her "antenna" ears to check for danger.

Again I ventured toward her. One step, two, then three steps closer I moved before the radar-like ears tensed and turned. One more step. *Zip!* She raced away and disappeared into a thicket of vines. The well-fed bunny with feet sure and fast fled to safety upon sensing a threat. I've always marveled at how well equipped animals are to find food and escape danger.

God's design of the cottontail echoes the miraculous blueprint He uses to ensure His children have spiritual food as well as protection from evil. He bestows encouragement and wisdom by uniquely gifting us to serve each other and provides the Bible for instruction. In addition to spiritual nourishment, God promises an escape route from sin's entrapment when we are tempted. Being alert to His provision keeps us in His thicket of safety.

. . . .

Heavenly Father, remind me to utilize opportunities for spiritual nourishment and to accept the routes of escape You design when I am tempted. Amen.

Banding Together

Though one may be overpowered, two can defend themselves. A cord of three strands is not quickly broken.

ECCLESIASTES 4:12 NIV

Black and white stripes might seem like a strange camouflage choice, but the distinctive coloring of zebras helps protect them against predators. A hungry lion might be able to spot a single zebra, but the crisscrossing stripes of a milling herd make it hard to distinguish one animal from another. From a distance, the stripes can also make them look like a single animal rather than a group of individuals.

Just like zebras, God encourages His children to band together in community because we are better able to fight our spiritual battles when we face them together rather than alone. We can remind one another to be on the lookout for Satan's schemes, encourage one another to grow, and support one another in difficult seasons.

One of Satan's favorite lies is to convince us that we are alone—no one cares, no one understands. Don't fall for it. God has placed people around you who care about you and want to encourage you, and He has put you in people's lives to encourage them. Take the risk. Pick up the phone. Ask for prayer. Look for friendship, relationship, and community. God has provided all of these so we don't have to be alone.

. . . .

Lord, show me how to take the risk of vulnerability so I can both give and receive the blessings of community. Amen.

Daffodil Dare

Trust in the LORD with all your heart, and lean not on your own understanding; in all your ways acknowledge Him, and He shall direct your paths.

PROVERBS 3:5–6 NKJV

Have you ever seen daffodils blooming in a blanket of snow? Their stunning presence is a picture of obedience and courage that mirrors the powerful impact we can have on the world around us, in ways far beyond what we may understand, when we immediately respond to God's leading.

"Just one more thing . . ." I said, before following God's leading, but then I never quite got around to doing what He asked me to do. My delay cost me regret as I missed visiting a dying friend. I was too busy to follow God's leading to stop what I was doing and spend time with her. How I wish I had taken my cue from daffodils that don't wait for everything to be perfect. They just do it!

When God prompts me to do something, it needs doing *now*—not later. As I submit to Him and trust His promises to keep me on track, I can dare to change my schedule and take the time needed to accomplish His purposes. Now, each time I see a daffodil, whether in the spring, on my white china mug, or on the yellow sun catcher that sparkles in the window, I'm reminded to dare to be a daffodil and do what needs doing—now!

Lord of all time, help me to hear and quickly respond to Your leading. Amen.

Deep Calls to Deep

Deep calls to deep in the roar of your waterfalls; all your waves and breakers have swept over me.

PSALM 42:7 NIV

Lake vistas, big and blue, dominate the scene as one travels the highway from Charlevoix to Petoskey in northern Michigan. The water of Lake Michigan can be enjoyed all along the route. You can walk sandy beaches searching for elusive Petoskey stones (rock composed of fossilized coral) and other "treasures" while the waves of Lake Michigan lap upon the shore. Some days, it is calm and smooth like a shimmering mirror reflecting all God's nature surrounding it. Other days, the waves are gentle, soothing and rocking like a lullaby of God's peace. Many summer days, dancing waves enticingly call to children of all ages, "Come play in me!" And there are days when the wind roars and waves crash onto the shore with great force, a reminder of God's strength and might.

Whatever the conditions, I am always aware of God calling to me. He calls to me from deep waters; He calls from the depths of His love—"Remember who I am. Remember what is important today. I am always here, calling from the depths of My love for you."

No matter what is happening on the surface of your life, peaceful calm, playful waves, or rough, choppy waters, God is there in the depths of your soul. He calls to you as "deep calls to deep" into communion with Him.

. . . .

Father, help me to remember that You are here, available each day. Amen.

A Hollow Existence

On the outside you appear to people as righteous but on the inside you are full of hypocrisy and wickedness.

MATTHEW 23:28 NIV

You did what?" I screamed into the phone. "Why did you cut down our big, beautiful tree?"

"Because it was dead," my husband said calmly. "I was afraid that if it stormed again, it would fall onto our house." He went on to explain that an expert evaluated the tree and, as it turned out, it was dying from the inside out. In fact, it was totally hollow. We had no idea that it had been slowly dying for a long time.

Every time I stare at that empty area in our backyard, I think about that big, beautiful, hollow tree and ponder— so many people in the world are just like that tree. They look great on the outside, but they are dying on the inside. And, what about me? How many times have I put on a happy face and faked my way through life, all the while dying on the inside?

If we're honest, we've all been like that tree before. But here's the deal—even if you fool everyone else, God knows! His Word says that He looks on the heart while others look on outward appearances. In other words, He knows if you're hollow on the inside, and His one desire is to fill you up with His love, goodness, and hope.

. . . .

Father, help me to stop faking my way through life and start being real with You. Amen.

When All Is Lost

Nothing will hurt or destroy in all my holy mountain, for as the waters fill the sea, so the earth will be filled with people who know the LORD.

ISAIAH 11:9 NLT

My friends Carole and Johnny evacuated their home moments before Hurricane Ike blew everything they owned into Galveston Bay. Fifty years of marriage and memories all swept away in an instant. You might call this total destruction.

But not Carole and Johnny. For them, it was only stuff. True, their kids had removed precious family photos during the evacuation. Still . . . *everything*, gone?

Carole's words during that crisis show how believers can respond when all seems lost: "The task that now lies ahead is simply to wait until God shows us the next step. We don't have a clue what the next step is, but we are at peace in the confidence that God is committed to bringing order out of the chaos of our lives."

That was nine years ago. Every year I spend time with Carole and marvel at her resilience. Even though Johnny has now gone home to heaven, her enthusiasm for life and trust in the Word of God have only deepened her desire to call others to trust and obey. She says, "Since Hurricane Ike, we have not wanted for a single thing that God has not provided."

* * * * * * * * * *

Lord, thank You for those who show us that even when the very worst happens, we can turn to You for peace, power, and provision. Amen.

The Flight of the Crane

Even the stork that flies across the sky knows the time of her migration, as do the turtledove, the swallow, and the crane. They all return at the proper time each year.

JEREMIAH 8:7 NLT

The crane was young, without its full plumage, gangly and top-heavy. It stood at the edge of the water, eyes focused on currents and the movements of fish only it could see. It plodded up and down on the shore, ignoring the cluster of people behind it, all of us snapping photos, eyes wide with delight.

What a joy to see its awkward nature on the ground turn to pure beauty once it took flight. We don't see cranes much in this area; they rarely stray this far west of their normal migration routes. But it wasn't lost, just pausing for food and rest, and it would be on its way again in a day or two.

Long before humans understood such things as "migration routes," God did. He imbued birds with the sense of when and where they should go, because He wanted the best for them. God also wants what's best for us, and He gave us a hunger for Him as well as His Word so we would know how to follow in His wise ways.

. . . .

Lord, our hearts crave You. Show us daily how to rely on Your care and love for us. Amen.

Powerful and Personal

On the glorious splendor of Your majesty and on Your wonderful works, I will meditate.

PSALM 145:5 NASB

I pulled my chair over to the large picture window. My hotel room had a view of the Blue Ridge Mountains and I didn't want to miss the beauty. Dusk settled, bringing an evening storm. Clouds moved over the mountaintops and streaks of lightning flashed. As I watched the spectacular light show, I marveled at the power of God.

The next morning, I noticed a tiny moth stuck to the outside of my window. I had a close-up view of its spotted wings, tiny mouth, and polished eyes. A gust of wind suddenly blew. The moth held onto the glass with all its might. As I studied it a moment longer, I thought about the intricate workings of God's creation.

God is powerful, as I witnessed in the storm the night before. But He used that tiny moth to remind me He is also personal. He set the stars in space, and yet He knows me by name. He marked off the heavens with the breadth of His hand, yet He wove me together in my mother's womb.

When storms rage and winds blow, God surrounds each one of us with His awesome strength and tender care. He knows us. He loves us. And whether through lightning on mountaintops or a tiny moth on a breezy morning, He displays His splendor.

. . . .

Lord, thank You for Your awesome strength and tender care. Amen.

Starlight vs.
Security Light

Be still before the LORD and wait patiently for him.

PSALM 37:7 ESV

Our neighborhood has no streetlights. Depending on how you look at it, this can be a blessing or a curse. Periodically I go out after dark to check on things and on a clear night the stars can take my breath away—until the motion sensor security light comes on.

In that moment I lose the theatrical view of the black velvet sky pinpricked with stars and the moon hung in one of its phases. However, I gain the ability to see the face-level spider's web and the frog oblivious to the danger of my approaching flip-flop. There is a bittersweet mix of gratitude for the safe passage to the recycling bin but also regret for the loss of God's magnificent display.

What I fail to grasp too often is the fact that if I just wait a few minutes the spectacular display can be mine again. When I'm not in a hurry and when I can settle into a spot free of gauzy webs and wary frogs, all I have to do is look up and be still. Soon the security light goes out and my eyes open up and the wonders of the heavens are mine again.

. . . .

Lord, help me to be still and wait on You. Your presence is both a beautiful and a secure light in the dark. Amen.

Paid Attention To

He cuts off every branch in me that bears no fruit, while every branch that does bear fruit he prunes so that it will be even more fruitful.

JOHN 15:2 NIV

I recently visited a friend who has a love for concord grapes. The mini-vineyard in his backyard looked pleased to be producing loads of grapes on every stem!

We got into a conversation about how to keep the vines healthy and encourage maximum fruit production. He told me the same principle that works for his trees works for his grapevines: shorten the distance between the branches and their source of life—the water and food collected at the root. It's called truncating. He told me if the vines are left to grow without care, they wander away from their life source and become weak, producing less and less fruit. I love what he said next: "The vines heavy laden with fruit are 'paid attention to' by the gardener. They aren't being left to their careless ways."

It's wonderful to know we're "paid attention to." Every day the Gardener of our lives is tending, doing what needs to be done to keep us close to our source of life. No matter how painful the pruning is or how hard it is to understand, God knows how to make the best fruit. Our hearts need only trust Him.

* * * * * * * * * * *

Dear Father, thank You for paying attention to me and producing fruit in me that brings glory to You. Amen.

Natural Mnemonic

May I never boast except in the cross of our Lord Jesus Christ.

GALATIANS 6:14 NIV

A common elementary science project challenges students to collect leaves, mount them on poster board, and identify them correctly. This exercise teaches students to differentiate between species based on certain characteristics. The variety of leaf shapes provided by the Creator certainly keeps these projects interesting and intriguing.

It doesn't take long for young collectors to notice the great variety of shapes found in the woodland leaves. Short, thin pine needles contrast with wide, round catalpa foliage. Compound and double compound leaves add even more diversity and keep young botanists on their toes.

Among the myriad of leaf shapes, that of the post oak is most interesting to me, for these unique leaves are formed like crosses. I'm sure there are biological benefits for such an unusual shape, but it's just like our imaginative Creator to set up subtle reminders of the cross throughout nature. On the third day of creation, He knew that one bleak morning centuries later, His only Son would be nailed to a cruel executioner's implement made from a tree, the very substance that He created that day. Perhaps He so designed this leaf to prophesy that future event in the years leading up to the crucifixion, and as a poignant reminder for all of us who live on the other side.

. . . .

Father, may the leaves of the post oak remind me of Your Son who willingly hung on a wooden cross in my place. Amen.

Preserving Our Core

If your hand causes you to sin, cut it off. It's better to enter eternal life with only one hand than to go into . . . hell with two hands.

MARK 9:43 NLT

Due to a record-setting summer drought several years ago, two things happened the following autumn. The oak trees in our yard produced an unusually large quantity of acorns, and they shed several massive limbs. Experts suggested the drought-stricken trees might be dying. As a result, in an effort to continue the species, the trees dropped a bumper crop of acorns. We were also told the shed limbs were a way for the trees to preserve their core.

I learned a couple of things from those oaks. First, the trees scattered acorns hoping those seeds would take hold and grow. I need to scatter seeds of truth from God's Word to those around me to give them a hope for the future. Secondly, our oaks survived because they willingly shed massive limbs to preserve their core. The Bible tells us that if our hand, foot, or eye causes us to sin, we are to cut it off or pluck it out. It may be painful and difficult to drop the unhealthy things that weigh me down and threaten to destroy me at my core, but if I want to preserve who God designed me to be, I must be willing to do whatever it takes.

. . . .

Father, help me sow the seeds You want planted, and discard the things that pull me away from You. Amen.

A God Beyond Understanding

Now to the King eternal, immortal, invisible, the only God, be honor and glory for ever and ever. Amen.

I TIMOTHY 1:17 NKJV

It doesn't take a master gardener to understand that to everything there is a specific time and place or season under heaven. Most people who plant flowers know that the wilting heat of summer is too much for pansies, but that the lantana will bloom in that time of extreme heat. Plants are limited to seasons and processes. All life has a beginning and an end on this earth. There is a general decay among us, for our bodies break down over time. In light of this, how awe inspiring it is to consider the character qualities of our God.

This passage in Timothy reminds us that God is eternal, immortal, invisible, and the only God. My friends, in this life we can never be eternal, for we have a beginning and an end. We are not immortal because our bodies—as evidenced on a daily basis—are decaying and dying. Lastly, we cannot be invisible because we have human bodies that are seen.

What is so formidable is that God is not limited by our limitations. What is so reassuring is that not only is our God all-knowing, all-powerful, and always present, but He is also merciful, compassionate, and holy.

* * * * * * * * * * *

Dear Lord, I just want to praise You for being a God beyond my understanding and comprehension. Amen.

From Death to Life

God told him, "I have made you the father of many nations."
This happened because Abraham believed in the God who brings
the dead back to life and who creates new things out of nothing.

ROMANS 4:17 NLT

On a visit to Olympic National Park in Washington State, I was struck by the sight of several tall, slender saplings growing out of a moss-covered log. These "nurse logs" are an important feature of the Olympic rainforest. The shade from tall spruce trees and thick ferns that cover the forest floor shut out the sunlight that seedlings need to sprout and grow. Nurse logs elevate seedlings above the ferns so they can germinate in better light, and nutrients from the fallen tree nourish the new trees as they grow. The death of one tree makes space for new life.

Sometimes we also have to experience death to make space for new life. In many ways we experience some kind of death—the death of a loved one, the death of a season in life, or the death of a dream. During these times, don't lose hope. God is in the resurrection business. What feels like an ending may be the seed of a new beginning—a seed that can flourish in the light and presence of our life-giving God. What might God want to plant in you?

* * * * * * * * * * *

Life-giving God, show me the new beginnings You want to birth in me. Amen.

The Fragrance
of the Lemon Tree

Thanks be to God who leads us, wherever we are, on his own triumphant way and makes our knowledge of him spread throughout the world like a lovely perfume!

2 CORINTHIANS 2:14 PHILLIPS

I once had a walled garden in the medieval heart of North Africa. It was a secret paradise, a refuge from the desert dust that blew in like fine talcum powder. An old mulberry tree sheltered the roof from the afternoon sun, and the broad-leafed rubber tree invited the children to hide within its branches. Fig trees, olive trees, and roses scented the air with heavy perfume.

The sweetest fragrance of all was the flowering lemon trees. Their delicate white petals opened like tiny gifts, releasing joy and peace into the air. During lemon blossom season I moved my work out to the garden just to breathe in the hope they spread throughout my soul.

For many, life is a desert, the winds of difficulty blowing like Sahara sand, covering hope with grit and disappointment. But there is a garden, a place where the lemon trees grow fragrant, their blooms opening to release a bouquet of joy and peace into the most parched heart. That garden is the body of Christ, people planted by the Lord to release His lovely perfume into the souls of others. Through our lives He has chosen to spread the knowledge of Him to the world.

* * * * * * * * * *

Lord, lead me today and make my life a lovely perfume, everywhere spreading the knowledge of Your love. Amen.

A Picnic with a Bear

God is our refuge and strength, a very present help in trouble.

PSALM 46:1 NKJV

We'd just unpacked our picnic basket in the Great Smoky Mountains, grilled some hot dogs, and enjoyed the first few bites on our plates when we noticed an unexpected guest headed our way to share the feast. We'd wanted to see wildlife on our trip, but we hadn't planned on a bear joining us for dinner; but there he was, meandering through the woods, heading straight for us.

We put our children in the van where they'd be safe, and then before we took refuge there, we gathered what food we could save before Mr. Bear got too close. We laughed as we watched that big furry guy guzzle the Pepsi, enjoy the mayonnaise, and eat the food we'd left on our plates.

Yes, it was a totally unexpected moment, but our lives are often full of them. We might not have growly bears headed our way, but we often feel like we're going to be devoured by health issues, heartache, family situations, and financial difficulties. That's when—just like we took refuge in the van—we need to run to our safe place, trusting the One who is our help in trouble, our refuge and strength in every situation. There is no need to fear whenever God is near.

* * * * * * * * * * *

Father, I'm so grateful that I can depend on You whenever I need help. Thank You for being my safe place. Amen.

After the Storm

༄ ◦°◦°◦°◦°◦°◦°◦°◦°

*Be merciful to me, Lord, for I am in distress; my eyes grow weak
with sorrow, my soul and body with grief.*

PSALM 31:9 NIV

You think it will never happen to you—and then it does.
The ruinous aftermath of a natural disaster leaves you
devastated and overwhelmed. Rioters destroy your business.
Your spouse walks away from you and the family.

On the day my husband told me to take the children and
leave, my whole world changed and no longer felt safe. The
loss, sorrow, and fear made me feel as if God was far away and
had left me to fend for myself. But I was wrong. God had
not abandoned me. The moment I cried out and reconnected
with the Creator of the universe, He rolled up His sleeves and
began moving in ways I could never imagine. Other people
offered helping hands, doors of opportunity opened, and—
over time—balance returned and my joy was restored.

The landscape of my life was changed forever by the storm
of deceit and rejection. But through it all, a new shoreline
has been formed, fortified with deeper strength, resilience,
and compassion for others. We may be powerless to stop the
storms of life but, despite our circumstances, we can cling
with certainty to the fierce and powerful love of God that
never changes.

· · · · · · · · · · ·

*Lord, be my strength after the storm; show up big and help me get
back on my feet again. Amen.*

Oasis in The Desert

Then they came to Elim, where there were twelve springs and seventy palm trees, and they camped there near the water.

EXODUS 15:27 NIV

The road stretched endlessly to the sun as we drove through the North African desert. There was no scenery to entertain our tired eyes, only miles and miles of brown, sandy earth. Even the lizards had taken refuge beneath the soil from the burning heat. Suddenly, like a mirage appearing on the horizon, an oasis of green palms rose to touch the faded sky. The landscape gently dipped, forming a green basin lined with lush grasses and bright flowering shrubs nestled along a flowing spring. It was a genuine oasis, right there in the middle of the wilderness.

I thought of the Israelites who had traveled for days in the burning desert. They were irritable and tired, brimming with complaints. The people needed an oasis to escape the driving heat. God brought them to Elim, the place of twelve springs and abundant date palms. From there they rose renewed and refreshed.

We sometimes march through life irritable and exhausted. We yearn for relief, a refuge from the relentless pressure. Where is the Elim? In the barren monotony of our circumstances we can easily miss the oasis rising like a mirage on the horizon. Stop your journey, nourish your bodies, and lay down your cares. God provides places of rest for His travelers.

* * * * * * * * * * *

Lord, bring me to the refreshing waters of Elim in my life today. Amen.

The Favor of the Lord

*Let the favor of the LORD our God be upon us; and confirm for us
the work of our hands; yes, confirm for us the work of our hands.*

PSALM 90:17 NASB

Beginning a new career at over fifty proved to be interesting, and thoroughly exhausting since the new job was farming and it exceeded all expectations of difficulty that I could have imagined. We planted, and weeds grew. We harvested, and had trouble selling. We fed chickens, and our dog ate them (at least a few of them). Sixteen-hour workdays got old after about a week.

But it has still been good. There's something special about planting a seed and watching it grow. Tasting the fruit of your hands makes any meal special—especially homegrown heirloom tomatoes. The first man and woman were farmers. The work they did had meaning, but because of their sin their work became difficult.

We all have our own work. It is established by God and just like it says in Genesis, it is good—but it's not necessarily easy. So when I'm complaining about the heat, I thank God for the work. When the weeds grow, I know there will be a harvest. And when my dog eats a chicken, well, I just remember the Creator made him too, and I give him a hug. But I don't let him near the chickens.

* * * * * * * * * * *

Lord, thank You for the work You have given each one of us on this earth. Amen.

Droplets of Honey

Whatever you do, work at it with all your heart, as working for the Lord, not for human masters.

COLOSSIANS 3:23 NIV

Most honeybees live only a few weeks. Faithfully they collect nectar from flowers, storing the sweet liquid in "honey stomachs." Then they carry the nectar to their hive and repeat the journey. In its life span, a bee only produces a twelfth of a teaspoon of honey, barely enough to sweeten a cup of tea.

Sometimes obedience to God seems like droplets of honey. A mother prepares meals for her family knowing she won't always be thanked. A teen doesn't know how to share Jesus but continuously invites friends to church. A professional takes extra time to mentor a new coworker although she'll never get credit in her annual review.

Jesus told us that our small efforts *do* matter. He said anyone who gives His disciples even a cup of cold water would not lose their reward (Matthew 10:42). When a widow gave just two copper coins to the temple, Jesus said she had given more than anyone because she'd given all she had to live on (Mark 12:42–44).

God has a purpose for us, just as He does for the bee. Using our time and gifts fully, and taking extra care to reflect His love—even if it goes unnoticed by human eyes—will be appreciated by the One who crafted your very soul.

. . . .

Father, help me to do every task—big or small—as working for You. Amen.

The Universe Testifies

The heavens declare the glory of God . . . . Day after day they pour forth speech; night after night they reveal knowledge.

PSALM 19:1–2 NIV

Everywhere we look, the grandeur and expanse of creation gives testimony to the glory of God and His role as Creator. Whether it is the sheer size of the Grand Canyon or the Great Barrier Reef, or the breathtaking beauty of the northern lights or Victoria Falls on the Zambezi River—each of these natural wonders are extraordinary reminders of the amazing God who designed them.

While we do not hear the audible voice of God, He has left us with a very clear imprint in nature. We recognize that this creation is vastly superior to anything we could ever think of or accomplish on our own. God's imagination is on display all around us.

Creation does not change its testimony either. It is a constant telling of how great our God is. In a world that is increasingly connected through the Internet and airline travel, there are not many regions left with limited access to information. But even in those remote locations, the inhabitants witness the glory of creation that testifies to the very reality of God without written word or spoken language. God speaks through nature, and all human beings can find and know Him no matter what. There are absolutely no barriers to His glory.

Dear Lord, may I always pay attention to what Your creation has to say about You. Amen.

The Storm

⁂ ○₀·₀°·○⁂ ○₀·₀°·○

*The men were amazed and asked, "What kind of man is this?—
even the winds and the sea obey Him!"*

MATTHEW 8:27 HCSB

The rain fell in blinding sheets, the wind roared and pushed the car, and what should have been an hour-long drive was stretching well into two. The headlights barely penetrated the darkness, and the wipers had little effect. My eyes burned, my shoulders ached, and my child slept, curled on the seat beside me. And so, I prayed . . . without ceasing. Nearing the lake and the most dangerous hill of our drive home, my prayers became increasingly desperate. *Please, God. Home is just ten minutes away. Please, stop the storm. Just ten minutes, Lord. Please.*

I crested the hill and began the steep descent as lightning turned darkness to daylight. *Please, God.* And the storm . . . stopped. No thunder, no wind, not even a single drop of rain. The stillness was so complete, I could hear my own breathing. God had stopped the storm.

Ten minutes later, I pulled into our drive and the heavens opened and the storm raged again. But my God had stopped the storm. For me. For my child. For His children.

Sometimes God does stop the storm, and sometimes He doesn't. It's impossible to understand His reasons—His ways are so much greater than ours. But we cherish those times He stops the storms, for they give us hope in the times He chooses to carry us through them.

. . . .

Whether the storms rage or whether they are silenced, I thank You, Lord, for being my shelter. Amen.

The Restoration of Spring

See! The winter is past; the rains are over and gone. Flowers appear on the earth; the season of singing has come.

SONG OF SOLOMON 2:11–12 NIV

Can you identify with the excitement found in this verse? *See!* Did you notice the use of an exclamation point? That's exactly how I feel after winter. So grateful that spring has sprung! The earth awakens from silent slumber and re-animates with beautiful growth, like sloughing off the cold and drab to don the warm and bright. Every aspect of nature contributes—the flowers bloom, birds coo, fruit trees bud, and the fragrant vines sweeten the air.

While spring transforms the exterior world, I like to evaluate my inner, spiritual world. Am I spending quality time reading and reflecting on God's Word? How's my prayer life? Have I shared my faith in words or deeds lately? Do I feel connected to the True Vine?

Spring inspires me to cultivate a fresh commitment to my spiritual side and nurture new habits of inner growth. I enjoy the birds singing outside my window as I probe deeper into the Word. Bringing vibrant flowers inside reminds me of God's generous abundance. And I can't help but offer prayers of heartfelt gratitude.

O, Father, as I enjoy the beauty of spring's restoration, create in me a deeper wisdom and love for You. Amen.

Fully Restored

The God of all grace, who called you to his eternal glory in Christ, after you have suffered a little while, will himself restore you and make you strong, firm and steadfast.

1 PETER 5:10 NIV

Year after year, I watched a Bradford pear tree—our harbinger of spring—bloom from my mother's front porch. From that porch, we sipped coffee and waited in expectation for the buds to burst into an explosion of white. Pear trees always command attention, creating a stark contrast to the grays and browns around them. Brightness breaking through the dullness.

When high winds severed several branches one day, my mom considered removing the tree. It seemed to have lost its purpose. The ornamental tree was now an eyesore, with gaping splits exposing the bare underneath. Thankfully, she decided to wait to cut it down. Though it looked dead, the tree was already at work healing itself.

Our spiritual healing often looks like this. We might think the cuts run too deep or the condition is too ingrained. Whether we face injury at the hand of others or incur wounds brought on by our own sin, God longs to heal us. No matter the source of our hurt, we serve the Great Physician who restores us from the inside out. The Lord sees every area where we need healing. Trust Him—He will heal and fully restore.

. . . .

Lord, I believe; help our unbelief and restore us today for the glory of Your name. Amen.

Following His Footsteps

Direct my footsteps according to your word.

PSALM 119:133 NIV

Black bears are some of the most popular mammals in North America. They are just as likely to appear at suburban bird feeders as at backwoods brush piles. These versatile animals will eat almost anything from insect larvae to bird eggs and from carrion to acorns, and they can thrive in most climates.

Bears possess the unusual tendency of stepping exactly in the tracks of other bears as they travel woodland trails. They avoid making unnecessary noise and will sidestep even the smallest of objects. While this minimizes the risk of breaking twigs that frighten potential prey, it was also used by nineteenth-century fur trappers to increase their take. Today, game biologists use this knowledge to tag and study bears. As they prepare their humane snares, they judiciously remove all sticks and rocks from each carefully constructed footprint that might cause a bear to hesitate.

This should be a warning for us to carefully watch whom we follow as well. Walking in someone else's footsteps is a very good thing if that person is following the steps of Jesus. On the other hand, tracks left by other humans may lead us right into sin. Let's examine our paths carefully and wisely and be sure to follow the Master's footsteps that lead away from spiritual harm and into joy and blessing.

* * * * * * * * * * * *

Maker of the black bear, help us to walk in Your footsteps today. Amen.

Controlled Burns

*That the genuineness of your faith, being much more precious
than gold that perishes, though it is tested by fire, may be found to
praise, honor, and glory at the revelation of Jesus Christ.*

I PETER 1:7 NKJV

My parents lived in the middle of a pine forest where fire
was a real threat, especially during times of drought. For
that reason they used controlled burns to protect their property. Controlled burns remove dead vegetation that can burst
into flames and burn out of control. It also helps release seeds
from pinecones. On top of that, the fire burns away shrubs
around trees that can provide snakes and other predators easy
access to woodpecker nests. It also reduces disease and insect
infestations.

I've realized that God uses controlled burns in my life,
removing the deadwood I've been carrying around, protecting me from exploding or burning out of control. After the
useless things are removed there is room for spiritual growth.
The fire of trials or tough circumstances can heat up my life,
but God uses those times to release spiritual seeds within me.
He's like a refiner's fire, burning away areas where predators
hide, waiting for me to let my guard down before they strike.

Though uncomfortable, God's controlled burns protect
me and help me flourish. He does this because I am His, and
He loves me.

* * * * * * * * * * * *

*Father, though it may be painful, please burn away everything
necessary so that I may please You. Amen.*

Sunrise Opportunity

The morning light from heaven is about to break upon us, to give light to those who sit in darkness . . . and to guide us to the path of peace.

LUKE 1:78–79 NLT

One morning at a red light, I observed a streak of vibrant color. The sky was painted in fuchsia, laced with orange, and punctuated with deep purple. What a magnificent testament to God's creative nature! The green light forced me to proceed. After traveling a short distance, I caught another glimpse only to discover the sunrise had transformed into an ordinary blue-gray sky. In minutes the dramatic spectacle had vanished, leaving not one remnant of vivid color. The morning sky reflected the glory of God yet only lasted a moment.

Just as our heavenly Father creates beautiful dawn snapshots, He extends opportunities to care for His children. Numerous needs surround us—a lonely widow, a discouraged coworker, a new neighbor. The offering of a warm smile, a kind word, or a more tangible blessing can reflect God's creativity in meeting human need. However, if we postpone our response to His prompting, the window of opportunity may disappear as quickly as a beautiful sunrise.

The works of God inspire awe, whether in a spectacular sunrise or in kind deeds. Daily evidence of His creative nature and glory can bless us and others when we take the time to stop, notice, and respond.

* * * * * * * * * * *

Father, call my attention to displays of Your glory that I might worship You, and then help me obey Your call to respond. Amen.

Above the Clouds

Set your mind on the things above, not on the things that are on earth.

COLOSSIANS 3:2 NASB

I love driving through the Blue Ridge Mountains, especially early in the morning. One day I left pre-dawn to photograph the sunrise in the midst of the mountains.

As I had hoped, the sun peaked over the horizon and the sky filled with a myriad of colors bouncing between clouds and cliffs. I snapped several shots, but continued farther into the mountains, knowing the more spectacular views lay at higher elevations. But as I drew closer to the summit, the car was engulfed in clouds. Black and white replaced color, and even the trees were indistinct.

I slowed the car to a crawl, tempted to give up and turn around. But something urged me on. Sure enough, just yards from my goal, the clouds parted and the sun returned. I pulled into the parking area and got out, stunned by the view.

The clouds that had impeded my progress now added to the richness of the scene below me. As I marveled at the beauty of God's creation, He spoke to me about my experience. No matter how the gray clouds of life close in, the Son is still there. My job is to keep moving toward Him, focusing my thoughts on His promise.

. . . .

Dear Lord, don't let me focus on the grayness of life; instead, keep my mind set on You and on the things above. Amen.

Charlotte's Web

I praise you, for I am fearfully and wonderfully made. . . . My frame was not hidden from you, when I was being made in secret, intricately woven in the depths of the earth.

PSALM 139:14–15 ESV

One of my favorite stories as a child was *Charlotte's Web* by E. B. White. I was fascinated by the talking animals and completely taken in by the sophistication and intelligence of Charlotte the spider. Over the years, however, my admiration wore off as arachnophobia set in.

Living in the woods, there is a tendency to come face to face with spiders and their webs all too often. I started carrying a stick around if I was the first one out in the mornings so that I could clear the way of any possible "hairnets." These webs are such a nuisance, and don't get me started on the spiders themselves.

Then, on one particularly dewy morning, I walked outside and there it was: the biggest, most intricately woven web I have ever seen. It was at least five feet in diameter and the webbing holding it in place spanned eight or more feet. And it was a perfect spiral.

From that day forward my fascination returned. I still go ballistic if I see one in my house, but outside I am drawn to their creative engineering and ingenuity. It reminds me that we are all a part of His miraculous creation, fearfully and wonderfully made, intricately woven by God.

· · · · · · · · · · · ·

Lord, thank You for paying attention to details. They are awe inspiring! Amen.

Breathing
Through a Tube

So God created the great creatures of the sea and every living thing with which the water teems.

GENESIS 1:21 NIV

Yes, the sand in Bermuda really is pink. And the water really is turquoise. And the best way to enjoy both is to snorkel in the sea. It took me awhile to learn to swim with fins and peer through goggles while breathing into a tube with my mouth. But once I got the hang of it—pure bliss!

Wonder. Color. Creativity. All of God's best handiwork on display right there under the sea. But don't hurry. Snorkeling is a slow activity. Breathe in. Breathe out. Kick and paddle with those fins and reach out to coral and underwater rocks nestled deep in the ocean floor. Eyeball the iridescent parrotfish and try counting the hundreds of tiny minnows. . . . Enjoy the moment.

The Hebrew translation of the word spirit is *ruach*, meaning "breath." Have you ever noticed that we use the words "breath" and "spirit" in similar ways today? If we say, "It took my breath away," we don't mean we literally stopped breathing. It means our spirit was deeply affected. That's how I felt when I finally got comfortable breathing through a tube. Relaxed and yet amazed.

Is it time for you to slow down and breathe deeply?

. . . .

Lord, since being in a hurry makes me miss life, enable me to slow down and just breathe. Amen.

Be Still

Come with me by yourselves to a quiet place.

MARK 6:31 NIV

It seems that every time we vacation by the ocean I am able to hear from God so clearly. I'll walk the beach by myself in the morning and I'll usually end my day sitting on a beach chair near the water, listening to the waves. I always look forward to our beach vacation—not just for the amazing key lime pie that you can only get in the South, but for the special times I share with God.

I've often wondered why I so easily hear from Him when I'm chilling by the ocean, and I think I finally know. First, I am intentional and expectant when I seek God on the beach. Second, I am not too busy to spend quality time with Him. And third, I am actually quiet before God as I listen to the ocean waves. (I've discovered that I'm otherwise rarely quiet.)

Since I can't stay on a beach vacation year round, I've determined to approach my daily quiet time with God the same way I do at the ocean, even as I'm sitting in my sunroom or chilling on the front porch swing.

I challenge you to do the same. Be intentional and expectant. Slow down and seek Him. And take the time to be still long enough to hear from God. He has stuff to share with you.

. . . .

Father, help me to be still long enough to hear from You. Amen.

Growing
Spiritual Muscles

*When I was a child, I spoke and thought and reasoned as a child.
But when I grew up, I put away childish things.*

I CORINTHIANS 13:11 NLT

When it's time for baby birds to learn how to fly, the mother will stop bringing food straight from her beak to their mouths. She will leave the morsels a short distance from the nest, forcing the babies to move around. At first, the babies stumble and lurch, but then they learn to flap their wings to hold themselves up. Eventually, they develop enough muscles to fly from branch to branch, preparing to fly on their own and leave the nest for good.

God teaches us to develop spiritual muscles. Once, when the disciples were out fishing, Jesus walked to them on the water. When they saw Him, they were afraid. But Peter asked to join Him. He took a few brave steps, but as the winds picked up he lost faith. Peter fell, but Jesus caught him.

Just like mother birds who don't give up on their babies after a few falls, Jesus wasn't done with Peter. Later, Peter denied Jesus three times, but Jesus still had great plans for His servant. Peter went on to lead thousands of people to faith.

God has a plan for your life as well. He's waiting to teach you the next step. Even if you stumble like the baby bird, He'll never give up on you.

. . . .

*Father, I'm ready for Your next challenge. Give me a willing heart
and a courageous spirit. Amen.*

Intimate and Precious

Consider the lilies of the field, how they grow: they neither toil nor spin; and yet I say to you that even Solomon in all his glory was not arrayed like one of these.

MATTHEW 6:28–29 NKJV

When the spring rains arrive, my yard erupts with tiny wildflowers in a riot of color. Wild strawberries and violets, miniature yellow blossoms, and delightful sprites my neighbor calls "bluets." Even though each bloom is smaller than a dime, they flourish so well that the grass almost disappears beneath their sprays. I dearly wish they could last all summer.

They are a glorious symbol of renewal, of the rebirth that spring brings to God's creation. They remind me to praise Him, grateful for the care He has for not only each of us but also the smallest flowers of the field, and that He is present in every aspect of His handiwork.

Sometimes I think of God only as the powerful Creator, huge and far away. How could He possibly be involved in the trivia of my life? But what I may consider small and unimportant, He sees as intimate and precious. The Creator who oversees the blossoming of a tiny bloom most certainly cares for me and for you.

* * * * * * * * * *

Lord, every part of Your creation is dear to You; let me not forget how wonderfully and intimately You care for each one of us. Amen.

Collecting Shells

Because of his great love for us, God, who is rich in mercy, made us alive with Christ even when we were dead in transgressions.

EPHESIANS 2:4–5 NIV

One of the benefits of living near the coast is an ever-growing seashell collection. It doesn't matter how many shells I possess, I can't resist the beauty of yet another one. Often I spot one appearing to be particularly attractive only to find it's broken. Still, it finds a worthy and useful place in my collection. Creative ideas are endless for discarded shells, even the broken ones. I recently covered a cross with broken shells to symbolize Jesus's brokenness for our sins (Isaiah 53:5).

God has many shells in His collection too, and He considers the imperfect ones beautiful and often the most useful of all. You may feel inadequate, but even when you were spiritually dead, God saw beauty and usefulness. You were found worthy to be included in His collection.

It takes time, effort, and sometimes money to collect shells; similarly, Jesus bought you with His life and has a purpose for you. My son was broken in drug addiction for years, but God gathered him up and is using him now as a pastor. God can use anyone, and He has the perfect idea for you. He's a master crafter with ideas beyond your wildest imagination (Ephesians 3:20).

* * * * * * * * * * *

Lord, You make beauty from ashes (Isaiah 61:3) so take my life and imperfections and make something beautiful and useful for Your glory. Amen.

Unshakeable Love

"Though the mountains be shaken and the hills be removed, yet my unfailing love for you will not be shaken nor my covenant of peace be removed," says the LORD, who has compassion on you.

ISAIAH 54:10 NIV

Enchanted Rock is a pink-granite batholith dome that rises 425 feet over the central Texas landscape. Legend says that the rock got its name because of the groaning sounds it made as it cooled in the evenings and because of the strange lights that sometimes appeared at the peak. Every weekend, hikers and campers make the trek to the top. It feels unshakeable.

Even if this rock could be shaken, God's love for us will never be shaken, nor will His covenant of peace be removed. In today's world it sometimes seems that contracts have an escape clause. But God does not do business that way. His covenant is a binding agreement, and was even ratified in our favor at the cross.

When we sin we may wonder if God still loves us, but our mistakes are not powerful enough to overwhelm the weight of God's love. We can't out-sin God's grace. Even if the mountains are shaken and the hills removed, God's love for us will not be shaken. When we stumble, we should fall into the arms of God. He redeems and restores us with His compassionate love.

* * * * * * * * * *

Lord, when I fear that my mistakes and failures can make You withdraw from me, remind me of Your unshakable love and draw me back to Your compassionate arms. Amen.

Cloud Messages

He covers the sky with clouds; he supplies the earth with rain and makes grass grow on the hills.

PSALM 147:8 NIV

Gorgeous masses of cumulus clouds recently caught my eye as they paraded across the bright blue sky. As cloud formations vary from day to day, their beauty amazes me each time I stop to notice. Do you remember finding pictures in the clouds? When our children were young, we would lie on a grassy slope, look up, and imagine that cloud shapes were bears, rabbits, and other animals.

In addition to pictures and beauty, clouds give us information. Meteorologists study these amazing sky features to formulate weather predictions. Do you glance skyward before grabbing an umbrella or packing a picnic basket?

Above all this, magnificent clouds can exemplify attributes of God. Dark nimbus clouds produce life-giving rain and remind us Jehovah Jireh is Provider. When clouds separate sunlight into individual beams shining toward the earth, they bring to mind how God opened heaven to send His Son as Savior. Sometimes the sun outlines the edges of gray clouds and brilliantly radiates outward. This glorious sight may prompt the thought: Jesus, Light of the World.

Clouds are remarkable creations that can turn our thoughts toward God. I think I'll grab a blanket, lie in the grass, and ponder His glory.

· · · · · · · · · · ·

Father God, may beautiful clouds lead me to praise You as Creator and Lord of all. Amen.

Planting Carrots

Everything should be done in a fitting and orderly way.

1 CORINTHIANS 14:40 NIV

Spring had arrived, and we'd decided to plant a garden. When I shook the carrot seeds out of the packet, I was amazed at how tiny they were in the palm of my hand. The man at the nursery had warned us to plant all our seeds sparingly, but these were so small . . . and I really wanted a large crop of carrots. So I sprinkled them thickly in the ground.

I think every single one of those tiny seeds took root and sprouted. As they grew, in a few short weeks they became a tangled mess. Each of them fighting for nutrients and space. Then, after lifting their green tops a couple of inches toward the sun, every single one withered and died, leaving me with only the bitter taste of disappointment and discouragement.

It was my overcrowded calendar that brought this memory to mind. God was warning me to plant fewer seeds and take time to nurture them. Otherwise I'd find myself with an empty garden and nothing but withered endeavors from pouring too many good things into my life.

* * * * * * * * * * *

Dear Lord, guard my time and give me wisdom to know where to spend my energy. Amen.

Toward the Light

You have been chosen by God himself . . . you are God's very own . . . so that you may show to others how God called you out of the darkness into His wonderful light.

I PETER 2:9 TLB

I once planted a sun-loving perennial on the north side of my house, hoping it would be happy getting late afternoon and evening sunlight. The saying that comes with perennials is: "The first year they sleep, the second year they creep, the third year they leap!" The flower didn't do much the first season, as I expected. The second year, it began to stretch, and as the summer progressed, it was clearly moving in one direction—toward the light it needed in order to thrive. The edge of the flowerbed enjoyed the most time in the sun, and that's where this flower was headed!

We do okay spending a little time in the light of God's presence, but do we want to survive or *thrive*? More time with God creates a brighter spirit, a bolder witness, a fuller blooming into all we were created to be.

The benefits of focusing on our Creator, leaning into His light, and spending time in His presence are countless and endless—peace comes, joy surfaces, hope emerges. Our hearts are strengthened and our spirits are nourished. We grow in the best possible way in the most important direction—ever closer to Him.

* * * * * * * * * *

Dear Father, today I'll stand in the light of Your presence, for strength, hope, wisdom, and growth. Amen.

Weeding Is Work

Cursed is the ground because of you; through painful toil you will eat food from it all the days of your life.

GENESIS 3:17 NIV

I finally had the garden I had always envisioned—tomatoes, cucumbers, and squash! I was so excited to see the plans start to come together. It wasn't easy. The ground was incredibly hard and clumpy. I turned it with a small hand spade for hours and achieved hardly anything! Thankfully, the next day my husband rented a large tiller and soon we had a lovely plot of ground thoroughly tilled. Still, every time I work in the garden, whether it's spring when I'm dealing with the hard ground, or mid-July when it's hotter than fire and the weeds are taking over, I'm always thinking of the curse.

The fact is, at creation the ground wasn't terrible to work with, but sin changed everything. The good news is that God designed us with the capacity to do the physical labor now required to work the land. The ground still produces the fruits and vegetables that we need for our survival. God reveals to us as we work that although we missed the mark for perfect conditions here on earth, He didn't abandon us without the resources to achieve the necessary results for our survival. God is good all the time and all the time God is good.

* * * * * * * * * * *

Thank You, Lord, that even as we live in a fallen world, You still care for us and meet our needs. Amen.

Neon Trees

He will be like a tree firmly planted by streams of water, which yields its fruit in its season and its leaf does not wither; and in whatever he does, he prospers.

PSALM 1:3 NASB

A creek runs through my neighbor's field. Even from a distance I can trace its winding path by the trees and shrubs flourishing along the banks. The fields parch during drought but the trees by the creek survive, nourished through deep roots spread into the moist earth.

When the psalmist sang of lush trees along a flowing river, he might have seen a creek like my neighbor's. The ever-present thirst in ancient desert dwellers prompted a perpetual search for an oasis. There were no road signs or flashing lights to draw them to a well. If vegetation flourished, they knew water flowed nearby. Even an illusion of an oasis motivated a nomad to change course toward a possible well.

I've watched deer and small animals traverse the field to gather at their watering hole. Like a drive-in neon sign, trees signal the presence of shelter and a source of cool refreshment. Nature's lowly creatures find provision and hear God's voice calling them to come and drink. To languish in a dry, parched field would be foolish when the source is so near. As the trees rustle and sway, God provides and speaks, beckoning the thirsty. I won't stay in the field and wither; I'll listen and run to the trees.

* * * * * * * * * *

Lord, thank You for both physical and spiritual nourishment. Amen.

Nightlight

You, LORD, keep my lamp burning; my God turns my darkness into light.

PSALM 18:28 NIV

Fireflies glittered in the pasture surrounding my daughter's home. As we strolled along the darkened path, she pointed to more fireflies sparkling in the trees like tiny Christmas lights. As a child, my friends and I spent summer evenings chasing the glowing bugs. If we caught one or two, we put them in glass jars with grass and drops of water and poked holes in the lid. When I spent the night in the upstairs room of my grandmother's house, I sometimes took a jar of fireflies caught earlier in the evening with me. The tiny bugs brought a comforting light to a little girl afraid of the dark.

What an awesome Creator we worship! He spoke light into existence on the first day of creation. He dwells in light. He loves us so much that He sent His Son to be the Light of the world. When we face difficult times—sickness, financial struggles, death of a loved one, loneliness—God is the One who can illuminate our darkness. The light of His presence brings peace and rest. We don't have to fear. Though the pain is real, the darkness will never extinguish the comfort of His light.

God's creation points us to Him. So when we see fireflies glow on summer evenings, may we praise the One who turns our darkness into light.

. . . .

Lord, thank You for shining the light of Your presence whenever I'm in the dark. Amen.

The Summer Storm

May the God of hope fill you with all joy and peace as you trust in him, so that you may overflow with hope by the power of the Holy Spirit.

ROMANS 15:13 NIV

I noticed the building clouds as I crammed supplies for the upcoming backyard Bible school into my SUV. The first fat raindrop plopped onto my head, and the sky darkened to gunmetal gray. The empty church seemed a better shelter to wait out the storm than my vehicle so I scurried inside. As thunder boomed and the foundation of the building shook, my heart felt heavy. *We'll have to cancel,* I thought. The canopy of trees swayed and webs of lightning illuminated the sky. However, in the quiet sanctuary, God spoke to my heart. *Be still and know that I am God.*

The storm diminished as quickly as it had appeared, and when I stepped outside, a fresh breeze met me instead of the sweltering humidity. I drove to the park pavilion and started unloading supplies while the other helpers arrived. Under the blue sky filled with songbirds, we played games with the children and told them of Jesus's love. I felt God's presence and I lifted a prayer of thanks. Maybe someday I'll learn to trust Him with everything. His plan is always so much better than mine.

* * * * * * * * * * *

Help me, Father, to trust You always. Please fill me with joy and peace so that my life may overflow with hope by the power of the Holy Spirit. Amen.

God Knows
What You Need

Your Father knows what you need before you ask him.

MATTHEW 6:8 NIV

As I filled my last hummingbird feeder right outside the sunroom where I spend most of my days writing, I could hardly wait to see my little feathered friends return. They are so cute and tiny and fast! I was so intrigued by these beautiful little birds that I wanted to know more about them, so I began my research and what I learned was fascinating.

For example, did you know that they are so little that five hummingbirds could fit in a person's hand? And, did you know that a hummingbird's beak is longer in proportion to its body than other birds' beaks? Neither of these unique characteristics is by mistake. You see, God made them tiny so they could fit inside flowers, and He gave them an extra-long beak so they could reach deep down into a tubular flower and get the nectar. God created them that way because He knew what they would need to not only survive, but thrive.

If God did that for the hummingbirds, don't you think He does the same thing for us? So no matter what you're facing today, you can rest in the knowledge that God knows what you need and has already provided it. What's more, you can count on Him being generous.

* * * * * * * * * * *

Lord, help me to see my needs as You do and be confident in Your care. Amen.

The Abundant Summer

Go to the ant . . . consider its ways and be wise! It has no commander, no overseer or ruler, yet it stores its provisions in summer and gathers its food at harvest.

PROVERBS 6:6–8 NIV

Nature advances the calendar from spring's restoration into summer's abundance. Longer days, brighter outlooks, refreshing rains, places to explore, and gardens to grow. Let's make the most of it! Get up and get moving.

I reflect on the ant's work ethic to become wise. Go, consider, store, and gather—a lot of action is required in the proverb's instructions. Wise advice warning me not to procrastinate. Like all seasons, summer is fleeting.

For the vegetable and fruit grower, summer creates the perfect opportunity to harvest a bounty of healthy food. Many generations of my family have preserved this abundance through canning and freezing. Like the ant, we are stocking away provisions for the winter. Tomatoes, green beans, squash, corn, relish, fruit jellies. I quickly learned you can't wait to can tomatoes when you feel like it. There is a limited time to preserve before ripe becomes rotten. Action is required on nature's timetable.

What do you enjoy about summer? Swimming, hiking, fishing, camping, gardening, biking. This season, immerse yourself into God's abundant nature and enjoy the beauty whether working or playing.

• • • • • • • • • • •

Lord, help me be like the ant, not only to take advantage of the abundance You provide this summer, but to also enjoy it. Amen.

Lily Clothes

Why do you worry about clothes? See how the flowers of the field grow. They do not labor or spin.

MATTHEW 6:28 NIV

Frantically, I swerved onto my street and sped down the hill mentally checking off all the items on my list. Make salsa for the farmers market, turn in the assignment for writing, call someone about the dryer, pick up chicken feed.

Suddenly, I see them: Wild tiger lilies on the edge of the property. Bright orange and red hues adorn elegant stems for the passerby's enjoyment. They're stunning. If I hadn't noticed them, they would still be there on the side of the road because our Creator—the Lord Most High—put them there.

Lately, I've been so worried about paying the bills that I've forgotten who spoke the world into being. He knows when a sparrow falls, and the number of hairs on my head. He even put all the stars into place just by a word.

Even more recently, I noticed white daisies in the pasture. Nearby, gigantic yellow blooms adorn thick green stems promising pattypan squash. The saucer-shaped squashes with the deep green center grow from the bottom of the bloom, pushing the bloom off and producing the fruit. Various bees swarm around them carrying their nectar to other places, making sweet honey for themselves. If God clothes the lilies and grows the squashes, He can handle my bills.

. . . .

Lord, forgive me for forgetting You are the great Creator and Sustainer. Amen.

The Path
of a Sand Dollar

*God created great sea creatures and every living thing that scurries
and swarms in the water, and every sort of bird—each producing
offspring of the same kind. And God saw that it was good.*

GENESIS 1:21 NLT

Most people are familiar with sand dollars—those round,
white disks available in a plethora of tourist shops
throughout coastal towns. Dried and bleached, they represent
pleasant, sun-drenched memories of wave-washed beaches.

Living sand dollars, however, are darker in color, from
beige to a deep purple. They mostly live in clusters on the
oceans' floor, where they eat by moving slowly across the sand.
In an area undisturbed by currents, a group of sand dollars can
leave extremely long trails, representing weeks, if not months,
of movement. While our lives seem to flash by, they plod along,
ending up only a few yards from where they were last week.
They do eat small animals, but they also scavenge, cleaning up
what others left behind.

God made "every living thing" in the ocean remarkable,
from the giant whales down to the microscopic plankton to
the plodding sand dollar. In each minute detail we can see the
glory of His work and the magnificence of His creative power.
Nothing is overlooked, in our lives or in the lives of the tiniest
of creatures.

. . . .

*God, we praise and thank You for the glorious creation around
us. Thank You for each loving detail You have put into the world
around us. Amen.*

Still Water Reflects

⸰⸰⸰⸰⸰⸰⸰⸰⸰⸰⸰⸰

Come to me. Get away with me and you'll recover your life. I'll show you how to take a real rest. Walk with me and work with me—watch how I do it. Learn the unforced rhythms of grace.

MATTHEW 11:28–29 MSG

What a great vacation we'd had, spending an entire week at the beach. There were long walks when we searched for shells and watched birds. My favorite part was hours spent lounging in beach chairs—feet in the sand.

One late afternoon, the blue sky mirrored the dusky blue of the ocean, and the tide began to turn. As the encroaching waves washed over my feet, I noticed something. When each wave receded, in its wake was left a a shallow film of water. It was so clear and calm I could see a perfect reflection of my face. This image was erased and replaced over and over again as rushing waves crashed upon the shore.

God used this visual wonder to remind me that when I get busy, rushing from thing to thing, it becomes harder and harder for my life to clearly reflect Christ. But when I slow down, living by His rhythm, His image is perfectly visible in all aspects of my life.

. . . .

Dear Lord, don't let me get caught in the pounding surf, but help me remember to refresh myself in the calm waters that reflect the light of Your Spirit. Amen.

A Song in the Dark

By day the LORD directs his love, at night his song is with me—
a prayer to the God of my life.

PSALM 42:8 NIV

As dusk settles across the land, wrapping the world in darkness, the whip-poor-will sings her song. This little winged beacon of God's glory reminds us not to be afraid of the pending darkness, for dawn will surely follow. Just before sunrise, while the world still sleeps, she patiently trumpets again, heralding the fulfillment of the promise. Light out of darkness. Her plaintive song sung in the night rises strong and sweet against a backdrop of silent anticipation, promising hope and the dawning of God's faithfulness upon all He has made.

Our God gives us songs in the night. His love reminds us that no darkness can prevent the coming of the light. Are you facing a long night in your life right now? Do your ears strain to hear the song of hope rising, signaling the coming of the dawn? Pour out your prayers to the God of your life and listen closely for the song He sings over you as you wait. Light is coming, His faithfulness speeds toward you like the rising of the sun.

. . . .

Lord, let me hear Your song in the night as I pour out my prayers
to You, the God of my life. Amen.

The Starry Sky

He determines the number of the stars; he gives to all of them their names.

PSALM 147:4 ESV

I stood, gazing at the starry sky. There were so many stars, and they were so beautiful. The new moon didn't give off much light, and there were no lights in the area to diminish the number of stars we could see. During my childhood on the farm, we had no outside lights nor did our neighbors who lived nearby. Most summer evenings were spent sitting on our front porch after supper, enjoying the coolness after the heat of the day. We listened to the whip-poor-wills' call and the katydids' chirp and the grown-ups' talk about the day.

My daddy joined us as we "star gazed" and pointed out the various constellations. He knew them all and told us their names and made sure we could see the outline in our minds. I remember the beauty of the stars and how pretty the dusty Milky Way was. I remember thinking about God and how big He must be to make all those stars so far away.

He is a big God, awesome in power and might! He made the beauty of the heavens and the earth and gives them to us to enjoy. He loves us so much that He surrounds us with incredible wonders. Just look around!

Gracious God, thank You for Your beautiful creation and for loving me so much that You gave it to me to enjoy. Amen.

Drink Up!

You, God, are my God, earnestly I seek you; I thirst for you, my whole being longs for you, in a dry and parched land.

PSALM 63:1 NIV

Our youngest daughter was never your typical girlie girl growing up so when she asked for a pet lizard, we weren't surprised. That's when Rocky, an African fat-tailed gecko, came into our lives. He was cute, I suppose, as lizards go, and Ally adored him. In fact, she loved him so much that she often took him out of his aquarium and played with him. Well, one night she forgot to put Rocky back in his habitat before falling asleep. The next morning, we couldn't find that little lizard anywhere. He was simply gone.

Weeks later, as I stumbled into the kitchen in the middle of the night to get a glass of water, I was instantly shocked out of my sleepy state, and so was my husband, when I screamed "SNAKE!" But it wasn't a snake. It was Rocky! We thought he was gone forever but apparently he was so thirsty he had risked his freedom to come out of hiding just for a drink of water.

That got me thinking. I should be so thirsty for the things of God that I would risk everything to drink them in. I should be so in love with His Word that I crave it—even in the middle of the night.

* * * * * * * * * *

Father, help me remember that I can satisfy my thirst by drinking in Your Word. Amen.

Unfortunate Encounter

Purify me from my sins, and I will be clean; wash me, and I will be whiter than snow.

PSALM 51:7 NLT

I found my husband out in the backyard one day, up to his elbows in a solution of baking soda and peroxide, leaned over our skunk-sprayed pup. Our dog, Bear, saw the skunk, refused to listen to his master's voice, and lunged headfirst into an unfortunate encounter. The consequences of his actions were repeated scrubbings and banishment to the garage.

Like Bear we can get ourselves into stinky situations when we refuse to listen to our Master's voice. When we chase after things we shouldn't, the consequences can be disastrous. When we allow the Devil to spray his foul odor on us, we carry his stench until it is washed away. We can't get the odor off on our own. Jesus is the only one who can make us clean.

Fortunately for Bear, he has a loving master who cares enough to endure the horrid skunk spray to wash him clean. Fortunately for us, we have a loving Master who willingly left His throne in heaven, came to earth as a man, endured all the hardships we endure, and paid the price for the debt of sin we owed but could never pay. He did all this to remove sin's stench and wash us whiter than snow.

• • • • • • • • • •

Jesus, thank You for enduring the cross to make me clean and whole. Amen.

An Invitation to Rest

So there is a special rest still waiting for the people of God. For all who have entered into God's rest have rested from their labors, just as God did after creating the world.

HEBREWS 4:9–10 NLT

When elephants sleep, the entire herd lies down to rest at the same time, flopping down one after another like a chain of dominoes. An elephant changing position in its sleep can send a rippling chain reaction through the herd as all the elephants adjust themselves more comfortably and slip back into their slumber. Few animals can sleep so securely in the dangerous African plains—but then few animals are willing to risk challenging an elephant, even a sleeping one. An elephant's secure position in the food chain allows it to rest.

Our secure position in Christ allows us to rest. Rest can seem hard to find in a world that drives us to produce, consume, and prove our worth. Spiritually, the pursuit of perfection or a sense that we need to earn God's favor can hinder our rest. Entering God's rest means that we can cease our efforts to earn our own salvation. Christ has already purchased it on the cross, freeing us to serve out of gratitude instead of guilt. We can stop our pointless pursuit of perfection and start enjoying the benefits of God's rest.

. . . .

Lord, thank You that I can enjoy the security and freedom of Your rest because of what Christ has done for me. Amen.

Unseen Dangers

May your love and faithfulness always protect me.

PSALM 40:11 NIV

Did you know that in the South, certain water snakes swim with only their head poking through the water? This small indentation becomes a warning sign of danger that the snake's body (often four feet long) is slithering beneath the surface.

There are many dangers that sneak into our lives, unseen at first—crumbling faith foundations, a breakdown of the family, seeds of violence, allegiance to terrorism. Suddenly we wonder how life got this way. Our cunning Enemy begins by revealing a small "head," just the tip of a fixation swimming our way. A suggestion that we don't need God after all, or that truth is whatever we want it to be. But the slithering tail can choke the life out of us before we know it.

Henri Nouwen prayed, "Do not allow evil powers to seduce me with the complexities of the world's problems, but give me the strength to think clearly, speak freely, and act boldly in Your service. Give me the courage to show the dove in a world so full of serpents."

In the midst of whatever comes our way, God is here promising His protection. He helps us to be wise to the ways of the world and to stand firm.

* * * * * * * * * * *

Lord, while I can't imagine all the lurking hidden dangers, I'm grateful for Your wisdom and protection. Amen.

DAY
196

Rushing Waters

I trust in God's unfailing love for ever and ever.

PSALM 52:8 NIV

A relentless roar could be heard as we approached the overlook. All other sounds were blocked out by the enormous rush of water descending almost fifty feet to the basin below. This was the upper Tahquamenon Falls of Michigan. The average flow of water over this waterfall is seven thousand gallons per second. It is one of the largest waterfalls east of the Mississippi. I couldn't help but be impressed by this mighty, seemingly unending flow of fresh water. We stood on the overlook enjoying the sense of power and strength that emanates from the falls. Many years ago, men had tried to dam up the flow of the mighty river but to no avail. The rushing waters would not be stopped.

God's love for us is like that. It cannot be stopped. It flows on unending and unfailing. He assures us that His love is constant, even when our lives seem to be in chaos. We may struggle for days or years; we may fail time after time; we may feel alone and abandoned. Yet Jesus is there with His eternal love for us. This promise is given in God's holy Word, and the bottom line of faith is to rely on that promise. We can count on the rushing waters of His love to fill us to overflowing.

. . . .

Father, thank You for Your unending, unchanging love for me. Amen.

Time Limitations

∘₀⸰₀∘∘O∘ ₀⸰₀∘∘O

Lord, you have been our dwelling place throughout all genera-
tions. Before the mountains were born or you brought forth the
whole world, from everlasting to everlasting, you are God. . . . A
thousand years in your sight are like a day that has just gone by.

PSALM 90:1–2, 4 NIV

As a child, I remember planting some flower seeds with
high expectations. I was quickly disappointed the next
morning when I returned to my garden bed. After spending
my previous morning carefully digging holes, planting seeds,
covering them with dirt, and carefully watering them, I fully
expected to see a beautiful row of flowers. Sadly, flowers don't
grow up from seeds overnight. It takes time.

Being limited by time, mankind works within the span
of a twenty-four hour day, a seven-day week, and a 365-day
year. The idea that God is not limited to that is awe inspiring!
How in the world has God always existed? Before time, God
was there. Before the earth was formed, God was there. After
time ends and there is no more time, God will be there. One
thousand years is like one day in God's sight. Astounding!

While we are limited by time and space, our creator God
exists beyond those boundaries, and so does His love. Our
boundless God has a boundless love for all of us. Unbelievable
but true!

• • • • • • • • • • •

Lord, I just want to worship You for being such a great God; time
and space have no control over You, but rather You have control
over them. Amen.

Sounds of the Species

Let the words of my mouth and the meditation of my heart be acceptable in Your sight.

PSALM 19:14 NKJV

As if the conductor's baton was poised in midair waiting to signal an orchestra to begin, the theater of my yard was silent. Then, the music began with a song from a gray-suited mockingbird perched on the holly bush. Cicadas performed several bars with the accompaniment of bamboo chimes. Occasionally, a wren's soprano notes or a woodpecker's rhythmic drumming joined in the chorus.

Many of these creatures are identified by sound alone. The unique voice of a species often draws our attention to God. For example, a sparrow's song can remind us of His care for the little brown bird and for us. Humans use their voices to identify themselves as well. Tone and volume say a lot about what we're feeling and our attitude. Sometimes we offer positive things that support and motivate; other times more negative things come out. When that happens I'm thankful for forgiveness and for the guidance Scripture offers us.

The Bible instructs us about speaking to our fellow man. We are to share the gospel and refrain from complaints and false statements. Ephesians 4:29 cautions us to avoid distasteful language and speak words that encourage. Our voice is a gift from God. What a joy to use our words to praise Him and lift up others.

. . . .

Lord Jesus, fill my heart with words that praise You and edify people around me. Amen.

God's Perspective

"For my thoughts are not your thoughts, neither are your ways my ways," declares the LORD. "As the heavens are higher than the earth, so are my ways higher than your ways and my thoughts than your thoughts."

ISAIAH 55:8–9 NIV

A couple of years ago my husband and I had the opportunity to visit Rocky Mountain National Park. We were there in October, just before the Trail Ridge Road—reaching elevations over twelve thousand feet—closed for the season. Already hemmed in by ice and snow, the vistas from this road were breathtaking. But as much as we wanted to admire the panoramas, the steep road with patches of ice kept us from taking in the beauty of God's creation all around us as we drove.

We pulled into every overlook, drinking in the amazing scenery. It was interesting to look back at the road we'd traveled. It had seemed much scarier when we were driving it than it did from our elevated vantage point.

This is so much like our spiritual lives. We travel through the stresses of life, aware of God at work around us. We know He's with us no matter how scary the journey, but it's only when we pause and pull over that we can look back with His perspective and see that He really did have a plan—a path through what we'd been experiencing.

* * * * * * * * * * *

Dear Lord, remind me to take time to stop and spend time with You so I can see things from Your perspective. Amen.

Leave the Leaves

Be truly glad. There is wonderful joy ahead, even though you must endure many trials for a little while. These trials will show that your faith is genuine.

1 PETER 1:6–7 NLT

For many people, raking leaves is an autumn obligation. Remember when it used to be fun? Pile them up, run, jump, repeat! My father used to hide a dollar in the pile for us to find. But for those who now have to rake, bag, and dispose of them, the memories are all we have. But do we really need to rake? Why not leave the leaves? Fallen leaves actually mulch the ground, providing important nutrients and protection from weed growth—a part of God's perfect providential design. Raking can take away their intended benefits.

Trials can be like those fallen leaves we'd like to rake and get rid of, but the verse above urges us to count it all joy, knowing that it will prove our faith genuine. Other verses assure us that adversity creates character and hope (Romans 5:3–4), peaceful results (Hebrews 12:11), and patience and wholeness (James 1:2–4).

Trials, just like fallen leaves, are but for a season. God will use your trials to your benefit, and then restore you strong and complete (1 Peter 5:10)—just like a tall, healthy, fruit-bearing tree.

* * * * * * * * * * *

Lord, help me trust You to work out Your plans using each trial to help me grow, and make me healthy, fruitful, and complete for all You designed me to be. Amen.

Stay Salty

You are the salt of the earth. But what good is salt if it has lost its flavor? Can you make it salty again? It will be thrown out and trampled underfoot.

MATTHEW 5:13 NLT

Salt, both today and in ancient times, has been used to add flavor and richness to food. It was, and still is, an integral part of life. Salt was so important that Jesus urged His followers to be like salt to the world, adding flavor and richness to it.

Yet Jesus warns that salt can lose its saltiness. In our modern world of processed and purified salt, that makes no sense. But the salt of the biblical world was different. It often came from the Dead Sea and was not pure sodium chloride, so it could indeed lose its saltiness. Then it was no longer good for anything except to be thrown out and trampled underfoot.

As followers of Christ, we must not lose our saltiness either. It is so easily washed away with harsh words, bitter ways, and selfish actions. Instead, we are to flavor our every word, our every action with the love of our Lord and the love of our fellow man—the two greatest commandments (Matthew 22:37–39). We are to be "salt" in a world that so desperately needs the flavor and richness of the love of Christ.

* * * * * * * * * * * *

Lord, show me how I may serve You and be salt to this world around me today. Amen.

Night Chorus

Each day the LORD pours his unfailing love upon me, and through each night I sing his songs, praying to God who gives me life.

PSALM 42:8 NLT

My family and I live in a neighborhood with an active nightlife. Now, this is not a case of noisy neighbors or disreputable establishments carrying on business at odd hours. No, this is nature's nightlife.

During the spring and fall when the windows are open more often than not, you can hear the critters on the night shift starting to assemble. To the restless ear this can be annoying; but to the person willing to listen, the seemingly chaotic fracas turns into the tuning of a terrestrial orchestra setting the stage for an evening of interdependent melodies and charming harmonies.

I was concerned at first about being able to sleep for I have been known to have a restless ear. And I also knew there was a possibility that I could let that concern grow into anxiety, which would increase the odds that I wouldn't sleep. So I took a deep breath and told myself that rain often lulls me to sleep, therefore this could too.

A funny thing happened when I took the time to listen: I didn't know whether to let it lull me to sleep or to stay awake and enjoy it. Either way, I found peaceful rest where I was least expecting it.

* * * * * * * * * * *

Lord, help me to be patient and willing to listen, and to pick up on the song You have for my life. Amen.

Two Bushels of Beauty

*The LORD doesn't see things the way you see them. People judge by
outward appearance, but the LORD looks at the heart.*

1 SAMUEL 16:7 NLT

The mountains of North Carolina are dotted with apple
orchards. I love picking the red orbs that hang from rows
of gnarled trees and visiting the stands that sell cold, sweet
cider.

Since I enjoy making my own jelly, I pick only the prettiest apples so I can produce beautiful jars of delicious fruit that
I give as Christmas gifts. Although it takes longer to inspect
each apple instead of picking randomly, I smile when my
baskets are filled with near perfect specimens.

Last fall, I had already put aside all my jelly for gifts when
a neighbor stopped by with two bushels of horribly blemished
apples. Assuming those apples would be blemished on the
inside as well, I did not want to peel the ugly green, spotted
apples. After preparing them, however, I discovered they had
a far better taste than the prettier apples.

Sometimes we feel blemished by our past mistakes. We
believe others look at us as though we are ugly, and we may
think we are unworthy to be used in God's kingdom. We have
all made mistakes, some producing notable scars, but our
Lord looks upon our repentant hearts and, like the spotted
apples, gives us grace to produce sweet fruit.

. . . .

*Thank You, Lord, for always seeing beauty, not blemishes, in Your
children. Amen.*

Safely Above

Those who hope in the LORD will renew their strength; they will soar on wings like eagles.

ISAIAH 40:31 NIV

Years ago I wrote an article on the bald eagle. My favorite discovery about them was how they deal with a coming storm. It is both magnificent and inspiring.

An eagle doesn't fly around it or hide away and wait for it to pass. It will sit out in the open and wait for the winds ahead of the storm and then take flight. Setting its wings, the eagle will allow the headwinds to carry it high above and beyond the tempest, safely and effortlessly.

Oh, to be able to handle life's battles with the same calm and courage. To resolve each and every time to wait on God, to let the wind of His Spirit lift us above the fight, to be certain our victory is in setting our hearts and minds on His unfailing love.

It's hard for us to make it that simple. We tend to dwell on circumstances and give in to worry. We like to get involved before realizing that ultimately we have little or no control over the outcome. Unless all our cares are put into God's able hands, they become a weight in our hearts; and instead of rising above the storm, we sink into it and become overwhelmed. *Everything* must go to God for *anything* to go right.

* * * * * * * * * * *

Dear Father, give me the courage to give everything to You. Amen.

Creation's Consistencies

I the LORD do not change.

MALACHI 3:6 NIV

God is neither boring nor plain. His diverse creation reveals an imagination that is boundless and intricate as well as practical and functional. The multitude of wonderful plants we call trees illustrates this truth.

We can learn of God's consistency in the way that trees of the same species conform to similar characteristics that allow us to depend on certain regularities. Eastern white pines, for example, consistently have five needles, their branches are borne in whorls, and the bark of all the specimens exhibit similar characteristics. Likewise, the lumber produced has comparable strengths, colors, and patterns that carpenters and woodworkers depend on for their projects.

Imagine if one tree of the species had two needles and another eighteen. Imagine if the wood of one was light while that of another was variegated. Such unpredictability would frustrate foresters, builders, and woodworkers. Similar common traits are shared by individuals within all species and demonstrate complex order and predictability.

Creation's consistencies reveal the dependability of its Creator. God is not compassionate one moment and vindictive another, and His plan for salvation doesn't change with clothing styles. Thankfully, we can depend on Him to be who He has always been.

* * * * * * * * * * *

Father, I praise You for Your creativity and I will rest in Your dependability. Amen.

Taking Flight

May your unfailing love be my comfort, according to your promise to your servant.

PSALM 119:76 NIV

The butterfly landed for a moment on the grave and then flew off into the sky. A calm came over me, and in my spirit I sensed that still, small voice: *She has earned her wings and is whole.*

The graveside service for my grandmother had ended and a handful of family members huddled together, searching for a way to say final good-byes. As the group broke to go, I lingered, praying for help in dealing with the loss of the lady who loved me more than anything. Out of nowhere, the butterfly made its appearance again, and I smiled toward heaven with the reassurance that my grandmother was at home.

The transformation from caterpillar to butterfly comes with much pain and struggle, but something beautiful emerges in the end. Life can be the same way, and ever since that encounter, God has opened my eyes to the beauty of this creature.

A few days ago I arrived early for an important appointment. I found a quiet spot outside and prayed for guidance. As I rose to go inside, a butterfly hovered in front of me for a moment and then went on its way. *I get the picture, Lord.* I knew the meeting would go well, and it did—not because of the butterfly, but because of the One who directed its flight.

• • • • • • • • • •

Father, thank You for butterflies and other creatures that remind me of Your loving care. Amen.

Trees of Old

The LORD is my rock, my fortress and my deliverer; my God is my rock, in whom I take refuge, my shield and the horn of my salvation, my stronghold.

PSALM 18:2 NIV

A number of trees standing on the earth today sprouted from the soil long before Christ was born. The Pando trees in Utah—a colony of quaking aspen whose trunks are linked underground—are thought to be the world's longest-lasting. In California's Sierra Nevada range, some of the sequoia trees—the world's largest trees—are older than three thousand years. These relics remind us of God's mighty, eternal hand. Through the ages, they have survived downpours, intense snow, droughts, and changes in the climate. The bark of the California redwoods is even resistant to forest fires.

As God preserves these amazing trees, He preserves us as we go through life's trials. He gives us spiritual nourishment when we hunger for wisdom, a tender heart when we thirst for love, and a shelter to survive the storms life brings. He is our rock, our stronghold.

The ancient trees remind us how short our lives are. Imagine all the generations these amazing trees have silently witnessed. God has chosen to number our years here on earth, but He promises everlasting life to those who believe and follow Him. Instead of perishing, our souls will remain in His hands—outliving the mightiest trees.

* * * * * * * * * * *

Father, grant me Your eternal perspective so I may stay hopeful about all You have in store for me. Amen.

Don't Give Up

With God everything is possible.

MATTHEW 19:26 NLT

In the Blue Ridge Mountains not far from Mt. Mitchell, a path winds steadily up. Hikers must maneuver a steep terrain and stop frequently to catch their breath. Many times, I thought I was at the summit. *Just a few more steps*, I told myself, only to arrive and see the path extend ahead. I thought of going back. The sun beat on my face and gnats swarmed me, but I pressed on. My calves and glutes burned and my heart pounded. I pushed myself just a little bit farther—to that next ridge, to that next tree, to that next bend in the path.

At times, we all experience similar life situations. Our strength wears out and the temptation to quit won't budge. We might even feel like we're walking alone. Jesus is with us and He cheers us on. We never walk alone. And sometimes He hides the top from view because if we were to see the distant peak, we would give up. Keep climbing. God will provide strength, encouragement, and respite for along the way. Even if it looks impossible, know that "with God everything is possible."

No matter what mountain you're climbing, making the summit is possible when God is your guide. When you finally reach the top, the view is pure euphoria.

. . . .

Father, please provide me the wherewithal to keep climbing and not give up when discouragement drags me down. Help me to sense You cheering me on. Amen.

Pumpkin Vine Runaway

༄ ༀ ༁ ༂ ༃ ༄ ༅ ༆ ༇ ༈

Before the harvest, when the blossom is over, and the flower becomes a ripening grape, he cuts off the shoots with pruning hooks and the spreading branches he lops off and clears away.

ISAIAH 18:5 ESV

My husband plants one of the prettiest gardens in our community. He enjoys inviting neighbors to pick baskets of tomatoes, cucumbers, and beans—at least until last year when I was given packs of pumpkin seeds.

I envisioned beautiful pumpkins for fall decoration on our farmhouse porch. My heart was happy as I dug the holes for the pumpkin seeds and mounded the garden soil—rich and dark as chocolate cake—around my plants.

A few weeks later, my husband made it clear he was not pleased with my handiwork. "Honey, these vines will soon take over the garden and choke out the other vegetables and fruits," he said.

I watered my rapidly growing plants with some dismay after discovering he was correct. The vines had taken over his garden. I was forced to prune my vines.

Sometimes we plant unhealthy habits in our lives and destructive thoughts in our minds. Like the pumpkin vines, they grow at a rapid rate and take over the good in our lives. Our heavenly Father prunes our lives to help us grow, not to punish us. The promise of greater fruitfulness outweighs the sting of the pruning shears.

• • • • • • • • • • •

Father, help me realize that You always have good in mind for me when I need You to prune. Amen.

The Swallow's Nest

Even the sparrow has found a home, and the swallow a nest for herself, where she may have her young—a place near your altar, LORD Almighty, my King and my God.

PSALM 84:3 NIV

The young swallow dipped behind the turret of the ancient northern gate of Fez, Morocco. Moments later, she hurried across the wall, returning again with a small insect in her beak. She was tending her young, and they were tucked safely in the heights far above the busy, crowded street below. I was a young mother myself, and we had just moved to a new and noisy place far from home. The image of the swallow caring for her young was a poignant picture of my own life at that time.

Wherever we go in the world, wherever we lay down our heads, we have a home that is unchanging. Our God is our home; He is our place of refuge and safe dwelling. If the sparrow knows this, if she can find security in the heights, above the dangers of the world below, can we not also find confidence in our God who is our strong tower? We can make our home near His altar, tucked safely right up next to the Lord, our King and our God. We will be safe there from the scuffle and bustle of the world.

• • • • • • • • • • •

Lord, be my dwelling place, my home, no matter where I am today. Amen.

The Rock That
Swam Away

෴ ෴

How many are your works, LORD! In wisdom you made them all; the earth is full of your creatures. There is the sea, vast and spacious, teeming with creatures beyond number—living things both large and small.

PSALM 104:24–25 NIV

Scuba diving brought me more pleasure than any other hobby I've had. Few places on earth so gloriously display God's bounty as a reef loaded with colorful plants and creatures.

On one particular dive, I drifted lazily around a reef, taking my time spotting fish and collecting a few shells. As I neared the end of my dive, I spotted a clam shell propped upright in the sand between two dark gray, mottled rocks. I paused and reached down carefully to pluck it free only to have one of the rocks shudder and scurry away. I jerked back, astonished, much to the amusement of my dive buddies. It was a rockfish, which feeds on smaller fish that live in the reef. Its bumpy surface and multiple colors make it look just like the reef to fool potential food . . . and the occasional diver.

What a glorious design! Every part of the reef, flora and fauna alike, fit together intimately, supporting all others, each life dovetailing into the other in a splendid whole. Form and function, beauty and practicality, all revealing God's remarkable creation.

. . . .

God, thank You for all Your gifts in nature, Your beauty and intricate design, which supports all of us and brings us joy. Amen.

Burning Bright

*You're here to be light, bringing out the God-colors in the world.
. . . If I make you light-bearers, you don't think I'm going to hide
you under a bucket, do you? I'm putting you on a light stand.
Now that I've put you there on a hilltop, on a light stand—shine!*

MATTHEW 5:14–16 MSG

One of the things I learned to do well in Girl Scouts was build a fire. A fire that will last begins with a layer of tinder—small dry twigs that catch fire when touched with a match. Once we have our tinder, we strike a match and set it on fire. As the flame begins to burn, we add kindling—dry sticks that snap in two. After the kindling becomes a blaze we feed the fire with larger branches. Thin branches of fuel are added first, then thicker ones.

As with building a fire, we all start out as dry tinder. Touched by the Holy Spirit, our flame ignites. The kindling of God's Word helps our fire grow. Old habits are burned away by its power. We feed the flame with solid fuel gained from digging deeper into the Bible and daily applying it to our lives. We surround ourselves with godly people who give good counsel and deepen our prayer life. Our once small flame becomes a blazing bonfire, burning bright within us.

* * * * * * * * * * *

Father, keep my flame burning bright for You, and let my light shine, drawing others to the Spirit who ignited a spark in me. Amen.

Blue Skies
and Clear Nights

*Praise him, sun and moon! Praise him, all you twinkling stars!
Praise him, skies above!*

PSALM 148:3–4 NLT

There's a lot of talk about North Carolina Blue where I live. You can hear about it in songs, you can see it on shirts and hats and at sports events. Since I've lived in the state for a while, I've seen a lot of North Carolina Blue skies turn into clear, crisp nights. In the summer, sometimes I lie on the grass and gaze up at the heavens. There are so many variations of green in the trees that frame the blue sky. The contrast is astounding.

September brings cooler weather and October promises colored trees and crisp nights. Often, we sit on the porch steps and gaze up at the stars. Our dogs sit next to us, and our kitty climbs on top of us, purring contentedly. We wear cozy jackets and stare starry-eyed at God's canopy—arms around each other and our animals, and we are content.

There is something about being in the country, away from all man-made lights, and viewing the stars. It makes me feel small and my God big. And that's the way it's supposed to be. Through the ages, people have gazed at the stars and have known there is a Creator. And those who are wise praise Him.

Lord, help me to embrace my insignificance so that I can understand my significance. Amen.

Go Deep to Find the Treasure

ஃ O∘˚o°˚O ஃ O∘˚o°˚O

It was to us that God revealed these things by his Spirit. For his Spirit searches out everything and shows us God's deep secrets.

1 CORINTHIANS 2:10 NLT

Our family once visited a ghost town with an abandoned gold mine. I don't remember the town well, but the mine is still clear in my memory. Going into the tunnel, the darkness enveloped us as the earthy smell surrounded us. I reached out and touched the sharp rocks that jutted from the walls, marveling at the effort it took to get to the mother lode that once resided deep in the earth.

As the guide explained the mining process, she shared that gold in the earth didn't look like what we might expect. The blue-toned rocks brought to the surface had to endure a purification process before they were recognizable as gold.

I'm struck by how many things God had to teach me in that mine. In our lives, the treasure we've been given isn't always easily accessible. We must go deep to dig it out. And what we find doesn't always reflect its value. Those dark places in our lives hold treasure. When we do go deep and bring out what we find, it's only in God's light and purification process that it becomes the treasure we seek.

. . . .

Dear Lord, help me be willing to go deep to find the treasure You've buried just for me. Amen.

Butterfly GPS

In your unfailing love you will lead the people you have redeemed.
In your strength you will guide them to your holy dwelling.

EXODUS 15:13 NIV

Monarch butterflies visit our garden every year on their long trip back to the forests of Mexico. But the butterflies that make the three-thousand-mile journey are not the same butterflies that made the journey the year before. In fact, only every fourth generation of butterflies makes the trip. This October it will be the great-grandchildren of the butterflies that made it the year before. God provides guidance for a new generation of butterflies to return to the same group of trees every year.

During the Exodus, God led His people with a pillar of cloud by day and a pillar of fire by night. He provided food for them to eat, water for them to drink, and protected them from the neighboring armies. God had redeemed His people from slavery, and despite their frequent failures, He continued to love and guide them until they reached their promised home.

God may not lead us with pillars of cloud and fire, but He still works to direct and guide us through the counsel of His Word and the prompting of the Spirit. Just as God guides the butterflies to a place of safety they have never seen, God guides us to find our safety and rest in Him.

. . . .

Lord, lead me to the place in our relationship where I find safety and rest in You. Amen.

Why the Donkey Speaks

The donkey said to Balaam, "Am I not your own donkey, which you have always ridden, to this day? Have I been in the habit of doing this to you?" "No," he said.

NUMBERS 22:30 NIV

Ever read something in the Bible that just makes you scratch your head? The story of Balaam and his donkey is that story for me. While the angel of the Lord blocking the road was visible to the donkey, Balaam did not see him. When the donkey refused to pass, Balaam beat him three different times. Finally, the donkey opened its mouth and spoke to Balaam. Stranger than fiction, Balaam answered him! The passage is clear, they had a conversation. Then the Lord—who opened the donkey's mouth—opened Balaam's eyes and he knew his donkey had saved him.

Has God ever used an unusual circumstance to get your attention? Perhaps He has used some form of His creation—a storm, a flood, a stray animal—to get you to turn around from a path He didn't want you to take. Perhaps not as dramatic as the story of Balaam and his donkey, but we know that God has used unusual means to reach out to us. When He needs to get our attention about something important, He may use a thing of nature to speak to us and, wonder of wonders, we might just speak back without surprise.

* * * * * * * * * * *

May I be aware, Lord, when You are trying to get my attention to change my direction. Amen.

Angry Bees

Woe to the earth and the sea, because the devil has gone down to you! He is filled with fury, because he knows that his time is short.

REVELATION 12:12 NIV

We were so enjoying the college football game. Our team was playing great, we had wonderful seats, and it was an especially sunny and warm afternoon for late October in Indiana. It was a perfect day . . . except for the pesky bees! They were everywhere, and they were aggressive!

I had been to a few football games earlier in the season and hadn't noticed the crazy buzzing bugs. I commented to my friend, "I think these bees are extra angry because it's about to turn cold and they know their time is short." I was just being snarky but as it turns out, I was right. In some bee species, the male bees die off in the winter months while the queen bee and some worker bees hibernate, rarely venturing out of the hive.

Later that night I was thinking about those annoying bees and I wondered if that's why Satan and his "worker bees" are so aggressive these days. He probably knows his time is short because the Lord is coming back soon. I believe we need to be aware of this fact so that we're not surprised by the increasing evil in the world today. The Devil may buzz, but Jesus has already taken his stinger.

* * * * * * * * * *

Father, help me to be aware of the Enemy's schemes while being ever mindful of Your presence. Amen.

So Long Snake

Then the LORD God said to the serpent, "Because you have done this, you are cursed more than all animals . . . . You will crawl on your belly, groveling in the dust as long as you live."

GENESIS 3:14 NLT

Recently, I saw a friend's post on Facebook that really caught my attention. A long, black snake had slithered onto her quaint little porch and set up camp in her quiet time area—the place where she reads her Bible and prays every morning. Initially, I was just horrified by the thought of that huge snake invading my friend's quiet time spot. I wondered if a snake could possibly slither its way onto my porch. And then I realized, it already had.

Okay, I haven't actually encountered a snake on my porch in my quiet time area. The Enemy usually comes in more sneakily than that to steal my time with God. One of Satan's favorite ways to distract me is by keeping me busy. And he is so sneaky that he will even keep me busy with godly activities such as directing Vacation Bible School or writing this year's Christmas program. Both of those ventures are worthy endeavors, but not if they take away from my quiet time with God.

It's not easy, but it's worth protecting my time with God above all else. And I really enjoy saying "So long, snake! You're not welcome here."

. . . .

Father, help me give You first place in my life. Amen.

Majesty and Might

⁂ ⁂ ⁂ ⁂ ⁂ ⁂ ⁂

Mightier than the thunder of great waters, mightier than the breakers of the sea—the LORD on high is mighty.

PSALM 93:4 NIV

My husband and I posed for a requisite photo in front of the Lower Falls in Yellowstone National Park. How could we resist? The backdrop was the epitome of majesty and might. Named "Artist Point" back in 1890, this *majesty* is indeed divine art. White foam spilling over spectacular canyon walls made up of many colors of rhyolite rock—reds, pinks, oranges, and yellows.

But the *might* is there as well. Twice as high as Niagara Falls, this marvel pushes over 63,500 gallons of water per second over its cataract. Standing there, we are speechless—in complete awe of God.

Do you ever feel that way? When He presents you with something so majestically beautiful that it takes your breath away? Or when He has done something so mightily powerful that you cannot even believe you doubted Him? Grandeur can make us feel small and unworthy. Why would the Creator of all this be concerned with my little life?

Because of love. He did it all for you and me because He loves us. All the beauty and all the power, the majesty and might are there just waiting for us to embrace them. It makes me want to sing.

* * * * * * * * * * *

Lord, truly all nature sings at the sights and sounds of Your creation; may I always embrace Your majesty and might, praising You forever! Amen.

Frost or Fruition

From whose womb has come the ice? And the frost of heaven, who has given it birth?

JOB 38:29 NASB

Each spring I watch and pray over the timing of the frost, knowing the outcome is entirely in God's hands. The Lord is in control and I am not. The dismal reality of frost on the budding trees brings great disappointment; there will be no pies. I can moan if the pattern repeats again the following year, but there will still be no pies.

God allows untimely frosts. Just as projects are ready to launch, plans are made, or achievements are anticipated, a brutal frost might descend with vigor and nip it all in the bud. There's no fruit from the efforts, no delicious aroma of baked success, and no stockpile of goods stored for future enjoyment.

Yet, I'm determined to wait. I'm confident the harvest will come and trust in God's faithfulness. A frost from heaven can be an opportunity to experience the Lord as my sustenance and His Word as my nourishment. I've learned delayed fruit still comes to fruition.

Eventually the blossoms produce and fruit is on my table again. I'm reminded by the heavy-laden boughs that God's timing is always perfect. Life may be put on hold but I remember I am held. When I wait on Him, the pie is delicious.

* * * * * * * * * * * *

Lord, teach me to use waiting times to deepen my relationship with You. Amen.

Taming Tongues
and Wild Horses

⁘ ☉∘°∘°☉ ⁘ ☉∘°∘°☉

*If we put bits into the mouths of horses so that they obey us, we
guide their whole bodies as well . . . . So also the tongue is a small
member, yet it boasts of great things.*

JAMES 3:3, 5 ESV

As a young teenager, my daughter was given her first
horse. For her, the idea of owning a horse was amazing!
Unfortunately, her joy quickly turned to despair because that
horse did *not* like taking a bit. Horses by nature are wild. They
have been domesticated through the centuries by humans.
Yet even trained horses can remain headstrong. Sweet and
docile animals don't necessarily need a bit that will grab their
attention with a bite of pain. For horses with more "spunk,"
however, the bit will inflict some "attention-grabbing" in
their lips.

This passage in James is fascinating in the way it sets the
stage for us to understand just how difficult it truly is to control our tongues. God created the horse with a wild spirit, and
we have learned how to train them into service for our needs.
Likewise, God's Word teaches us here also that indeed our
tongue can be controlled by the Spirit, or a bit, that He gives
us. When we allow the Holy Spirit to control our tongue, we
are in a better position for God to use us for His service.

• • • • • • • • • •

*Father, please fill me with the Holy Spirit's power to control my
tongue today! Amen.*

Surrounded by God

If I take the wings of the morning and dwell in the uttermost parts of the sea, even there your hand shall lead me, and your right hand shall hold me.

PSALM 139:9–10 ESV

One of the scarier moments I've had while scuba diving happened when I broke all the rules. I began following a fascinating fish that led me away from the dive site—and all common sense. The fish was colorful and cute and it lured me away from safety. When I finally stopped and looked around, a slow sense of dread settled over me. There was nothing in sight but blue water. Nothing. No bottom, no boat, no divers. With no sense of what was east or west, I had no idea where the boat lay. If not for my bubbles, I wouldn't have known which way was up.

I fought panic and remembered my training, which told me to go to the surface. But first I needed to do a safety stop. Hanging in the water, I once again looked at all that blue. And I remembered my favorite verse from Psalms. "Even there . . . your right hand shall hold me."

Everyone gets lost sometimes, although not usually in the vastness of the sea. We wander away from God, from our families, from our church home. But He is always there, holding our hand. And He'll be there until we find our way home.

* * * * * * * * * * *

Father, never let us forget that You are always with us, comforting and guiding, until we return to You. Amen.

Rain in the Rockies

*Praise GOD from heaven, praise him from the mountaintops . . .
praise him, sun and moon . . . praise him, heavenly rain clouds;
praise, oh let them praise the name of GOD.*

PSALM 148:1, 3–4 MSG

As we drove through the pine-spired foothills on our way to Mount Robson, I noticed a rainstorm on the horizon like an artist's brushstroke sweeping a downpour out of the billowy painted clouds.

My first thought was, *Aw, nuts! We won't get to hike up to the lake.* This was one of the places we wanted to show our kids on their first trip to British Columbia where their dad grew up. It was disappointing to miss the up-close-and-personal view of this majestic place. I remember hiking there years ago and catching my breath because of the beauty, and losing my breath because of the high altitude.

We entered the storm and rain pelted the car. It was discouraging, but at the same time it was a reminder that life comes with both sunshine and rain. After the hard rain passed, we saw sharper colors and gleaming contrasts. And when the sky started to clear, the blue behind the clouds was fresh and promising. It reminded me of how God's promises always make things clear. The rain stopped in time for us to enjoy a hike, and the uniquely beautiful storm that God painted became a crystal clear memory for our family.

．．．．．．．．．．

Lord, in the sunshine or the storm, help me to continually praise You. Amen.

Light in the Darkness

Your word is a lamp to my feet and a light to my path.

PSALM 119:105 NASB

Our family loves to camp, but we began as camping snobs, preferring the hardship of tents rather than trailers or other RVs so we could be closer to the out-of-doors. Being willing to rough it is a good thing, at times. At other times, not so much.

One moonless night we were making the inevitable trek to the bathhouse when my flashlight died. The darkness closed in, leaving us essentially blind. My son thought it was great fun, but for me it was a hair-raising five minutes before we managed to get close enough to see the welcome lights of the restroom. In the dark, what I thought had been a clear path became an obstacle course as I ran into trees and stumbled over roots and rocks.

I face the same dilemma spiritually when I wander too far from God. Without His light showing me the way, small things become huge obstacles as I stumble around in the dark. A once-clear path becomes a navigational nightmare. It's only when I plot my course with His light that I find my way.

* * * * * * * * * * *

Dear Lord, illuminate my path and don't let me wander far from Your light. Amen.

Mistaking Dolphins for Sharks

꙼ ᪣᪣᪣ ꙼ ᪣᪣᪣

Let my cry come before you, O LORD; give me understanding according to your word!

PSALM 119:169 ESV

My husband and I spent the last day of summer vacation at the beach before I headed back to my classroom to teach. A broken foot left me with little to do but dangle from my boogie board. As I dangled and twirled in the water, a school of silver bait fish jumped over my head and sparkled in the sunlight. My first thought was *Beautiful.* My second thought was *Oh no!* When my husband saw the fish jump, he drew the same conclusion. SHARK!

I knew none of the ripples that passed for waves that day would carry me to shore. I also knew I'd never outswim a shark (but surviving a shark attack might interest my incoming fifth graders). As my husband rushed to reach me, the shark got closer and closer . . . and turned out to be a dolphin.

Although I thought I knew a dolphin from a shark, I was wrong. I made a judgment without all the facts. Similarly, it's easy to look at situations, circumstances, or people and make judgments that turn out to be incorrect. The Bible tells us God gives wisdom and discernment to those who ask. Before I jump to conclusions again and mistake a dolphin for a shark, I plan to seek out that wisdom.

. . . .

Father, give me wisdom to see and understand situations clearly. Amen.

Daisies on a Mountaintop

You are the hope of everyone on earth, even those who sail on distant seas. You formed the mountains by your power and armed yourself with mighty strength. You quieted the raging oceans with their pounding waves and silenced the shouting of the nations.

PSALM 65:5–7 NLT

When we view the world from a mountaintop, the glory and grandeur of God's power spreads out before us in every direction. We stand in awe of the strength that moved slabs of stone and populated them with life. But God is also in the small things; He is the Lord of hope.

Once, standing on such a mountaintop, I saw a glimpse of that hope. In an area where the trees had been devastated by fire, a cluster of daisies had pushed up through the ashes near the base of a tree. Their white petals stood out starkly against the ruin, a reminder that even in the bleakest of times, God provides a sliver of hope, as if to let us know that all is never lost. When I returned the next year, more growth surrounded the daisies.

Hope can be hard to cling to when the world seems to press in on every corner of our lives. But in all of creation, God reminds us that He is not only a God of power and strength but also one of hope.

Father, I know that hope lies within You. Remind me through Your creation that Your power and strength also brings the hope I can depend on. Amen.

Fireflies in the Darkness

꙳ ꙳꙳꙳꙳꙳꙳꙳꙳꙳꙳

It is you who light my lamp; the LORD my God lightens my darkness.

PSALM 18:28 ESV

There's one! Get a jar! Turn the porch light off!" When I was a child, these exclamations announced the sighting of lightning bugs, or fireflies as they are often called. Our youthful summer game involved catching enough lightning bugs to turn an empty jelly jar into a lantern and then quickly releasing the amazing insects without harming them.

Due to bioluminescence, these winged beetles glow conspicuously. The yellowish light they emit shines in stark contrast to encroaching darkness. Observers simply cannot miss the tiny sparkling flashes that enhance summer evenings.

A light in the midst of darkness changes the environment. Have you ever felt relief after lighting a candle during a storm or after finding a flashlight when your car malfunctions at night? When we use a tool for illumination, beams of light provide safe passage through the darkness.

God uses the Bible as His tool for shining truth into our hearts, to light the way and change our lives. As we study, we can be assured He will use the truths therein to demonstrate His love for us, to guide us through life's challenges and to show us how to respond to His call. How comforting to know that we have a loving heavenly Father lighting the way for us.

. . . .

Father, increase my thirst for Your Word, which You use to shine truth into my heart and light onto my pathways. Amen.

The Baobab Tree

When you open your hand, you satisfy the hunger and thirst of every living thing.

PSALM 145:16 NLT

The baobab tree left me speechless as I took forty steps to circle its trunk. The Kenyans with whom I traveled explained that some of the trees might be more than three thousand years old. These trees absorb and store water after a rainstorm. During drought, people and animals can collect life-giving water from its branches. For this reason, it's called the Tree of Life.

As we gathered under the shade of this ancient tree, one of the women stood and started singing a praise song in a language I did not know, but I still understood. I could feel God's presence as I stroked the gray bark and listened while my new friend sang and caressed my Bible. She seemed indifferent to the tree and more in tune with God, and that's when I realized I'd taken His holy Word for granted.

God designed the baobab to sustain His creation during drought. His provision, however, goes beyond satisfying the physical thirst for water. Our souls were made to thirst after God, and here again He provided the thirst quencher, Jesus Christ.

It left me awestruck to consider this tree might have been alive when Jesus walked the earth and shared His life-giving water. I'm thankful that I'll never thirst again.

* * * * * * * * * *

Father, thank You for the living water of Jesus. Help me to share it with others. Amen.

Pool in the Desert

*Let anyone who is thirsty come to me and drink. Whoever believes
in me, as Scripture has said, rivers of living water will flow from
within them.*

JOHN 7:37–38 NIV

There is an oasis in the near-desert conditions of far West
Texas: the springs at Balmorhea State Park. The park is
home to the world's largest spring-fed swimming pool. The
pool—twenty-five feet deep in some areas—is deep enough
that scuba divers use it for training and practice. Fish swim
in the cool waters, and the spring invites wildlife and water-
fowl to find shelter nearby. Despite the lack of rain, the spring
makes the pool a source of life.

Sometimes it can feel like we are living in a spiritual
desert with few places to restore our soul. But Jesus promises
that if we believe in Him, rivers of living water will flow from
within us. If we are in Christ, our source of life comes from
the Spirit of God. Like a pool in the desert fed by a constant
spring, we can enjoy God's abundance in a world of spiritual
drought. When we look to Christ as our source, He fills us
with His love and power. We become channels of water in a
thirsty land, overflowing with life and abundance that enables
us to bless the world around us.

- - - - - - - - - - -

*Lord, fill me with Your presence, power, and love so I can be a
channel of blessing in a dry and thirsty world. Amen.*

Desert Garden

The grasslands of the wilderness become a lush pasture, and the hillsides blossom with joy.

PSALM 65:12 NLT

During the early years of our marriage my husband and I had the opportunity to move several times and experience new places. One such move, however, did not look like an opportunity to me. No matter how hard I tried, I couldn't see the opportunity or the adventure. Still, I sensed God sending us there. My husband felt His leading and I felt a gentle coaxing, like a parent encouraging his child to try out the big pool for the first time.

Even though we obeyed the calling, I didn't take the right attitude along with me. First of all, we moved to the desert. We had rocks and bricks for a backyard. How were our boys supposed to play? Plus, we were far away from our family and friends. My support system vanished! I cried out to God: "What were You thinking!?"

I wallowed in that attitude for a time, but then the Lord led me to Psalms. I dove into it like a fish gasping for water. David's voice became mine when he complained or begged for understanding. God allowed me to vent and He continued to hold my hand. Slowly I joined in on the verses of praise and thanksgiving. Before I knew it, His joy filled my heart and I started to see the desert in a whole new light.

* * * * * * * * * * *

Lord, surprise me with beauty and joy wherever You lead me. Amen.

Shrewd as Snakes

*I am sending you out like sheep among wolves. Therefore be as
shrewd as snakes and as innocent as doves.*

MATTHEW 10:16 NIV

Have you ever noticed that some people just aren't, well,
nice? Even downright cruel? And it's not just the obvi-
ously despicable citizens either. It's that sweet-looking lady in
the pew who uses razor-sharp words to carve out your heart
and hand it to you with a sugary smile. Or it's that guy who
plots an elaborate scheme at work designed to destroy you on
his way to the top. How on earth can we be like Jesus to these
joy-stealing, spirit-shredding wolves in our midst?

The answer lies in the marching orders Jesus gave His disciples as He sent them out to be light in a dark world: "Be as
shrewd as snakes and as innocent as doves."

As shrewd as a snake? That's hard advice after the whole
Garden of Eden episode. But the fact is, snakes have highly
honed senses and are able to detect even the slightest distur-
bance. This gives them time to either prepare for battle or flee
from danger. Like the snake, we are to be ever alert to signs
of danger, giving us time to flee to our Father or prayerfully
prepare for battle.

But until danger comes, we are to be "as innocent as
doves"—kind, compassionate, and loving one another—just
as Jesus did.

. . . .

*Lord, help me to love as Jesus did while being ever alert to the
dangers around me. Amen.*

The Bald Eagle

God said to them, "Be fruitful and multiply and fill the earth and subdue it, and have dominion over the fish of the sea and over the birds of the heavens and over every living thing that moves on the earth."

GENESIS 1:28 ESV

A regal bird sat on an oak limb overlooking the pond. I gasped when I recognized it—a bald eagle. Its snowy head, ebony body, and bleached tail feathers were unmistakable. God equipped the majestic bald eagle with strength and tenacity. Impressively, the male and female mate for life and work together to build their nest and raise their young.

Over four decades ago, a wildlife conservationist warned my sixth-grade class that bald eagles were an endangered species. I never dreamed I'd see one in Kentucky, but thanks to diligent efforts and the ban of harmful pesticides, the bald eagle is thriving and no longer threatened. The image of the eagle has been used to symbolize courage, power, and freedom, but when I witnessed the glorious bald eagle perched in an ancient tree close to home, my heart surged with hope for the future.

The Lord gave us dominion over the creatures of the earth. Even so, He knew humanity would make mistakes so He gave the planet and His creatures the ability to heal. God always had a plan to save us and His world.

Father, thank You for Your wondrous world. Help me to be a good caretaker of Your creation. Amen.

Purified Water

Jesus answered, "Everyone who drinks this water will be thirsty again, but whoever drinks the water I give them will never thirst. Indeed, the water I give them will become in them a spring of water welling up to eternal life."

JOHN 4:13–14 NIV

Do you remember learning in school about the water cycle? Water evaporates from the earth's surface, turning into water vapor that forms clouds that later produce rain or snow that falls back to earth. Over the years, pollution has degraded the quality of the earth's water supply. And yet, nature's purification system will take unclean rain, filter it through layers of soil, and produce a flowing spring with clear and pure water. From polluted to pure.

Similarly, Christ is our purification system. He takes our polluted lives of sin, filters them through His sacrificial death on the cross, and produces eternal life through His resurrection. From stagnant in sin to welling up in endless life.

The things of this world will always leave us thirsty and unsatisfied. Only Jesus can end perpetual thirst and quench our hearts' desire. Do you still feel parched deep down inside? Try the living water that Christ offers. Not only will He fill you up, you will overflow. Your life will be a conduit of His abundant love, drawing others in who are dying of thirst.

* * * * * * * * * * * *

Thank You, Jesus, for filling me up with Your living water and satisfying my soul. May Your love overflow in me, drawing others to You. Amen.

Spiritual Adventure Awaits

By faith Abraham, when called to go to a place he would later receive as his inheritance, obeyed and went, even though he did not know where he was going.

HEBREWS 11:8 NIV

God likes to evict us out of our comfort zones. Just ask Abraham. God called him to move to a new place, destination unknown. Did Abraham anticipate an adventure or did he grumble as he went? I imagine Abraham embarking on the quest with gusto, traveling unmarked roads, witnessing panoramic views; a skyscraper-less world, unmarred by man.

Is God calling you to a similar spiritual odyssey, into the unknown rugged terrain of deeper faith? In Christ, an adventure awaits us akin to no other. We're made for so much more than nine-to-five work weeks. God created us for more than a ho-hum existence, safely hedged inside our four walls. Just as God called Abraham, He calls us up from our couches, into the unknown—to explore, create, and risk our lives for something greater.

Here's the thing with stepping out to follow Jesus—it won't be easy. Sometimes the journey gets rocky and the terrain grows treacherous and we question God's navigation skills. Abraham didn't know where God was taking him, but he trusted. We too must trust God. He is calling us to step out in faith. And He will give us the courage to do so.

* * * * * * * * * * *

Father, please grant me audacious faith like Abraham and help me to see stepping out in faith as an adventure. Amen.

Water of Life

In the beginning God created the heavens and the earth. The earth was formless and empty, and darkness covered the deep waters. And the Spirit of God was hovering over the surface of the waters.

GENESIS 1:1–2 NLT

On the first day—the *very* first day—of the creation of the earth, God created water. In our retellings of the creation story, we usually focus on the earth and sky, the light from darkness. But on that first day, God made the waters.

On the second day, God separated those waters from the sky. And on the third day, He separated the waters themselves, forming oceans and dry land. For three days, God focused much of His creative attention and power on water. Before plants, before animals, before us. *Why?* Because the Lord God knew the plants, the animals, the people would all need water. So He provided it *first.*

That's what God does. He provides for His children, especially when His children seek Him: "But seek first his kingdom and his righteousness, and all these things will be given to you as well" (Matthew 6:33 NIV). God knows exactly what we need—even before we know we need it—and He sets about providing exactly the right thing, at exactly the right time, and in exactly the right way, when we seek Him first.

Lord, I thank You for the many ways You provide for me— even before I know what I need. Amen.

Light Spilling Through

He has made the earth by His power, He has established the world by His wisdom, and has stretched out the heavens at His discretion.

JEREMIAH 10:12 NKJV

There are days in life when I just need time alone with God. One of my favorite places to pray is in my car. Driving to work one day, I was praying about some things and some people in my life. I felt a tangible connection with God and I "had church" right there in the car. As I rounded a curve, I looked up and witnessed a brilliant display in the sky. There was cloud cover but the sun was peeking through, forming streaks of light descending from the clouds.

I experienced the Lord's presence during that prayer time in my car, and the scene outside mirrored what my heart was sensing, as if God's glory was spilling out of heaven and overflowing through the clouds. Through all my indecision, doubt, and stress, I want God's light to shine through the "clouds" in my life. When I open myself up to Him, that light can shine through.

I enjoyed the view on the rest of my drive, feeling refreshed and basking in the glory. I desire that feeling, that sense of God's presence filled to overflowing, more and more every day, like the sun spilling out through the clouds.

* * * * * * * * * * *

Father, fill me with Your presence to overflowing. Amen.

Magnificent Mountains

I lift up my eyes to the mountains—where does my help come from? My help comes from the LORD, the Maker of heaven and earth.

PSALM 121:1–2 NIV

Usually, I'm rushing into town to run errands in order to get back to work on the farm. Driving the hilly roads and hairpin turns often makes my riders nervous. But I always slow down and gape at the Blue Ridge Mountains as I round the last curve to town. The view never ceases to amaze me and I hope it never will. "Awesome!" is an expression commonly used now to describe just about anything, but the sight of the misty mountains over the hilly horizon is in its truest sense *awesome.*

Not only does the sight make me worship the Creator, it makes me think of my grandmother. Psalm 121 was her favorite Bible passage. This woman loved the Lord and her family. Born in a sod hut, married at a young age, she followed her husband to homestead in Colorado. The dust storm blew them back to Detroit where she raised her children. She passed down her love for the Creator to her daughter, who in turn passed it down to me. That is truly awesome.

The same Creator who made the heaven and earth and mountains sustained her and ushered her into God's presence. When I view those mountains, I think of my grandmother with her Lord.

• • • • • • • • • •

Lord, You are the maker of all things, and that is truly awesome. Amen.

Rock-Solid Peace

Trust in the LORD forever, for in God the LORD, we have an everlasting Rock.

ISAIAH 26:4 NASB

When we go hiking, I always try to choose a trail that meanders near a stream or river. There's just something about flowing water that draws me in. I could sit for hours watching water rush by, tumbling over rocks and pooling in quiet eddies.

One day we were hiking beside a river near flood stage. Those waters weren't calming, but a little bit frightening. As I gazed across the river, I spied a boulder in the middle with three smaller rocks balanced on top of it, perched as if there wasn't even a breeze blowing, much less a river raging.

My first thought was of the irony pictured there. In the midst of possible flooding, a picture of peace. Then my mind turned to Christ. Wasn't that exactly what God promises— and delivers—when we turn to Him?

As we observe the life of Jesus, we see Him engulfed in a flood of need. Yet He was the very picture of peace. I realized then the truth of what I was seeing. Peace is an interior thing, untouched by the exterior life. The world promises peace in many ways but fails to deliver. God offers us one way to peace—Jesus Christ—and always makes good on His promise.

Dear Lord, when life rages, remind me that peace is found in You. Amen.

Even the Stones

∴ ○∴°○∴○∴ ○∴°○∴○

Some of the Pharisees from the crowd told Him, "Teacher, rebuke Your disciples." He answered, "I tell you, if they were to keep silent, the stones would cry out!"

LUKE 19:39–40 HCSB

Do you ever wonder why Jesus chose stones to cry out? Of all the things He could have chosen, why rocks? The full Scripture passage provides details of the triumphal entry of Jesus into Jerusalem. He had been prophesied in intricate detail and promised for centuries, but they missed the signs and rejected Him as Savior. He came quietly and humbly, riding a donkey, and only His disciples stopped to praise Him. Even the Pharisees—those who knew the Scriptures best— missed the signs. Even as He was preparing to lay down His life for their sins, they still did not see it. Would we have missed the signs as well, or would we have believed and followed Him?

The Bible doesn't specify, but I wonder if Jesus picked the stones, something hard and unmovable, for their likeness to the hard hearts of those to whom He spoke. We know that one day every knee will bow and every tongue will confess; those small and great and even the hardest of hearts will one day recognize Jesus as King of Kings and Lord of Lords.

* * * * * * * * * * * *

Lord Jesus, I praise You today for the gift of salvation made possible by You fulfilling the prophecy of the coming true King. Amen.

Storms and Shipwrecks

I urge you to keep up your courage, because not one of you will be lost; only the ship will be destroyed.

ACTS 27:22 NIV

I didn't panic until I saw the furrowed brow and white knuckles of our ship's captain, who only days before had taught our ragtag crew how to sail. We were on a mission trip en route to one of the islands "behind God's back" in the Bahamas when the storm blew in and the sky turned dark. This was the sort of storm that makes a person feel small and stand in awe of the raw power of nature. We braced ourselves as rain pelted our fifty-four-foot sailboat, and the mutinous waves threatened to capsize us.

When storms of life roll in, sometimes the only thing you can do is to hold on and endure. In the Bible, a similar scene unfolds. The ship's crew didn't see sun or stars for days. Completely lost in the storm, they abandoned hope until the apostle Paul, a prisoner on board, makes this declaration, "I urge you to keep up your courage."

If you're weathering a storm today, don't lose your courage. God knows how to preserve your life even in the midst of a shipwreck. He knows how to turn the situation around for your good and for the good of others.

• • • • • • • • • • •

Father, don't let me drown in the storms of life, but give me the courage to endure so I can live to honor and serve You. Amen.

Eyewitness to Majesty

We were eyewitnesses of his majesty.

2 PETER 1:16 NIV

*E*yewitness: a person who has personally seen something and is able to give a firsthand account of what happened. An eyewitness to majesty—that's what Peter declared himself to be in this passage. And what did he witness? The majesty of the Christ, the very Son of God. Majesty in hands that touched the untouchable, wonder in words that washed away sin, and might in the Son of Man who defeated sin and death to offer life, love, and salvation to all who would follow Him.

What must it have been like to have seen all that Peter saw—to have witnessed with our own eyes—this majesty, this face of God?

And yet, we *are* witnesses, each and every day. We only have to open our eyes to see, to witness, the majesty of the eagle that mounts into the sky, the wonders of the wildflowers that dot our paths and carpet our ways, the might of the mountain carved out and built up from the depths of the earth.

His majesty. His wonder. His might. It is everywhere, all around us. For in His creation, we see the Creator. And we are eyewitnesses to the majesty, to the face of God.

. . . .

Lord, I see the wonders of Your creation all around me, and I know that You are the one true God! Amen.

Back to Life

Jesus said to her, "I am the resurrection and the life. The one who believes in me will live, even though they die."

JOHN 11:25 NIV

My heart sank. The beautiful bird lay still. Sleek gray-brown with bright orange wing tips, it had evidently hit a window and fallen. This was a cedar waxwing, not common in our area. Hopeful that this bird was only knocked out temporarily, I laid it in a sheltered warm spot, intending to check on it later. In my mind, it seemed so disconcerting and useless for this exquisite creature to lose his life unfairly.

Jesus's disciples were confused and dismayed at His death on the cross. They had expected His kingdom to be an earthly one with the Roman rulers driven out, and their nation restored to greatness. They did not understand. They couldn't believe that their precious Lord could be killed so cruelly and unfairly.

I looked awhile later for the cedar waxwing. It was not there in the sheltered spot. I never knew for sure if it regained its breath and flew away or not. Unlike me looking for the bird, the disciples did see their Lord again. Jesus defeated death and offers eternal life to all who believe in Him. They now understood, and they couldn't wait to share the good news: He is the resurrection and the life!

. . . .

Father, thank You so much for Your Son who has opened the way to life eternal. Amen.

Rain for the Roots

The earth trembled, and the heavens poured down rain before you. . . . You sent abundant rain, O God, to refresh the weary land.

PSALM 68:8–9 NLT

Upon every life rain must fall—sometimes as a gentle shower; other times as a tumultuous thunderstorm; and every so often in sudden, unexpected cloudbursts that shatter our calm and send us scrambling for cover. No matter how the rain comes, it is a necessary element for growth, cleansing, refreshing, and renewal.

Just as the earth benefits from rain, our spirits grow by watering. It's impossible to produce a clear reflection of love, a true example of kindness, or a genuine likeness of Christ without allowing the Word of God to take root in our hearts—and roots need moisture. It's often during the rainy seasons that we press in closest to Him for shelter, comfort, and security. Even when rainy days become prolonged periods of gray skies and we wonder how much "watering" is needed for us to grow, one thing is certain: God in His wisdom will provide the delicate balance that is essential to our growth and His glory.

God knows we can't grow in sunshine alone. He's the rain that washes, waters, and renews . . . the refuge that shelters, warms, and protects . . . and the Bright Morning Star that dawns brilliantly when the rain ends.

. . . .

Dear Father, I choose to see Your will through the rain, knowing every drop passes through Your loving hands. Amen.

An Early Frost

The trees of the LORD are well watered.

PSALM 104:16 NIV

I've often heard that spring can be a picture of the Resurrection. From dormant plants that look dead comes a rebirth, a riot of color that brings the earth back to life. But what happens when spring is short-circuited?

Every year, I look forward to the blooming of our tulip magnolia tree. Its abundance of pink and white blossoms fills the yard with beauty. As it turns green, the petals drop and cover the yard like snow, letting the loveliness linger just a bit longer.

One year, however, an early frost killed the buds. No pink petals appeared, and I worried that the tree had been killed by the cold snap. But a few weeks later, tiny, pale green leaves appeared, and the tree stayed healthy and green all summer.

What a glorious reminder that everything God has made, the nature we look at everyday, continually demonstrates the depth of God's provision for us. No matter how bleak the world seems, God will eventually bring growth back into our lives.

* * * * * * * * * * *

Lord, who You are is revealed in all Your handiwork and in everything You've done for me, and I thank You for Your blessings and Your love. Amen.

Ultimate Powerlifter

❃ ০˚০˚০❃০❃ ০˚০˚০

Go to the ant . . . consider its ways and be wise!

PROVERBS 6:6 NIV

Ounce for ounce, tiny ants are some of the strongest creatures in creation. Certain species of these miniature powerlifters can carry over five thousand times their own weight. That would be like an adult human hoisting 425 tons. The thought of such a burden is crushing to even consider.

This may help us comprehend the weight of Jesus's cross, however. Although the wood didn't weigh that much, the weight of the sin He carried is impossible to estimate. How much does a lie weigh? Or one foul word? Once you know, multiply by the times we've committed each. How many pounds of pride, greed, and selfishness have we amassed? Throw in all the wars of history along with all the racism, betrayal, murder, and mayhem. Even if each sin weighed a fraction of an ounce, added together for all humanity, the tonnage is staggering.

Looking ahead to that day when Jesus would carry the cross, Isaiah said, "Surely he took up our pain and bore our suffering. . . . He was crushed for our iniquities; the punishment that brought us peace was on him. . . . The LORD has laid on him the iniquity of us all" (Isaiah 53:4–6 NIV). Imagine the sheer crushing force that one soul endured. No wonder He sweat great drops of blood and prayed for the cup to pass as He shouldered our burden in the Garden.

. . . .

Dear Jesus, thank You for bearing the weight of all my sin. Amen.

Ahoy, Mateys!

Then He arose and rebuked the wind, and said to the sea, "Peace, be still!" And the wind ceased and there was a great calm.

MARK 4:39 NKJV

One day when my sons were young, we were visiting my parents' home located near a creek in an eastern Kentucky hollow. Following a delicious supper, we settled in to rest as rain began to fall. My boys went to play in a spare bedroom, and after a while I noticed they were being very quiet. I entered the bedroom and found them looking out the window.

"Dad, we're riding a ship!" Noah gave me a salute.

"I'm the captain! We're sailing down the sea!" Ethan pretended to steer.

I peered out the window, and the yard was flooded. Even though we were basically trapped, my sons saw the flash flood as an adventure. I said a quick prayer for protection, for the rain to stop, and for continued calm in my children.

I left the captains at the helm of their "ship" and informed the adults of the situation. We kept a watch on the yard, and thankfully the rain ended shortly and the waters receded. The boys were disappointed that their ship was docked, but I assured them we could now explore the shore.

Jesus talked about the faith of children, and that day I learned to consider life as an adventure even in tense situations. The ultimate Captain is in control.

• • • • • • • • • •

Lord, help me to have the faith and sense of adventure of a child. Amen.

A Different Kind
of Beauty

༝ ༺ ༝ ༺ ༝ ༺ ༝ ༺ ༝ ༺ ༝

Charm is deceptive, and beauty is fleeting.

PROVERBS 31:30 NIV

Mama's front yard was the envy of the neighborhood, if not the whole town. Situated on a main street, it seemed that everyone had to pass our home on their way to church. It was Easter morning and the azaleas and camellias were in full bloom along with the pink Japanese magnolia and several deep red rose bushes. Surely our yard was wearing its best and most beautiful Easter finery!

Mama, however, was so busy getting three little girls dressed in Easter bonnets and white gloves that she missed what Daddy had secretly planted at daybreak. A flock of tacky, hot pink flamingoes was assembled on our lawn, front and center.

Now this was in the 1960s, back when pink flamingoes were not considered "funky chic" but more like something relegated to vacation trailers in Florida. They were certainly not Mama's idea of beauty. Hysterical laughter (from those three little girls) and abject horror (from Mama) ensued as Daddy dutifully pulled them up before church.

Beauty really is in the eye of the beholder, and what God thinks is breathtakingly stunning is a heart that loves and honors Him. It's not what you wear or what's on display at your house. It's the beauty of Christ in your heart.

• • • • • • • • • • •

Lord, may I also see the wide variety of beauty found in the people I meet along life's journey. Amen.

Really Resting

*Come to me, all of you who are weary and carry heavy burdens,
and I will give you rest.*

MATTHEW 11:28 NLT

The day on the island was so picture perfect that I almost expected to see Gilligan and Mary Ann come strolling by. The view of crystal-clear, turquoise water was like something on a postcard, and the sand was so white it looked like God had taken a powdered sugar sifter and shaken it over the bay.

Not one bit of civilization could be seen from my vantage point under a shady umbrella. Well, except for the snow cone boat bobbing near the shore. Oh my, that was some icy-cold deliciousness on a hot day! And one of the best parts was having fun with my children and grandchildren, watching them splash in the waves and listening to their laughter as it echoed across the water. I'd been so exhausted when we got there. But on that day, I rested, soaking in the sheer beauty of God's creation, and thanking Him for the gift of a day shared with my loved ones.

Sweet friend, when's the last time *you* rested? Truly rested? Those be-still moments are the times that refresh your soul, the moments when you are quiet enough to hear God's whisper. And you don't even need an island or a snow cone to rest and spend time with Him.

. . . .

Father, remind me to rest. Refresh my heart and soul so that I can serve You more. Amen.

Faithful to the End

⸙ ◦°◦°◦°◦⸙ ◦°◦°◦

*Greater love has no one than this: to lay down one's life for one's
friends.*

JOHN 15:13 NIV

With the skill and precision of elite aviators, the Canada geese arrive. Barking orders through the cool, crisp air of early spring, they swoop low, glide above the pond, and alight in a synchronized touchdown. We love it when they choose our home for their home. Our anticipation grows as each pair selects the perfect nesting place. Along with it comes the anticipation of woodland predators.

I'd heard of a fierce battle that ensued one night when a ruthless raccoon attempted to drive a female from her nest. During the onslaught, first one and then the other of her wings were broken. Wounded and no longer able to defend herself, she faithfully maintained her post, never leaving the nest unprotected. The determined raccoon continued to return until, in a final display of valiant loyalty, the female goose gave up her life protecting her unborn chicks.

But that's not the end of the story. Her sacrificial faithfulness saved the nest, and with the continued care of her mate, the next morning six downy goslings were hatched. Soon, under their father's care, they were safely protected in the water.

The faithfulness of God's creatures in saving their young—at the cost of their own lives—is a vivid reminder of Christ's faithfulness to sacrifice His life that we might have eternal life.

• • • • • • • • • • •

*Thank You, precious Jesus, for loving me so much that You died
for me. Amen.*

Born Climbers

God saved you by his grace when you believed. And you can't take credit for this; it is a gift from God.

EPHESIANS 2:8 NLT

Squirrels frolic above the carpet of grass, always preferring the canopy of trees, like gutsy trapeze artists, twirly through branches and scampering across power lines. One thing I know—they're happiest climbing. Walking on the ground makes them skittish, nervous like, and always eyeing who's around the corner.

Like squirrels, we humans are born climbers, latching onto every ladder we can find. We're happiest when we're fixing ourselves, tugging up our own emotional and spiritual bootstraps. And oh, how we want to work at faith. Like squirrels, we dash and skitter, toil and dig all day. We're reluctant to receive the gift God offers.

Because of Jesus, we don't have to climb anymore. Cloaked in human flesh, He chose to climb down to meet us on our own dusty turf. At the cross, God emptied His hatred of sin onto Him. Jesus's sacrifice cleansed us from all our past and present sins, and purged from us all our future sins. "For God made Christ, who never sinned, to be the offering for our sin, so that we could be made right with God through Christ" (2 Corinthians 5:21 NLT).

We can quit our climbing and turn our ladders into lanterns—shining the light of grace for all to see.

* * * * * * * * * * *

Lord, help me to comprehend Your gift of grace so that we can give You all the praise. Amen.

Sun Peaks

I am with you always.

MATTHEW 28:20 ESV

All were filled with anticipation of a glorious sunrise symbolizing Jesus's resurrection from the dead that Easter morning. But rain clouds covered the sky, allowing only a few peaks of sun to shine through. Perhaps some were disappointed that there was no visible sunrise that Easter. But for me, the clouds preached a message clearer than any bright, clear sky: the sun is still there, and even when the rains of life come, the *Son* is still there.

Sometimes it rains, sometimes it storms, and sometimes it's an all-out hurricane. Dark clouds come—pain, despair, and even death—but Easter's message is, no matter what we face, nothing in all creation can separate us from the love of God (Romans 8:35–39).

Clouds do not change the fact that the sun is still shining, just as storms of life do not change who God is or His purpose—to bring good out of them. As the sun continues to shine behind clouds, God's Son is still Savior in all circumstances. He is merciful, comforting, and in control. He is Lord of all, and our only hope is in Him.

Remember, the beautiful, sweet-smelling flowers cannot grow with sunshine alone. They need the rain too.

. . . .

Thank You, Jesus, for going to the cross and sending Your Holy Spirit to be with me always. Help me to see You and Your love through every cloud or storm in my life. Amen.

Talking Trees

The mountains and the hills will break forth into shouts of joy before you, and all the trees of the field will clap their hands.

ISAIAH 55:12 NASB

After being a city dweller most of my life and then moving to sixty-six acres of mostly wooded land, things can get, well . . . quiet. Lazy dogs lounge on the porch. My cat yawns and curls up in the sun's rays while I listen to silence. The longer I listen, the louder it gets. Birds chatter in trees. Dogs bark in the distance. A rooster crows. Occasionally, I hear bees buzz or a hummingbird zip up to sip from my bright red feeder.

But the sound that surprised me most came from the trees. In fantasy movies they move around and even talk. I've never conversed with an oak, but I've heard one. One day soon after we moved to our farm, I walked through the woods. At first I thought someone called out, but as I sought out the sound, I realized it was all around me. Wind whistled through the stately oaks. They creaked and groaned as their branches ground together. The natural music played a heavenly tune. The Creator's tune.

The book of Isaiah speaks of a day when trees will clap at the announcement of their King. In fact, it states that the mountains and hills will sing for joy. That will be a concert I won't want to miss.

. . . .

Lord, help me to listen to silent sounds of creation and give You praise. Amen.

We Are Not Alone

*The young lions lack and suffer hungry; but those who seek the
LORD shall not lack any good thing.*

PSALM 34:10 NKJV

T he hunting prowess of lions comes from their ability to
attack cooperatively. Most hunting animals concentrate
on vulnerable members of a herd, but lions working together
can successfully take down large and healthy animals. While
lions hunt well together, they are less successful on their
own. Only 17 percent of solo hunts yield a kill. Nomads—
lions without their own pride—have to travel longer distances
and work harder for their food. Territorial prides chase nomad
lions away. Without the security of a pride, a lone lion can
go hungry.

Lions may grow weak and hungry, but we who seek the
Lord lack no good thing. We are not facing the world without
the security of a pack. If we seek the Lord, then we are never
truly alone. We are not lions, carving out our own survival in
the harsh African plains; we are sheep, lovingly tended to by a
shepherd who makes sure we have what we need.

When fear rises up, we can respond with thanksgiving,
and trust in the God who blesses us with all good things. We
don't have to fear that someone else's success threatens our
own or worry that there's not enough to supply our needs.
God, owner and creator of all, makes sure we have enough.

* * * * * * * * * * *

*Lord, I praise You because You meet my needs and bless me with
all good things. Amen.*

Every Gift

Just as a body, though one, has many parts, but all its many parts form one body, so it is with Christ.

1 CORINTHIANS 12:12 NIV

Tomatoes are a versatile fruit. When you bite into one, it tastes both sweet and savory, juicy but firm. Cultures all over the world use them in their dishes, enriching salads, pastas, and sandwiches. Long before you eat a tomato, many helpers have aided in its growth. Sunshine, water, and soil all play a role, but perhaps the most fascinating is the bee. Several kinds, including the honeybee and bumblebee, move from plant to plant collecting nectar. As they do this, pollen is spread around, allowing the flowers to be fertilized. Without this pollination, tomatoes can't grow.

God calls His followers to many unique helping roles too. Moses led the Israelites out of Egypt, but Joshua led them into the Promised Land. David was God's warrior king, but Solomon was tasked with building the temple. Within families there are important roles for parents, siblings, and caregivers. Most jobs fill a vital need—from the nurse working late into the night, to the computer expert keeping an office running efficiently.

Imagine your delight if a mentor said to you, "You'll be great at this. It's what you were born to do." That's what God says about you. Just as you are, you are one-of-a-kind, handcrafted for His purposes.

. . . .

Father, thank You for my role in Your kingdom; help me to use my gifts wisely and cheerfully. Amen.

Transformed
in the Storm

⚬ ○ᵒ•ᵒ°○ ⚬ ○ᵒ•ᵒ°○

*As the Spirit of the Lord works within us, we become more and
more like him.*

2 CORINTHIANS 3:18 TLB

The mighty, uncontrollable nature of storms is fascinating
to me, and at night they can bring a breathtaking light
show. But they also come with a potential for destruction—
as do the storms in our lives.

Recently, lightning struck a tree in front of my house,
breaking off one of its largest branches. Sadly, it revealed the
inside was plagued with something that was destroying it,
even though it looked fine on the outside.

Likewise, we don't always see or know what is hurting us.
God loves us completely, but He's most passionate about our
innermost being. In His flawless love He allows storms in our
lives for perfect reasons. Brokenness hurts, but often God's
greatest purposes emerge through the things He reveals to us
during, or following, a storm.

When God picks up the broken pieces of our lives (and
He will always be there to pick up the pieces), we are re-
made. Memories of how it felt, what God revealed *to* us and
in us, how He put us back together—these are life-changers.
Although we're whole again, we're transformed. We become
more like the One who *chose* to be broken for us and chooses
every day to watch over, pray for, and love us.

• • • • • • • • • • •

*Dear Father, I will embrace Your will in every storm, thankful to
become more like You. Amen.*

Early Warning System

Preach the word; be ready in season and out of season; reprove, rebuke, and exhort, with complete patience and teaching.

2 TIMOTHY 4:2 ESV

This morning I heard a call. I first thought it was a juvenile hawk, only to have the call give way to an incessant squawking. That's when I realized it was actually an irritated blue jay. It didn't surprise me to hear the jay, but it did surprise me to see where it sat. The jay was perched on a branch not far from a red-shouldered hawk, apparently unafraid of the much larger predator.

Knowing hawks eat other birds, I wondered why that jay wasn't afraid. More puzzling, I wondered why the hawk didn't chase after the blue jay. In researching to find answers I learned that whenever predators like the red-shouldered hawk are around, jays squawk a warning in an effort to keep others safe. You might say God created the jay as an early warning system.

The courageous blue jay stood its ground in the presence of the much larger hawk. It wasn't afraid to sound the alarm and warn others of the potential danger. Like the jay we need to be courageous, stand our ground in the presence of our adversary, warn others of possible attacks, and speak the truth in love.

. . . .

Father, You are the Master Designer who created blue jays as an early warning system. May I also care for others in the same way, speaking the truth in love. Amen.

Lessons from
the Sheep

๛ ๐ؚ๐ٚ๐ ๛ ๐ؚ๐ٚ๐

My sheep hear my voice, and I know them, and they follow me.

JOHN 10:27 ESV

Moving to Mississippi was an eye-opening experience for this Florida family. Leaving a subdivision near the beach, we moved to Mississippi and rented a house with several acres and a barn. We learned a lot that year about country living, not the least of which involved raising sheep. Rearing baby lambs from birth is hard but fun work. As the lambs receive care from their human "mommies," they begin to run and play and identify which child to follow based on who gave them bottles and cuddles. It was beautiful to experience these living creatures because of the great lessons we learned from them.

Each interaction with the sheep drew my attention back to Scripture. After all, Jesus talked a lot about how we are like sheep in the New Testament. This particular passage caught my attention because I remember so clearly how the lambs would chase after the voice that belonged to the child who had been caring for its needs—feedings that occurred around the clock, fresh water daily, stalls that were cleaned out, and safety for sleeping. What a beautiful picture this was for me as I think about how my Savior cares so carefully for me in my neediness just as a lamb, and how I, in turn, should follow hard after Him when I hear His voice.

. . . .

I praise You, Lord, for knowing and meeting my every need. Amen.

Go with the Flow

In the same way, faith by itself, if it is not accompanied by action, is dead.

JAMES 2:17 NIV

When I had the chance to tour the Everglades by airboat, I loved the loud, noisy ride. On top of that, listening to our guide tell us about the swamp was just as fun.

I'd thought swamps were full of still and stagnant water. That's not exactly accurate. Most swamps are connected to other bodies of water, and although it's slow, the water in them does flow. It's that movement that keeps the environment healthy. However, there are places in every swamp where the water is truly stagnant, and there we find almost no life. There are many reasons why water is cut off from the flow; environmental barriers like the roots of vegetation are the most common.

I couldn't tell the difference between the two types of water until the guide drew my attention to the odors around me. Although swamps are rich with strong, earthy smells, they aren't unpleasant. In contrast, stagnant water stinks. It carries the overwhelming odor of decay and death.

We can be like that swamp. When we let our lives get clogged with the roots of sin and disobedience, things get foul. To avoid the stink, we can allow the Holy Spirit to flow through us, bringing life to our lives and to others.

• • • • • • • • • • •

Dear Lord, help me clean out the roots clogging my life and once again let Your Spirit flow through me. Amen.

Win-Win

Love each other with genuine affection, and take delight in honoring each other.

ROMANS 12:10 NLT

Every so often, hunters find two bucks with their antlers tightly locked together. One or both are already dead from starvation or thirst. What causes otherwise healthy animals to become inseparable and die? Their desire to be dominant.

Males of most deer species engage in these battles every mating season. Because both are strong and virile, each is convinced he can bully the other into submission. But once they become entwined, they both lose. If they simply walked away, or agreed to disagree, or settled on clear boundaries, they both could pass their genes along to their offspring.

Are whitetails prone to pride or are they simply obeying instincts? Do they attempt foolish feats to save face or are humans the only ones who do so? Are deer capable of reasonable discussion and respectful disagreement or do their hormones demand all or nothing? We may never know, but we humans can do better, for we too try to intimidate others, only to become embroiled in bitter, winner-less duels.

Although some causes are worth dying for, it is usually more advantageous to part company without either party surrendering. Before we clash, let's evaluate the risks and search the Bible for wisdom. To avoid locking horns, let's resolve conflicts by enabling all to walk away with dignity and respect.

• • • • • • • • • • •

O God, please reveal my foolish pride and help me resolve my conflicts in ways that glorify You. Amen.

Dinner for the Deer

Therefore do not worry, saying, "What shall we eat?" or "What shall we drink?" or "What shall we wear?" For . . . your heavenly Father knows that you need all these things.

MATTHEW 6:31–32 NKJV

At the end of every day, I watch my husband trudge to the place behind our house where the field meets the woods, shaking a bucket filled with corn as he walks. For several years now, Paul has fed the deer there. He's placed a salt block in the yard, and sometimes adds some apples because he knows they enjoy them. The deer stand in the clearing until he's almost there and then they retreat just out of sight in the woods and wait. Most nights before Paul's back to the house, they're already munching away on their dinner.

It's taken awhile, but as time has passed, they've come to trust him. They've learned from experience that he's supplying their need. God does the same for us, walking to us as He shakes His bucket of mercy and grace, faithfully providing everything we need. And often He adds extra things we didn't ask for just because He knows we enjoy them.

I've wondered to myself, Do I forget that I am provided for and worry about the future, or am I like the deer that stand there in anticipation waiting to see what God will do?

· · · · · · · · · · ·

Dear Lord, I am so grateful that I can trust You to supply all my needs. Remind me to trust You whenever my faith is weak. Amen.

Snow Storm Symphony

*Wilderness and desert will sing joyously . . . a symphony of song
and color. . . . God's resplendent glory, fully on display.*

ISAIAH 35:1–2 MSG

Growing up in the great white north, I was used to winter
and snow storms. As a family, we would hunker down
and wait them out. When I went away to college, I actually
went even farther north to a small-town Bible college. Most
of the students there were also used to large helpings of winter
and so a snowy night locked in the dorm wasn't a big deal.

On one snowy evening in particular, several of us had
gathered in the lounge on the second floor, the one with the
comfy couches. A few had homework or a book. Conversations
were low-key, and someone turned on some classical music. I
was enjoying the whole atmosphere, staring absentmindedly
out the window.

I'm not sure how long it took before I noticed a syn-
chronistic link between the whirling fantasia outside and the
musical composition inside. I had to do a double take. Sure
enough, the collaboration was not only now and then, it was
constant. An upward sweep of the melody was accompanied
by an upward sweep of snow. A calming lull in the wind
attended the quiet phrases in the music. It was incredible.
God, the Master of all seasons, conducted winter to the tune
of *The Four Seasons* by Vivaldi. His orchestrations are there if
we just take the time to notice.

. . . .

*Lord, thank You for the breathtaking ways You capture my at-
tention. Amen.*

Community

To him be glory in the church and in Christ Jesus throughout all generations, for ever and ever! Amen.

EPHESIANS 3:21 NIV

The Great Florida Reef is the only living barrier coral reef in the continental United States. The coral polyps live in colonies, secreting their limestone exoskeletons from their base. Over time the colony creates a coral skeleton—a living and growing reef that provides shelter and food for a diverse collection of marine life. Altogether, the fragile coral polyps create a place of beauty, strength, and life.

Like the reef, the church is made up of individuals who build community together that is stronger than the sum of its parts. As we minister together, each using our gifts, we create a place of beauty, strength, and life that testifies to the glory and power of God. Who else but God could bring together people from different ethnicities, backgrounds, and walks of life, and unite us into one living body?

Just as the coral polyps all have their part in building up the living reef, you have your part in building up the living body called the church. When we join together in love to share the good news, we also proclaim the power and strength of our God, and He gets all the glory.

· · · · · · · · · · ·

Lord, help me be a vibrant and living part of Your body as I join in the community of faith and use my gifts to lift others up. Amen.

A Coconut
by Any Other Name

Jesus Christ is the same yesterday and today and forever.

HEBREWS 13:8 NIV

The first week of every December my father brought home a large coconut to encourage my mother to make her six-layer, wrapped-in-a-cloud-of-seven-minute-frosting coconut cake. "Here it is," he would announce. "The biggest coconut for the biggest cake ever to be seen on Christmas day!"

Until cake-baking day arrived, I claimed the coconut as my pet. After all, it appeared to have two eyes, a mouth, and lots of fur. I enjoyed my imaginary pet, but I happily returned the coconut to my mother when she was ready to incorporate it into the luscious frosting.

One night, I rolled over and unconsciously touched the coconut I had left by my pillow before falling asleep. My parents rushed to my room when they heard my screams. What had been familiar and enjoyable to me in the light was unknown and terrifying in the dark.

Our circumstances can change so fast. Political leaders come and go, sunny days turn stormy in a flash, relationships wax and wane. How freeing it is to know that Jesus's words are certain and unchanging. If the ground on which we stand feels like shifting sand, we need to turn our eyes to Him and remember that He has always been, is always, and will always be there.

. . . .

Thank You, Jesus, that in a world of constant changes and un-certainty, Your love and faithfulness are the same forever. Amen.

Wings

Those who hope in the LORD will renew their strength. They will soar on wings like eagles; they will run and not grow weary, they will walk and not be faint.

ISAIAH 40:31 NIV

An elegant, mature eagle flew over my car and landed in a field nearby. I was driving on a country road and I stopped to watch this amazing bird. After months of lying in bed, unable to walk and in severe pain, I was finally able to drive. However, it was a day of struggle—both physically and emotionally. To keep myself from discouragement, I was reciting Scripture. This helped me focus on God's perspective. Isaiah 40:31 had become very important to me during my struggle. That day, the moment I recited the verse, the eagle flew over. As I watched, two pesky crows attacked the eagle on the ground. They were no match for the mighty bird, however. He easily fought them off. Unfurling powerful wings, he rose into the sky and soared away. I was stunned. What an amazing message from God, sent directly through one of His wild creatures.

God hears our sighs, our cries. He cares enough to send one of His creations to fly over at the perfect moment. That experience was a gift meant to be shared. When pesky crows of discouragement plague you, remember the verse from Isaiah. Remember God is there to lift you up.

* * * * * * * * * * *

Father, thank You for glimpses of You through Your creation. Help us remember Your great love for us. Amen.

The Snow-Covered Landscape

It is not what you and I do. . . . It is what God is doing, and he is creating something totally new, a free life!

GALATIANS 6:15 MSG

Few things are more stunning than the sunrise after a fresh winter's snow. The crisp air is clean, and there is a stillness while all nature seems to pause to take in the splendor of creation. The glory of the Lord surrounds us, perfect and new, where nothing is left untouched by His hand.

The ugliest of landscapes, even a trash heap, can be transformed into something stunningly gorgeous when covered with fresh snow. The same miracle happens when Jesus enters our hearts, and our ugly trash heap of sin has been covered forever by His cleansing sacrifice. We are left whiter than the most pristine snow. Our hearts can be as peaceful as the winter landscape, and our lives as fresh as crisp, clean, winter air.

When Satan throws his arrows and we recall the trash heap of sin that smeared our lives, it's easy to doubt God's love. But Satan is a liar. God loves us so much that He gave His only Son to redeem the world. When we believe in Him, He will create something totally new in us—the beautiful creation we were always meant to be.

* * * * * * * * * * *

Thank You, Lord, for Your Son who made me more lovely and perfect than a spotless snow-covered landscape. Amen.

Hidden Jewels

Jesus told the crowd all these things in parables, and He would not speak anything to them without a parable.

MATTHEW 13:34 HCSB

Longhorn Cavern State Park in Burnet County, Texas, is a hidden jewel. While most caves are formed as limestone slowly dissolves through erosion, Longhorn Cavern was carved out by the tremendous pressure of underground rivers. The force of the water carved the cavern into fantastic whorls and swirls of rock, and over time flowing crystalline structures formed throughout the cave. Walking through the cavern is like stepping into another world.

Why would God go to the trouble of creating such beauty deep underground where so few people see it? Perhaps it is a reminder that there are things in God that we have to search out in order to understand. This is one reason Jesus taught in parables. Parables are stories containing spiritual truths that must be pondered to be understood.

God invites and desires us to seek Him. Just as caves hide their beauty beneath the earth, there is beauty in the depths of God that we discover as we earnestly seek Him, taking time to ponder God's power and love. God also promises that when we seek Him, we will find Him. God reveals His treasure to those who take time to search it out and devote themselves to the study of His Word.

. . . .

Lord, I desire to seek You. Help me plunge deep into all the wonder and beauty of knowing You as Savior and Lord. Amen.

Faith in the Waiting

March around the city, all your soldiers. Circle the city once.
Repeat this for six days.

JOSHUA 6:3 MSG

As we pulled into Masai Mara National Reserve, we waited in anticipation to see one of Kenya's greatest treasures—Simba the lion. We spied elephants and zebras and gazelles, all as ubiquitous as the acacia trees that dotted the savannah. We spotted cheetahs and leopards, difficult to tell them apart from far away. I knew I could differentiate between them and a lion once I finally saw one. We waited and waited, and even stared down a black rhino, but Simba never appeared. Our best chance would happen when they hunted, either at dawn or dusk. That meant more waiting.

Joshua, one of Israel's greatest warriors, knew about the waiting game. He proved his courage in battle many times, so imagine the day God told Joshua, *Don't fight—wait.* God didn't tell Joshua to storm the fortress of Jericho, but to march around it, waiting. Was Joshua tempted to start tearing down the walls? Probably. Did he make a back-up plan? Maybe. But his faith in the waiting prepared him for the victory once Jericho's walls began to crumble.

In Kenya, we finally saw a lion. Days later, in the most mundane of circumstances, we glimpsed Simba sprinting in the distance. The beauty was worth the wait.

* * * * * * * * * * *

Lord, teach me to wait on You today, to surrender to Your timing in all of life's circumstances. Amen.

Small Beginnings

Do not despise these small beginnings, for the LORD rejoices to see the work begin, to see the plumb line in Zerubbabel's hand.

ZECHARIAH 4:10 NLT

Our plum tree bore fruit for the first time this year. When I first went out to see the fruit, it didn't look like much. The tiny plums were only the size of the head of a pin. But over the next few months they grew into round balls the size of a child's fist. In summer they ripened into sweet, purple fruit. Those tiny plums were a reminder to me not to despise small beginnings. God makes small things grow.

After the Babylonian exile the Jewish people returned home and began to rebuild the temple. For those who remembered the glories of the former temple, the new construction must have seemed a poor imitation. But through the prophet Zechariah, God told the people not to be discouraged. It might seem like a small beginning, but God was pleased with their obedience and would rejoice when the structure was completed.

Sometimes when God calls us to step out into a new adventure—moving to a new location, starting a business, or planting a church—we can be discouraged by small beginnings. But God is pleased with our obedience, and our small acts of faithfulness will reap a fruitful harvest in time. God makes small things grow.

. . . .

Lord, when I am discouraged by small beginnings, remind me that You are the God who makes small things grow. Amen.

The Garden Spider

I want you woven into a tapestry of love, in touch with everything there is to know of God. Then you will have minds confident and at rest, focused on Christ, God's great mystery.

COLOSSIANS 2:2 MSG

During the summer, I often study the garden spider's intricate web. It's a mystery to me as to how this creature weaves delicate threads into a circular pattern that brandishes a zig-zag. The spider's gold and onyx body is camouflaged amid the plants where her web captures mosquitoes and other insects I consider pests. The garden spider has a purpose, and God designed you for a purpose too.

Consider your life as a tapestry, spun with delicate threads. As intricate as the spider's web might be, it cannot compare to the complex design that's created as God weaves together the fabric of your life. It too may have a zig-zag, but God even has a purpose in that. Our lives may be stained with sin, but because of God's grace, we can be transformed into new creations. Just as the garden spider repairs her web each night, God restores our lives.

God gifted the garden spider with the ability to create something unique and beautiful. Likewise, you are made in His image, unique and beautiful, and He sacrificed His only Son, Jesus Christ, so that you may have eternal life.

Father, as You weave me into a tapestry of love, help me trust You always, and thank You for my unique design. Amen.

The Coming
of the Rains

*The LORD will open the heavens, the storehouse of his bounty,
to send rain on your land in season and to bless all the work of
your hands.*

DEUTERONOMY 28:12 NIV

The rains came in sudden deluge. With a deafening roar, water pounded against the tin roof. Our entire African village was dancing with joy in the downpour. Children giggled and rolled on the once-hard ground, reveling in the mystery of mud. Old ladies threw their heads back as the free water poured over them like baptism. Men and boys danced under the dripping palms.

Behind our house I found a laughing throng, clamoring to capture the overflow from our roof. In discarded tin cans and plastic buckets, every drop would be stored and treasured. The dry season was past. The promise of planting and harvest had come.

Dry seasons of life can seem unending. The soil of our heart grows parched and hardened. We see no growth, only wilted dreams. We become sluggish in our prayers. But there is a day coming when the skies will surely open. From the storehouse of His bounty, the Lord will send the rain we have been longing for to our weary hearts. The promise of planting and harvest will fill us with celebration as we lift our faces to the rain, refreshed and renewed.

. . . .

Lord, fill me with hope during the dry seasons of life and help me fix my eyes on the coming harvest as I trust in You. Amen.

Fuel to Live By

Abide in me, and I in you. As the branch cannot bear fruit by itself, unless it abides in the vine, neither can you, unless you abide in me.

JOHN 15:4 ESV

The complex process of photosynthesis occurs each day. Plants convert light from the sun into energy, which then provides continued life for plants and all living organisms on the earth. Without sun or water, the process is interrupted and a domino effect occurs that impacts the rest of the planet because of the lack of oxygen.

In just the same way, if I disconnect with Christ, I detach from the source of my spiritual growth. Sadly, I sometimes become complacent in my walk with Christ and I don't realize how important it is for me to remain connected to Him. When I go through times that are comfortable, I don't always seek God's face. Or I stop at times when I decide that the way is too difficult. There are many excuses to skip regular times with God and His Word, but when I don't have a vital connection with God, I can tell that I'm missing out. When I walk closely with the Lord and I'm in His Word, I can count on that relationship to fuel my life.

* * * * * * * * * * *

Dear Lord, help me remain connected throughout my day to the source of life that is You. Amen.

The Beach Cleansing

*He saved us through the washing of rebirth and renewal by the
Holy Spirit, whom He poured out on us generously through Jesus
Christ our Savior, so that, having been justified by His grace, we
might become heirs having the hope of eternal life.*

TITUS 3:5–8 NIV

People young and old come to the beach to enjoy the hot
sun, warm sand, and of course the majestic ocean. By
the end of the day, the sand has dents, holes, and tracks from
footprints, sand castles, and beach coolers on wheels. And
then overnight, nature does its cleansing.

The tide rushes in and covers the footprints, fills the sand
castle holes, and removes all the tracks. The early morning
crew—joggers, walkers, and surfers—have a fresh and pristine
beach to enjoy.

The cleansing tide reminds me of God's grace. Every
day we can suffer from negative footprints across our hearts,
sand castle–sized holes from painful betrayals, and cooler-like
tracks of unresolved wounds on our souls. God comes to the
rescue and justifies us by His grace like the tide cleanses the
beach. But He doesn't stop there. He also bestows gifts—
rebirth and renewal from the Holy Spirit and the hope of
eternal life.

* * * * * * * * * * *

*Father, thank You for nature's example of the cleansing tide on the
sandy beach, for generously pouring Your justifying grace into me
and giving me eternal life. Amen.*

Forced Evacuation

He fills my life with good things. My youth is renewed like the eagle's!

PSALM 103:5 NLT

Baby eagles do not just begin to fly because they want to be adventurous. Instead, they are forced from the safety of their nest . . . by loving parents. They actually begin to starve their little fledglings so that the comfort of provisions and protection is increasingly removed. As they burrow around for pieces of bone or meat embedded in the nest, they inevitably lose weight. Their first clumsy efforts at flying often end in crash landings. Still, as they lose their baby fat and become more playful, they also find it easier to catch a draft and soar a bit while trying to use their wings.

Although it seems the eagle parents are being cruel in withholding food and comfort, they are actually doing their fledgling a service by forcing it to want more and eventually take the great risk of leaving the nest in order to find it.

Do you ever feel stuck? Is your familiar "nest" becoming increasingly uncomfortable, perhaps forcing you to look for more? Quite possibly your heavenly Father is nudging you forward to something new. He will provide the necessary strength. You may be holding back, hesitant. . . . Send up a prayer and then leap out "on wings like eagles." God is with you!

* * * * * * * * * * *

Lord, when I feel Your ways are candid and harsh, help me to remember that You always know what will help me to soar with strength. Amen.

Resilience

᛭ ᚩ᛭ᚩ᛭ᚩ᛭ᚩ᛭ᚩ᛭ᚩ᛭ᚩ᛭

You know that the testing of your faith produces perseverance.

JAMES 1:3 NIV

Blizzards are not supposed to arrive in October. Even here in New England. That's when our trees usually show their finery—an abundance of leaves in a palette of rust, cranberry, green, and gold. So when the snow and ice arrived with a fury early that autumn, each individual leaf on every tree was encased in ice. The weight was incredible. The limbs on our little front yard tree bowed low to the ground with the heavy, unexpected burden.

We went without electricity for a week and I cringed every time I heard the snap of another branch finally succumbing to the harsh elements. Huddled under two blankets, wearing three wool sweaters and long johns, I mouthed a silent "good-bye" to our little tree. I just knew it could not survive.

Have you ever felt so weighed down that you think you're breaking apart? Will the suffering you're experiencing now be what finally wrecks you? Or will it be what gives you new hope? Sometimes God uses storms to strengthen us, to build our character. Three years after that October blizzard, my little tree still stands proudly in our yard. It's not as beautiful as it once was. It carries scars. But it is there, a testimony to resilience. It never lost hope; nor shall I.

. . . .

Lord, when I feel beaten down, please remind me that I can call on Your strength to help me persevere through any storm. Amen.

Trapped

❁ ❁ ❁ ❁ ❁ ❁ ❁ ❁

Therefore if the Son makes you free, you shall be free indeed.

JOHN 8:36 NKJV

The gray morning light provided a perfect backdrop for the giant spider web that stretched like a banner from one side of my office window to the other. The gossamer strands almost looked like the spider had spun a hammock there. Then I saw the weaver of that fancy web, a large wicked-looking black spider tucked into the corner of the window, lurking there, waiting for its next prey. As I leaned closer, I realized that there were already numerous victims caught in the web—smaller spiders, flies, moths, and even a mosquito or two. Once they flew into the web, they were trapped.

I don't know about you, but I've often had that trapped feeling. Trapped in despair. Trapped in heartache. Trapped in difficult circumstances. There have been so many times when it seemed like there was no escape, no way out. Can you relate?

The victims in that finely woven spider web couldn't free themselves—and we can't free ourselves either. But the good news is that we have a Rescuer who is there whenever we need Him. He excels in squashing the circumstances that trap and defeat us, setting us free—with true and lasting freedom—so that we can serve Him with great joy and delight.

• • • • • • • • • •

Dear Father, I'm grateful that You are my rescuer whenever I feel trapped, and that true freedom is found in You. Amen.

Cat Eyes

Even the darkness will not be dark to you; the night will shine like the day, for darkness is as light to you.

PSALM 139:12 NIV

Cats have an incredible ability to see in the dark due to cells behind their retinas that reflect the incoming light into their eyeballs. This brightens the images and enables cats to resolve them in surroundings seven times darker than what humans can see in and greatly enhances the success of their nighttime prowls.

This remarkable capability was replicated by scientists who developed night vision goggles for soldiers that protect troops in nighttime operations. Although current models are bulky, their advantages are significant.

God also has night vision capabilities. In the Psalms, David declares that darkness is as light to Him. This is a great comfort for those who rest in God, for not only can He spot invisible hazards, He's able to protect us from them.

Although this Almighty attribute is true physically, it is more of a blessing spiritually. During dark periods in our lives when we can't even see the pathway beneath our feet, it is especially comforting to know that we have a God who can. He will direct our steps and see us safely through as we follow Him in obedient faith. I'm thankful for a God who sees, and can resolve any situation regardless of the light level.

* * * * * * * * * * *

God of perfect vision, enlighten my pathway and grant me grace to follow You even when my way is dark. Amen.

Mysterious Travelers

You guide me with your counsel, leading me to a glorious destiny.

PSALM 73:24 NLT

When birds migrate south for winter, they don't need a compass to point them in the direction of warmer climates. When they head back north the following year, some birds return to the exact same location. Scientists can't fully explain this uncanny sense of direction. They say landmarks are a key part of it, but much of it is simply instinct—an instinct human beings can't seem to fathom. One species, the cuckoo, is especially skilled at it. Cuckoos often lay their eggs in the nests of other birds so when the babies hatch and mature they must find their migration route without the help of parents or siblings.

Likewise, God is a compass for our lives. When we face important decisions, He will guide us if we will listen—"Whether you turn to the right or to the left, your ears will hear a voice behind you, saying, 'This is the way; walk in it'" (Isaiah 30:21 NIV). Along the path, we'll see His love in action, His promises fulfilled, and His wisdom proved flawless again and again. The destination is eternal life, and Jesus is the Way.

God wants to be our guide. Not only are His instincts more perfect than those of the migrating bird, He cares about where we go and He'll always point us to the right coordinates.

Father, help me to turn to You first for direction so I can follow You home. Amen.

Lessons from
the Flamingo

Man shall not live by bread alone, but on every word that comes from the mouth of God.

MATTHEW 4:4 NIV

Flamingos are fascinating. They're graceful, peaceful, and beautiful. Born white and gray, they change to their bright pinkish color from eating beta-carotene–rich foods. They are monogamous and take excellent care of their young. Interestingly, both males and females produce milk, which is fed to their chicks through their bills. On top of all this, flamingos are friendly and stick together in flocks. I've heard they make nice pets, but I'll settle for the low-maintenance plastic ones.

Scripture tells us we are to live by every word from God's mouth, His daily bread. Just as flamingo chicks reach up and open their beaks to receive nourishment from their parents, we are to lift our hearts and open our spiritual mouths wide for our heavenly Father to fill (Psalm 81:10).

Like the flamingo that grows pink from the beta-carotene in their food, a diet rich in God's Word will show throughout our whole being. When Moses came down from the mountain, his face shone—evidence he had been with God (Exodus 34:30). As we spend time with God in His Word, our lives will begin to change color and shine with His grace, peace, and beauty.

• • • • • • • • • • •

Thank You, Lord, for the daily bread You provided to nourish me spiritually and color my life with Your love. Amen.

The Preparation
of Autumn

*When you are harvesting in your field and you overlook a sheaf,
do not go back to get it. Leave it for the foreigner, the fatherless
and the widow, so that the LORD your God may bless you in all
the work of your hands.*

DEUTERONOMY 24:19 NIV

Leaving behind the abundance of summer, nature cools
the earth, ripens the harvest, and shortens the daylight
hours. Autumn provides the opportunity to get ready for the
long, cold winter. God knew what would be coming and gave
instructions on how to prepare for ourselves and also help
others.

First of all, we are expected to do the harvest for ourselves. The verse doesn't say, "If you are harvesting . . . "; it
says, "When. . . ." Secondly, share. Remember those who are
less fortunate.

What about us today? Few of us have fields, trees, or vines
ready to be picked. However, we are now nine months into
the year and surely we have received a harvest of something
along the way. Maybe it's financial gain or a new skill. Maybe
we have accumulated extra winter coats, blankets, or canned
goods in our homes. These items or services will not only bless
those who receive them, but they will bring a blessing to the
giver as well. God promises that it goes both ways.

*Father, I am grateful for the harvest You have sown into my life
this year and ask that You open my eyes to how I can share with
others in my community. Amen.*

A Simple Nudge

Jesus . . . said to them, "All authority in heaven and on earth has been given to me. Go therefore and make disciples of all nations, baptizing them in the name of the Father and of the Son and of the Holy Spirit, teaching them to observe all that I have commanded you. And behold, I am with you always, to the end of the age."

MATTHEW 28:18–20 ESV

When I looked into the backyard one morning, my heart sank. A large hawk rose from the ground with a squirrel in its claws. I pounded my fist and screamed, but it was too late. Moments later the hawk's mate arrived; this time, however, when I pounded and screamed, the predator flew away. I stared at the hawk's nest, mourning the squirrel who just became a part of the circle of life.

While I stood there, I felt God nudge me. Several tough questions came to mind that required thoughtful honesty to answer. Am I as concerned over a lost human soul as I am over the hawk's prey? Do I pound at the door and scream to save those caught in Satan's evil schemes? Am I vigilant to pray for those who don't know Jesus? Do I support efforts that reach out to the world for Christ?

I thanked God for those tough questions; they opened my eyes to purposes and possibilities all around me.

. . . .

Jesus, give me a deep concern for those who haven't heard about You, to share the truth of who You are with them. Amen.

Where the Wheat Blows

The grasslands of the wilderness become a lush pasture, and the hillsides blossom with joy. The meadows are clothed with flocks of sheep, and the valleys are carpeted with grain. They all shout and sing for joy!

PSALM 65:12–13 NLT

The summer crops had been harvested, sold to a waiting market. The rich, brown loam left a pungency of freshly turned soil in the air, and a gentle breeze brought the promise of rain. The coming showers would soon set free the tiny green sprouts of winter wheat just waiting to burst through the earth.

Around the house, fall flowers had popped forth, their red, orange, and yellow covering the ground in a striking array. Even as the trees dropped their leaves and so many plants and animals prepared for winter, a lush bounty still remained.

Few things are as peaceful and soothing as a field of wheat undulating in the breeze. Light dances over the field, as appealing as the ocean shore, but only a whisper, sweet and calm, echoes back and forth through the waves of grain.

God's gifts to us abound in nature, both in the grandeur of the mountains and in the gentle wind through a wheat field. They surround us in every moment, a present to appreciate—the flowers, the turning leaves, and the glory of a simple field. He is, indeed, Jehovah Jireh, the One who provides.

· · · · · · · · · · ·

God, may I always find time to stop, look around, and appreciate the glory and abundance You have created on this earth. Amen.

Clear My Vision

I will lift up my eyes to the hills—from whence comes my help?
My help comes from the LORD, who made heaven and earth.

PSALM 121:1–2 NKJV

I'm sorry about this weather—you can't see our mountains!"

My son and I had just met my friend for dinner after our flight into Utah. It was a gray, cloudy evening, and a dense fog had settled in the sky. The visibility was low as we drove to our hotel in Provo.

After a much-needed restful sleep, I awoke the next morning and opened the curtains. The view outside the window took my breath away. The clouds and fog had lifted to reveal Mount Timpanogos, and I could definitely tell I wasn't in Kentucky anymore.

The mountains were tall, rocky, and awe-inspiring. I took in the view for a while and thanked God for His beautiful creation.

Though the fog had obscured my vision that first night, the weather was clear for the rest of the trip, and I stood amazed at the mountains every time they came into view.

Sometimes my problems engulf me in a "fog" that clouds my vision, and I forget that the Creator of the universe holds my life in His hands. When I remember who holds the future, the fog lifts and I can enjoy the view, despite my circumstances.

. . . .

Father, clear my vision so I can keep my eyes on You. Amen.

Behold the Beauty

The heavens declare the glory of God; the skies proclaim the work of his hands.

PSALM 19:1 NIV

My girls love to tease me because every time I see a gorgeous sunset, I have to take a picture. You know the kind of "gorgeous" I'm talking about, right? When the sky is several shades of pink, or when the sun is an enlarged orange orb as it dips below the horizon. I can't help myself; I simply have to snap a picture.

The other day, we were headed home from Nana's, and as we topped the hill near our local high school, the view literally took my breath away. The sun was fiery orange, with touches of pinks and purples dotting the horizon. I squealed with excitement like a little girl, fumbled for my cell phone camera app, and frantically pointed it out the window just in time to capture God's masterpiece.

I realize that my infatuation with sunsets is a source of entertainment for my friends and family, but I don't mind. I hope I never lose that overly enthusiastic appreciation for God's handiwork. After all, God is good and worthy to be praised. If it's been awhile since you've watched the brightly colored sun sink below the horizon and appreciated the majesty and beauty of that daily event, I suggest you grab a camera and await the marvelous show. I promise, you won't be disappointed.

. . . .

Father, thank You for creating such beautiful sights to behold every day. You are an amazing artist. Amen.

How Far Is the East from the West?

As far as the east is from the west, so far has he removed our transgressions from us.

PSALM 103:12 NIV

Calculating distance from one spot to the next can be overwhelming. While we tend to comprehend short distances fairly well, longer spans tend to give us some trouble. The nineteen nautical miles across the English Channel or the ten to eighteen miles across the Grand Canyon (depending where you measure) are reasonable. But what about trying to gauge the distance across our galaxy? Because the number is so large, it is measured in light years, but if we did measure in miles, it would be approximately six hundred quadrillion miles. A quadrillion, by the way, has fifteen zeros!

Similarly, the concept of distance between the east and the west is incomprehensible. North to south measurements are logical because the poles delineate actual north and south. There is never such a point from east to west. You would have to make a 180-degree turn and go the opposite direction to create a "point" where east would meet west.

When we have confessed and abandoned our sins, God removes them "as far as the east is from the west." What a consolation to know that once He removes sin from our lives, it is remembered no more. There's no distance further apart that could be expressed.

. . . .

We praise You, Lord, for Your son Jesus who had the power to conquer death and remove my sins so completely. Amen.

Rain

°°O°°O°°O°°O°°O°°O

*Consider it a sheer gift, friends, when tests and challenges come at
you from all sides. You know that under pressure, your faith-life is
forced into the open and shows its true colors.*

JAMES 1:2 MSG

I sat watching the rain in disappointment. It had started as a
gentle shower but was soon a downpour. Family plans for
the day were washed out in the storm. New arrangements were
made and, as it turned out, this actually made way for a better
option, drawing family closer. The rain had become a blessing, providing an opportunity to build family relationships.

I am trying to see the "rain" in my life like that. When
faced with unplanned, difficult circumstances, trials, or disap-
pointments, I am trying to see them as drops of God's mercy
inviting me to grow. After the rain, plants, grass, flowers all
burst forth with new growth. This is evident in many ways in
nature. Changes in color, size, blossoms, and fruit attest to the
benefits of life-giving water.

Growth is hard work. No doubt about it. I want to resist, to put up my umbrella or run for cover. Difficult as it is
to absorb, I need to consider hardships as an opportunity to
trust God more. He wants to see my true colors, and the only
way that happens is if I put down my umbrella and receive
the rain.

. . . .

*Father, help me to see the rainy times as an opportunity to grow
closer to You. Amen.*

Chronic Overpacker

Come to me, all you who are weary and burdened, and I will give you rest.

MATTHEW 11:28 NIV

One of the things I've learned about hiking is the need for a backpack, even on a day hike. We never know when we'll be caught out longer than expected and need first-aid supplies, water, or even a snack to renew flagging energy.

I've always been a chronic overpacker, and it turns out that my tendency toward stuffed suitcases and purses extends to backpacks. One day I filled my pack to overflowing without once considering how strenuous the hike would be.

It didn't take long before the straps of my pack dug into my shoulders and my muscles began to cramp. Fortunately, my husband is a patient and generous man. We redistributed the contents of my pack and made it through the hike. But my lack of forethought weighed everyone down.

I couldn't help but draw the comparison of the spiritual weight I carry with me daily—the expectations I take up without reason, the stress and worry I add to my load—and how it affects those around me.

Now, whenever I see that I'm overloaded, I come back to these verses and hand over all the extra stuff to Jesus. I exchange what I thought I wanted for what He knows I need. And it's *always* a more manageable load.

. . . .

Dear Lord, teach me how to always come to You for help with the load I'm carrying. Amen.

Even in the Fog

꙳ ꙳°꙳°꙳°꙳ ꙳°꙳°꙳°

*Though the fig tree does not bud and there are no grapes on the
vines, though the olive crop fails and the fields produce no food . . .
yet I will rejoice in the LORD, I will be joyful in God my Savior.*

HABAKKUK 3:17–18 NIV

The fog thickened till my car was shrouded in a gray blanket. I slowed down, peering ahead for any sign of tail-
lights or obstacles. Just when I was wondering if it was ever
going to lighten up, the sun shone through a veil of cloud. It
was shrouded, but still there.

Life can sometimes feel like we are driving through fog.
There are times when we live with unanswerable questions.
Why does God allow such suffering? I have been faithful—
why am I having to deal with this? We can lose our way in the
fog of doubt.

Habakkuk lived in such a time of struggle. He longed
for God to intervene and put an end to the evil he saw
around him, but he dreaded the cost: invasion from Babylon.
Habakkuk questioned God, but at the end he vowed trust.
Even if the worst happened, Habakkuk promised to trust in
the God of his salvation.

In places of mystery we have to trust in who we know
God to be even when we can't see Him at work. Even in the
fog, the light of God's presence still shines.

. . . .

*Lord, help me trust in Your faithfulness even in the places of
mystery and doubt. Amen.*

Off with the Old

Do not lie to each other, since you have taken off your old self with its practices and have put on the new self, which is being renewed in knowledge in the image of its Creator.

COLOSSIANS 3:9–10 NIV

Snakes are some of the most provocative creatures in the animal kingdom. Nearly everyone reacts strongly in some way to these legless reptiles. Even their discarded semi-transparent skins often accelerate heart rates and induce goosebumps.

Those skins, however, generally indicate a well-fed serpent. As the animal's girth increases, it is unable to purchase larger waist sizes; instead, as it outgrows its old layer of scales, it develops a new one. When the new skin is ready, it simply peels the old one off on a rock or tree trunk, revealing its brand-new, vibrant, skintight outfit. The more it consumes, the faster it grows, and the more it leaves behind shed skins to needlessly frighten unsuspecting humans.

Although Eden's serpent gave all of his descendants a bad reputation, snakes can help us understand our own spiritual growth. The more we consume the Bread of Life—God's Word—the faster we grow. As we do so, the Holy Spirit convicts us of sins that inhibit even greater development, which we must leave behind if we are to become all God created us to be. If we feast on His Word regularly, we will shed continuously.

Lord God, reveal what limits my spiritual growth and enable me to "shed" it with Your power. Amen.

Unbelievable
Natural Power

Who believes what we've heard and seen? Who would have thought GOD's saving power would look like this?

ISAIAH 53:1 MSG

Discoveries of thermal features in the earth—"fire and brimstone"—in the western territories were considered wild tales. Yet trappers, explorers, and miners continued telling stories about boiling pools of water, using the term "geyser" for the first time in 1842. They also told of petrified birds and trees. But no reputable magazine would publish such "frontier fiction" until an expedition included professional photographer and renowned artist Thomas Moran. Finally, his pictures were irrefutable proof!

I saw it with my own eyes last year—the wonders of Yellowstone National Park. And still it was hard to believe. Old Faithful geyser erupts about every ninety minutes—shooting as much as 8,400 gallons of hot water up to 184 feet. That's a lot of thermal power. And it's all from our Creator.

Some people are still waiting for God to "prove" He is sovereign. They still wonder if He knows what's best for their life or if He has the power to make it happen. The signs are all around us in nature, sometimes as big as a geyser. God is here and active. We may not recognize His gifts and guidance at first, but trust Him. He will deliver.

. . . .

Lord, when I have a hard time believing, help me widen my expectations for Your goodness and power. Amen.

A Broad Place

He brought me forth also into a broad place; He rescued me, because He delighted in me.

PSALM 18:19 NASB

What a heart-warming verse. After all, who doesn't need a little rescuing? And who doesn't long to be "delighted in"? But the significance of being brought forth into "a broad place" became apparent to me while on—of all places—the back of a horse.

Now, this particular horse much preferred the barn to the trail and was quite determined to scrape me off its back, utilizing every available tree. Since our ride was through a forest, he had approximately 312 opportunities to do so, give or take a couple.

After forty-five minutes of ducking, dodging, and clinging, we finally emerged from the forest and trotted into a broad, open space. And the full meaning of the Psalm became so very clear. Yes, I was still on that horse, I still had to get *off* that horse, but I was rescued from the trees. I could breathe. I could focus on what needed to be done: get back to the barn and off that horse!

When we call out to God, He may or may not remove the root problem (in this case, the horse), but He delivers us from those things that scrape away at our faith so we can breathe, so we can focus on what needs to be done.

. . . .

Lord, lead me to a broad place so that I may clearly see You and what needs to be done. Amen.

Hidden Gems of Grace

I will make rivers flow on barren heights, and springs within the valleys. I will turn the desert into pools of water, and the parched ground into springs.

ISAIAH 41:18 NIV

On a recent hike in the mountains, I bowed over in exhaustion. Heart pounding, I could walk no farther. But as I faced the ground I smiled in surprise. Tiny sparkles were embedded in the rocks! They glittered like gold. Later, I learned minerals caused the rocks to shine like that, but before this day I had never seen the ground glisten. My eyes were set on the mountain, not on the ground beneath. I almost missed the beauty beneath my feet.

God hides tiny nuggets of His grace everywhere. All we need to do is open our eyes and recognize them. His grace sparkles from every angle. We see His grace in the glory of nature. We see it in the way the wind blows through the trees or the bird's melody. That day, grace nuggets glowed at me from a place I never thought to look. He delights in causing His grace to flow to us from unexpected places.

When I'm discouraged and down and out, I begin to hunt for nuggets of grace. Instead of keeping my eyes glued on the problem, I'm learning to take delight in the hidden gems of God's grace.

* * * * * * * * * * *

Jesus, open my tired eyes to see Your grace surrounding me; show me Your mighty strength and let me rest in You today. Amen.

Powerful and Personal

He heals the brokenhearted and binds up their wounds. He determines the number of the stars and calls them each by name.

PSALM 147:3–4 NIV

One night during a camping trip we went out to look at the night sky. The heavens glowed. The Milky Way was so thick it looked like you could drink it. As we looked at the innumerable stars, I remembered that God knows them all by name.

The heavens declare God's glory and power, but they also reminded me of God's intimate care and concern. If God knows the stars by name, I can trust He also knows mine. And though God is powerful enough to determine the number of stars and set them in motion, He is also intimate and personal enough to know my tears and to heal my heart. The God who calls the stars by name also binds up the brokenhearted.

God is powerful, but He is also personal. God is not too busy with the cosmos to care about me. He knows my name. He sees my tears. He loves me enough to heal my wounds, and He is powerful enough to intervene on my behalf. I may feel small standing out under the night sky, but the uncountable and unknowable stars remind me that I am perfectly and powerfully loved.

* * * * * * * * * * *

Lord, thank You that You who know the stars by name also know mine. Amen.

A Rock Where
We May Stand

Then the LORD said, "There is a place near me where you may stand on a rock."

EXODUS 33:21 NIV

The Rock of Gibraltar rises out of the ocean like a beacon of strength. The waves crash against its stony cliffs only to shrink back again, unable to scale the heights. As I climbed the peak, I was prepared for fierce wind and the noise of the crashing sea. What I encountered instead was stillness, quietness, and a tangible sense of strength and power. To stand on the summit of that mighty rock made me feel invincible. It was as if the strength beneath me had become an extension of my own stature and I was safe, secure, victorious over anything.

Moses was struggling with insecurity. He wanted to do God's will but he knew that alone he could never accomplish the great task before him. He experienced the strength and promise of the living God only when he stood upon the Rock. Moses would not go forward alone; the Lord would be with him and he would be victorious.

Are you struggling with insecurity? Is the task before you too great? There is a place near the Lord where you may stand upon a rock. In that place you will be invincible through the name of our great and powerful God.

. . . .

Lord, I come to today as my Rock, bringing to You the tasks just too big for me, asking You to equip me with strength. Amen.

Perfect Rhythm

I am the vine; you are the branches. If you remain in me and I in you, you will bear much fruit; apart from me you can do nothing.

JOHN 15:5 NIV

There's a fantastic German word that describes the beauty and freedom of a horse when it fully trusts its rider—*losgelassenheit*. It speaks about the way a horse's body moves when it fully relaxes, totally devoid of tension. Almost like a dance, horse and rider achieve *losgelassenheit* when the horse's back swings in perfect rhythm with its neck and back muscles moving together with its legs. The closest English word is "looseness."

Something similar happens when believers fully trust the Master, when we relax into Jesus's presence and trust His sovereign reign over our lives. We experience joy and peace, and we manifest His grace and power to overcome our weaknesses.

Jesus uses the metaphor of the vine and branches to describe His abiding presence in us. He wants us to bear fruit, but He never expects us to do it apart from His presence. As the horse needs to trust the rider, we must rely on God's supply—His grace. For spiritual growth, we need Him. For patience, we need Him. For power to overcome sin, we need Him. This amazing gift is available by opening up our hearts to His Spirit. He wants to walk with us through each day, hand in hand.

. . . .

Jesus, I confess my need for You in every way, and I ask You to fill me with Your Spirit today. Amen.

The Woodland Stream

He restores my soul.

PSALM 23:3 NKJV

Sometimes the troubles of this world threaten to overtake me. When that happens, I seek the balm of the woodland stream. Seasons come and go, but the sound of water caressing stones washes a sense of peace over me. During spring, the bank is carpeted with purple creeping phlox, wild violets, and a myriad of plant life. On a steaming summer day, I can plant my feet in the cool waters where tiny minnow kiss my toes while dragonflies hover. In autumn, all I need to do to feel refreshed is glance up. Starbursts of sunlight filter through the orange, crimson, and green canopy. Bleak winter days don't daunt the woodland ferns thriving at the water's edge. Their green fronds teach me to cling to the rock and seek the warmth of the living water.

The melody of birds serenade me through every season and prompt me to sing with joy. Fossils amid the pebbles remind me God has always been and will always be. I have nothing to fear from the troubles of today. Breathing in the beauty of God's presence restores my troubled soul. There are blessings through every season at the woodland stream.

. . . .

Father, thank You for Your quiet waters that restore my soul through every season, and may I refresh others now that You have refreshed me. Amen.

Release and Return

*The eyes of the LORD move to and fro throughout the earth that
He may strongly support those whose heart is completely His.*

2 CHRONICLES 16:9 NASB

My late friend, Suzi, was a certified raptor rehabilitator.
Spectacular views of the Colorado Rockies could be
seen out her window through a giant net that covered the
entire backyard, hung to protect the birds. Her devotion out-
weighed a distasteful practice of raising mice in the garage
as food for the captive birds—a practice I did not hold in
high regard. She won my admiration, however, by demon-
strating the activity of release and return, the tethered hawk
returning to her outstretched gloved hand. She would determine the proper time to carry her bird to a wide open field,
look into the massive western blue skies, and set the healed
creature free.

At times I find myself in need of care from the Great
Rehabilitator. Broken and weak, in need of nourishment,
I thirst for His resources. Like a lost bird that soars above,
I search for the Healer's hand of safety and care. Yet God
searches the whole earth for me too. He stands in default position, arms outstretched, waiting for me to return. He attends
my wounds and in His perfect timing I am healed and set
free. The cry of the hawk makes me think of how the Lord
has sought and found me. I am safe under His love and care.

*Lord, tether me to You so I may receive healing in my times of
need. Amen.*

Artichokes

No one's ever seen or heard anything like this . . . what God has arranged for those who love him.

1 CORINTHIANS 2:9 MSG

She carefully laid the flowery vegetable on a plate in front of me. I stared. Where to begin? My eloquent hostess carefully explained, "Simply pull each petal off, dipping the end into melted butter, and then scrape the soft tender flesh off into your mouth with your slightly clenched teeth. When you reach the heart, scoop out the fuzzy choke with a spoon. That's where the sweetest taste is."

Exploring these exotic edibles left me incredulous. Having just moved to Boston, all I could think was *I wonder what the folks back home in Georgia would think of this?* Who knew such treasures lay inside this prickly plant? Today one of my favorite recipes is artichoke dip. I laugh when I remember that adventure of discovery, glad I was game to try anything.

God is far more creative than we can possibly imagine. He is the One who thought up the anteater, dressed the zebra in stripes, and decided that porcupines were a good idea. We cannot even imagine all He has planned! Are you willing to try something new, daring, or exotic? Perhaps now would be a great time to "taste and see that the LORD is good" (Psalm 34:8 NIV).

* * * * * * * * * * *

Lord, I'm grateful that there are always new realms of Your creation to discover and pass along if we just take time to notice. Amen.

Do You Know
His Voice?

Blessed are those who listen to me, watching daily at my doors, waiting at my doorway. For those who find me find life and receive favor from the LORD.

PROVERBS 8:34–35 NIV

Whether a bird, a horse, a donkey, a sheep, or a dog, animals know their master's voice. In fact, I recently read a study by scientists at the University of Tokyo that revealed even cats can tell their owner's voice from a stranger's voice. (Being all catlike, they may still choose to ignore their owners.) No doubt, the reason that our animals can distinguish our voices from others is because they spend so much time with us. And it's the same way with God.

Have you ever heard someone say, "I heard God speaking to me . . . "? And, have you ever wondered how they were "hearing" from God? Well, typically they aren't hearing a booming voice from heaven; rather, they are referring to that small, inner voice that they know is God because they know His voice. How do they know His voice? From spending time with Him—reading His Word, conversing with Him in prayer, and taking time to be quiet and listen.

Every now and then I ask myself how well I am hearing God's voice. Sometimes the answer is "not well," and that's when I know it's time to connect more with my Master.

. . . .

Time with You is so precious, Father. Help me to covet it more so that I know Your voice over all the others in my life. Amen.

Things That Go
Bump in the Night

Turn your ear to me, come quickly to my rescue; be my rock of refuge, a strong fortress to save me.

PSALM 31:2 NIV

In sixth grade an intruder made its way down our chimney and into my room where I lay in my bed reading the latest Nancy Drew mystery. At first I wasn't sure what flapped its wings near my head, but on its second flyby I knew. I threw the covers over my head and as wings beat around me, I repeatedly screamed, "There's a bat in my room!"

Within minutes my father appeared at the top of the stairs. He glanced into my room and the bat buzzed his head. Assuring me he'd be right back, he instructed me to stay absolutely still and quiet. My father quickly returned with a broom in his hand. He charged into my room and exterminated the bat. Because my father loved me, I knew if I called he would come to my rescue. I didn't know what he would do. I only knew that with him battling the bat I would be safe.

God is our Father who loves us with an unfailing love. When we call, He will come to our rescue. We may not know what He will do, but with God battling the things that go bump in the night, we know we will be kept safe.

．．．．．．．．．．

Father, I need not fear when the things of this world threaten to harm me because of Your unfailing love. Amen.

Good News

Always be prepared to give an answer to everyone who asks you to give the reason for the hope that you have. But do this with gentleness and respect.

I PETER 3:15 NIV

Chickens have their own language. They "talk" to each other with more than two dozen chirps and calls, each with a distinct meaning. These vocal talents begin at an early age. When baby chicks find morsels of food, they call out with short, high-pitched chirps as if to say "Come eat this, everybody!" Just as chicks trumpet their discoveries through their tiny beaks, we can share God's love with anyone willing to hear.

Imagine a life without the chance to know God. Nothing offered by the world comes close to His everlasting, unchanging heart. No person can give you hope for eternal life, which is found in Jesus alone. Family, friends, neighbors, and coworkers all need the chance to experience that hope.

No matter where you stand in your walk with God, you can share what you know. If a neighbor is grieving, they may need a comforting verse. A friend burdened by guilt might need to hear how you felt God's grace and forgiveness. As we do this, God's Word says we should be gentle and respectful, and just like the baby chicks, excited to share.

* * * * * * * * * * *

Father, because You have given me so much hope, give me opportunities to share that with others. Amen.

Silly Monkeys
and Grinning Goats

Then God saw everything that He had made, and indeed it was very good.

GENESIS 1:31 NKJV

Have you ever thought about the amazing detail of God's creation? I thought about that recently when my son posted a photo of an adorable raccoon by his barn. I've seen lots of raccoons over the years, but I'd never seen a completely white one before. And think about the variety of birds— parrots in rainbow colors, doves in muted gray, pink flamingoes, and spindly-legged herons. God designed zebras in black-and-white, leopards with spots, and goats that grin as if they've just had a whitening treatment on their teeth. He made monkeys that swing through the trees by their tails, alligators with leathery hides, and cuddly kittens with oh-sosoft fur. One doesn't have to look far to realize that He's a God of great detail.

If God cares about detail so much that He puts stripes on a tiger and pockets on kangaroos, why would we ever doubt that He cares about the little moments of our lives? He notices when the pantry shelves are bare. He sees the tears in our eyes when our hearts are broken. He knows when the doctor calls with scary news. And we can trust Him to take care of every detail.

* * * * * * * * * *

Dear Lord, I'm so grateful that You care about every little detail of our lives, and for creating such beauty for us to enjoy. Amen.

Known by Name

He counts the stars and calls them all by name.

PSALM 147:4 NLT

To be truly known—and to be truly loved in spite of being truly known—isn't that what we all long for? Isn't that what we search for in friends, in spouses, even in worldly possessions? Though we may search both near and far, there is only One who truly knows us, inside out and soul deep. And who truly loves us—inside out and soul deep!

Impossible! we rationalize. How could it be possible for God to individually know so many people through so many centuries? How could it be possible for Him to know each of us? *To know me?* Ah, but remember, "With God all things are possible" (Matthew 19:26 ESV). For God—who flung galaxies across eternity, who set planets spinning into motion, who spoke and made stars fall from His fingertips—nothing is impossible. He not only created and counted the uncountable stars, He calls each of them by name!

And who are we? The crown of His creation. He created us and counts us and calls each of us by name. Our names are written on the palm of His hand. *Your* name is written on the palm of His hand (Isaiah 49:16). You are known by name, and you are loved.

· · · · · · · · · ·

Lord, You know me, inside out and soul deep, and I'm so grateful that You call me—by name—to be Your own. Amen.

God Is Always There

Trust in the LORD with all your heart, and do not rely on your own understanding.

PROVERBS 3:5 HCSB

I grew up traveling across America in the back of a Volkswagen bus. I've been out West in a blizzard so fierce we scraped ice from the *inside* of the windows. I've cooked an egg on the pavement in Death Valley and spent several nights camping on top of what used to be Mount St. Helens. But only a small percentage of our time on the road was spent on major highways, Daddy preferred the scenic route.

One day, he headed down a dirt road and we got stuck in the mud. No matter what Daddy did, we stayed stuck. As the sun was setting, a truck—complete with towing package—appeared.

He pulled us out in no time, refusing money. When asked why he'd come this way, he tipped back his cowboy hat and scratched his head. "I can't really say. It just seemed like something I needed to do."

This was the day I learned that God is always there for me. Whether He's using a cowboy with a pickup truck, or a close friend, His presence and provision always surround me. Truthfully, it's in the mud that my hardest lessons and greatest joys have been realized.

* * * * * * * * * * *

Lord, lead us down the paths we need to go, strengthening our faith in the muddiness of life. Amen.

Innumerable Stars

When I look at your heavens, the work of your fingers, the moon and the stars, which you have set in place, what is man that you are mindful of him, and the son of man that you care for him?

PSALM 8:3–4 ESV

Do you remember the first time you tried to guess how many gumballs were in a jar at a store or bank? Did you try to make an educated guess by analyzing how many rows you could count and multiply how many gumballs were in each row or did you just wildly pick a number?

Even more so, when we consider the stars of our galaxy, we have to acknowledge that they are beyond counting. The Psalmist reminds us that just looking at the night sky with its magnificent stars, planets, and moons reminds us that we are tiny by comparison. Contemplate for a moment the earth's position in the planetary mix. It is the perfect distance from the sun—any degree closer or farther away and Earth could not sustain life.

Planets that move in perfect order and stars that are innumerable to our eyes expand across our sky. Our God who can manage all of creation is more than capable to care for me and my needs. It's so reassuring to know that such a big God cares for me.

. . . .

Thank You, Lord, for showing me Your vast creation; it fills me with peace to know that You hold it all together in Your hands. Amen.

Snowflakes

Have you entered the storehouses of the snow or seen the storehouses of the hail?

JOB 38:22 NIV

Have you ever suffered writer's block staring at a blank screen or struggled to paint a new picture or invent a new gadget? Sometimes human imagination is exhausted, especially after having been drained by some rigorous workout. We all look forward to vacations and weekends to recharge.

Our heavenly Father, however, never has this problem. His creative capacity knows no limits. As we look at the plant kingdom, we see unbelievable creativity and ingenuity. The animal kingdom is even more diverse as we recognize the infinite number of possible DNA combinations just within humans. Even astronomers struggle to comprehend the variation among the stars of the night sky.

There's probably no better example of God's endless design capability, however, than the tiny snowflake. Scientists estimate the number of snowflakes falling from the clouds at one followed by twenty-four zeros annually. And yet, each of these miniature artworks bears its own unique shape and form. Some have even said it's probable that the number of snowflake shapes on earth exceeds the number of atoms in the universe. That's a lot of shapes.

We have an infinitely creative Creator who is still at work expressing His endless originality. He deserves all the adoration and worship His creatures can give Him.

* * * * * * * * * *

Designer of snowflakes, I worship You for Your infinite creativity. Amen.

Life Out of Darkness

Truly, truly, I say to you, unless a grain of wheat falls into the earth and dies, it remains alone; but if it dies, it bears much fruit.

JOHN 12:24 NASB

The seed lies like a fragile embryo in the darkness beneath the soil. The shell that once grew hard on the vine now lies softened, cracked open, a doorway to life. Unfolding from this shell is a tender shoot pressing its way toward the light above. In just a little while it will emerge strong, growing tall and bearing many seeds of its own.

The paradox of life out of darkness is a mysterious wonder. But this mystery is exactly how our creator God has ordained our growth and multiplication. Like seeds sown upon the souls of men, our lives carry the potential of love multiplied.

How will you sow your life, your one seed? You were designed for multiplication. It is in the dark places of life our hard hearts can be transformed, giving way to new, tenacious life. It is here that love emerges miraculous, delightful, invigorating.

Does darkness envelop you today, threatening to crush your hope? The Creator invites you to trust Him as he brings life from death, fellowship out of loneliness, multiplication out of your one life, surrendered to Him.

· · · · · · · · · · ·

Lord, show me where to sow the seed of my life that I may not remain alone, but that I may bear much fruit. Amen.

The Cedar Tree

The godly will flourish like palm trees and grow strong like the cedars of Lebanon.

PSALM 92:12 NLT

The scent of cedar is one of nature's most memorable fragrances. When Mama told me the story of King Solomon's temple where the walls were lined with cedar, she gifted me with a New Testament encased in a box made of the same material. I opened the lid and inhaled the woody scent. "The same cedar aroma filled the temple where King Solomon worshiped God," Mama said.

From a small pinecone, God designed this unique tree to reach soaring heights. Its wood is valued for strength and endurance, and its branches provide a haven for wildlife. They thrive in rocky soil on mountaintops, but to grow to their extreme heights, they must dig their roots deep into the mountain and cling to the rock. If we dig deep into the Word of God and cling to our rock, we too can possess strength, and endurance and reach for the heavens.

The cedars in my region are scraggly compared to the cedars of Lebanon, but the same perfume fills my home each holiday season. When I close my eyes and breathe in the distinct cedar fragrance, I'm reminded of God's greatest gift—His Son. It's Jesus who lifts me higher and makes me stronger than the cedars of Lebanon. With Him I can endure any storm.

· · · · · · · · · ·

Father, help me be like the cedars of Lebanon, strong, with deep roots, wrapped around You—my solid rock. Amen.

When the Pines Sing

Let the heavens rejoice, let the earth be glad; let the sea resound, and all that is in it. Let the fields be jubilant, and everything in them; let all the trees of the forest sing for joy.

I grew up in a pine grove, and pines make a different sound in the wind than do other trees. Maples, oaks, elms, and fruit trees rustle when their boughs sway and shiver. Magnolias almost clatter when their stiff leaves pop against each other.

Pines, however, sing. The wind through their supple needles results in a whispery, serene sound that calms the soul. It's a sweet melody that would dance through the grove, announcing the arrival of a cool breeze long before it reached my face. Even in the harsh gusts of an approaching storm, pines sounded more reassuring than alarming.

I have seldom felt as close to God as I do among the pines, and Psalm 96 almost always come to mind. In His presence, even the earth revels in the splendor He has spread before us. How can I not rejoice when surrounded by His beauty, marveling at the glory of His creation? Why, even the trees "sing for joy."

* * * * * * * * * *

Lord, You surround me with a magnificent beauty that reveals Your love and care. May I always remember to sing Your praises. Amen.

God Makes
All Things Possible

What is impossible for people is possible with God.

LUKE 18:27 NLT

It snowed our first Christmas in South Texas. The snow started at dusk on Christmas Eve. It sprinkled powder along the power lines and branches, then glazed the hoods of our cars. We weren't sure it would stick, but the snow continued to coat the ground and kept falling. By the time it stopped, the ground was blanketed in three inches of snow. It was a Christmas Eve miracle. Once in a hundred years, the weatherman said. We went for a walk in the pristine white, marveling at the incongruity of palm trees covered in snow.

If you'd asked me before it happened, I would have called it inconceivable. Snow in deep South Texas? And at Christmas? Impossible. But then, we serve a God who makes the impossible possible: A virgin bearing a child? No problem. A dead man coming back to life? Not hard at all for the one who holds the keys to the grave. And previously condemned sinners, now repentant, restored, and made whole? Impossible—except for the God who made it possible at the cross.

What looks impossible in your life? The salvation of a loved one? Getting out of debt? Finally conquering that sin that's kept you tangled and trapped for years? Persist in prayer, and don't lose hope. All things are possible with Him.

* * * * * * * * * * *

Lord, when the struggles in my life seem impossible, remind me that all things are possible with You. Amen.

Creator
of Constellations

Ever since the world was created, people have seen the earth and sky. Through everything God made, they can clearly see his invisible qualities—his eternal power and divine nature. So they have no excuse for not knowing God.

ROMANS 1:20 NLT

We've come a long way from believing the earth is the center of the universe, but a 1990 photo from Voyager 1 still shocked people. The space probe famously captured our planet as a pale blue dot, a pinprick on the canvas of the vast expanse of space. The photo revealed just how small our planet really is. Blink and you miss it.

The Bible, however, doesn't pull any punches when it comes to this fact. We are small, and God is big. But we humans have been known to get this backwards, choosing to see ourselves as the larger part of the universe. Today, in our fast-paced, me-centered culture, we run the risk of forgetting who hung the stars and set the earth's foundations. We're in danger of losing the wonder that leads to worship. Knowing our smallness teaches us God's greatness and leads us to praise Him.

Sure, we live on a pale blue dot in the middle of expanding space, but even in our smallness God sees us and loves us. Our big, big God is also our good, good Father.

. . . .

Father, open my eyes to see Your power and might, and free me from myself so I can praise You with my whole heart. Amen.

Homeward Bound

Return to the LORD *your God, for he is gracious and compassion-ate, slow to anger and abounding in love.*

JOEL 2:13 NIV

Some mysteries in nature are truly touching, such as the phenomena of animals finding their way back home after being separated from their families, sometimes hundreds of miles apart.

For example, I once read about an indoor cat named Howie who belonged to the Hicks family in Australia. They loved their kitty very much so while they were on an extended vacation overseas they left him with relatives instead of taking him to an animal boarding establishment. When the Hicks family returned to retrieve Howie, they were sad to learn that he had run away. An entire year later, when one of the Hicks' children returned home from school, she discovered a mangy, skinny cat waiting outside their house. It was Howie! It had taken him twelve months to cross a thousand miles of the Australian outback, but Howie had found his way back to his beloved family.

Animal behavior experts can't explain how some animals are able to navigate their way back home, but I believe it's a powerful, magnetic love that draws these pets back to their families. It's a beautiful illustration of how God's supernatural love draws us back to Him. No matter how far we might roam in life, or how lost we might become, our heavenly Father's love draws us back to Him.

. . . .

Father, thank You for loving me and drawing me to You. Amen.

Get Me Outta Here!

God has not given us a spirit of fear, but of power and of love and of a sound mind.

2 TIMOTHY 1:7 NKJV

Move over. You're driving too close to the edge!" My voice rose. "Move *over*!" I don't usually nag my husband about his driving (well, not *too* often), but as we drove up the winding mountain road, the warnings were warranted because Paul couldn't see what I saw out my window. The narrow road to the Cataloochee Valley is packed dirt with gravel. Storms have rutted the road, causing the sides to crumble. And then there are scary three-hundred-foot drop-offs on my side of the road.

But once we made it to the valley, the scenery was absolutely gorgeous—meadows filled with elk, babbling brooks, and a quaint old church and schoolhouse. The bugle sound of the elk echoes through the valley, as if they were praising the God who made them. Each time that we visit there, I'm grateful that I didn't let the fear of that dangerous road keep me from enjoying His creation.

Fear can be crippling, and if we let it control us, it can keep us from experiencing those special moments that God has for us. The Bible has almost four hundred "Fear not!" passages—verses that encourage us to find strength in God. See. He's got you covered.

* * * * * * * * * *

Father, don't let fear hold me back from serving You. Thank You for the courage and faith You provide in Your Word. Amen.

Beside a Still Lake

He leads me beside still waters.

PSALM 23:2 ESV

The name alone was enticing—Lake Pleasant. Add the surrounding Adirondack Mountains, clear sparkling water, and summer sunshine, and I had the perfect setting for recalling stories from my life. With a looming deadline, I had hastily shuffled all four kids off to summer camp and nestled into a small cabin to write. Sitting in silence, I dug deep into unfiltered memories for appropriate stories to open each chapter of my first book. Each day I sat by the water and listened to God's whispering voice reminding me of the many years of His faithfulness. I used "STILL" as my guide:

Sit in silence with open hands. Listen with a receptive heart. **T**hink back to times of God's faithfulness through answered prayers. **I**dentify your current concerns and struggles, offering them to God. **L**ist the gifts God has given and thank Him for His graciousness. **L**ook forward with hope to what God will do in and through you.

Today, twenty years later, I am sitting by the same lake. The kids are grown and my twelfth book has just been published. This morning I was a speaker sharing from God's Word, my favorite calling. And now I sit in quiet serenity. My heart is full of gratitude.

. . . .

Lord, since You created us to need silence and stillness, help me incorporate those restorative spiritual disciplines into my busy life. Amen.

Sails Set Anew

Oh, that you had listened to my commands! Then you would have had peace flowing like a gentle river and righteousness rolling over you like waves in the sea.

ISAIAH 48:18 NLT

Nothing spells summer to me like an afternoon spent under an umbrella, soothed by continual tides lapping at an ocean beach. Since any ocean is over a day's drive away, the beach sands usually have to lodge in my dreams instead of between my toes.

The prophet Isaiah may have reflected on his own travels to the Mediterranean Sea when the Lord recapitulated Israel's story of stubbornness just before they were released from slavery. If only they had listened, the sands between their toes would have been from the beach, not the desert.

Disobedience in my own life has caused me to miss a few peaceful rivers and the comfort of ocean spray. Though I've ridden some sad seas after failure, the never-ending tide of His mercy washes over me and I am clean again. I think of immeasurable oceans that perpetually hold wonder, life, and resources, offering a grand opportunity to travel to new destinations. Like the continual tides, God never ceases to offer His loving guidance, providing a new path back on course. With the anchor of defeat aweigh, I hoist the canvas and set sail once more on a limitless pool of grace as deep as the ocean.

. . . .

Lord, teach me to map out a new direction with You when failure blows me off course. Amen.

Retreat from the Heat

How wonderful and pleasant it is when brothers live together in harmony!... Harmony is as refreshing as the dew from Mount Hermon that falls on the mountains of Zion.

PSALM 133:1, 3 NLT

For a season we lived in the Nevada desert. We were in a city, but even in the midst of modern civilization you cannot dial down the sun. It was hot! So, like northerners in winter, we withdrew indoors to escape. That worked for a while until the four walls started closing in. The boredom was intensified by the baking temperatures and we were overdone.

Thankfully, a friend suggested we take a day trip to the mountains nearby. It was only an hour away, and the wind was to our backs like a hair dryer on the hot setting, blowing us out of town. We had a vision of an oasis and made a run for it.

It wasn't until we arrived on the mountain and stepped out of the air-conditioned car that we noticed the climate change. The temperature had grown cooler, fresher, and oh so much more tolerable. We spent the day hiking the wooded slopes and enjoying each other's company for the first time in weeks. The day became a reboot for all of us. Even though we had to go back to the sweltering valley, our outlook on life had been refreshed.

• • • • • • • • • • •

Lord, may we be refreshed not only by Your creation but also by Your Word that revives us whenever and wherever we are. Amen.

Fishing in Mud Puddles

∴ ○ ○ ○ ○ ○ ∴ ○ ○ ○ ○ ○

My God shall supply all your need.

PHILIPPIANS 4:19 NKJV

My grandchildren love to fish. That's always one of the much-anticipated events when our family goes to Hilton Head Island each year. We look a bit like the *Beverly Hillbillies* as we strap little ones and fishing gear onto our bicycles and ride around the island to our favorite fishing ponds. With six young fishermen, we sometimes get hooks in our clothing and catch a variety of stumps, rocks, and tree limbs way above our heads. But oh, the excitement when one of my sweet grandbabies reels in a fish!

That led to an interesting moment at my son's house recently when my daughter-in-law discovered her three-year-old twins sitting side by side, fishing in a mud puddle by their driveway. Eden yelled, "Mama, I caught a shark!" as she reeled in a leaf.

I laughed at those two cuties, but then wondered, *Don't I do the same thing?* Instead of going to God with my needs, I cast my line in water where there are no fish and come up with leaves instead of sharks. My life would be so much easier if I'd quit fishing in mud puddles and trust the One who can supply every single thing that I need.

· · · · · · · · · · ·

Father, thank You for supplying all of my needs. Remind me to come to You first next time instead of stressing over things. Amen.

The Blues

As the mountains surround Jerusalem, so the LORD surrounds his
people both now and forevermore.

PSALM 125:2 NIV

D o you recall your first glimpse of mountains? The initial
view for my brother and me occurred while traveling to
a cabin beside the Amicalola River, which served as home base
for memorable excursions into the Blue Ridge Mountains.
Beautiful waterfalls and the occasional sighting of a black bear
filled vacation days with wonder.

These gorgeous landforms are part of the ancient Appalachian chain and seem to be veiled in blue, partially due to
chemicals released by trees as a protective measure during
severe heat. Many of the stately peaks reach heights of over
five thousand feet and appear like powerful uniformed sentinels holding a commanding view of the valleys below.

Like magnificent mountains encircling farm-dotted valleys, God's presence and provision surround us. He reigns
with an all-knowing view of the world and understands the
innermost parts of the heart. He supplies peace and wisdom
in joy-filled mountain moments as well as in despair-laden
valleys. Just as stressful high temperatures contribute to the
pretty color of the Blue Ridge range, our heavenly Father uses
the stress of tough times to bring out the color in our lives.
Indeed, God surrounds us with His wise and powerful arms,
bringing comfort in the mountains or the valleys.

. . . .

Father, thank You for Your provision and power and presence,
which surround me. Amen.

Deep Roots

Your roots will grow down into God's love and keep you strong.

EPHESIANS 3:17 NLT

In the middle of the Sahara Desert of northeastern Niger stands a metal sculpture. It commemorates a single acacia tree known as the Tree of Ténéré, which stood there for most of the twentieth century. It was the last survivor of a group that grew there before the desert became so harsh. Standing alone for decades, it was the most isolated tree on earth and became a landmark on caravan routes and later a tourist attraction until it was destroyed not by the heat but by a drunk driver.

What allowed this tree to flourish in the midst of the harshest conditions on earth? In the 1930s, a well was dug nearby and the roots of the tree were discovered in the ground-water over one hundred feet below. The roots had sought out precious life-giving water ten stories beneath the sand dunes.

We all go through difficult dry spells. The secret of surviving and even thriving in these desert-like times is to tap into the Water of Life, Jesus Christ. His Spirit will nourish and refresh our souls, and keep us from withering under the scorching heat of life. A shallow, superficial association won't cut it. We must develop a deep, abiding relationship through prayer, worship, and time in His holy Word.

. . . .

O God who refreshes all living things, enable me to grow and flourish as I sink my roots into Your eternal water source. Amen.

Am I Caught in a Crab Bucket?

The world would love you as one of its own if you belonged to it, but you are no longer part of the world. I chose you to come out of the world, so it hates you.

JOHN 15:19 NLT

We used to live near the ocean and occasionally we'd be invited to go crabbing. We'd lug big plastic buckets filled with water to house our catch. My first time out, I questioned our leader about the lack of lids on the buckets. Surely the crabs would just crawl out after we would put them in, I said.

He shook his head at my ignorance. "We only have to watch the first one we put in. After that, they keep each other down."

Turns out that when there's more than one crab in a bucket, if any try to escape, his buddies pull him back. I was skeptical, certain no group of animals could be that stupid. But I watched it happen over and over again all afternoon.

It struck me that the world treats us just like those crabs. Those who embrace this world will pull us back if they can, keeping us from the freedom found in serving God.

. . . .

Dear Lord, don't let me be dismayed by those who long to see me fail; instead, keep my hope centered on You. Amen.

Is It a Weed or a Flower?

The earth brought forth grass, the herb that yields seed according to its kind, and the tree that yields fruit, whose seed is in itself according to its kind. And God saw that it was good.

GENESIS 1:12 NKJV

The old man, a master gardener, had a "truck farm" behind his house—rows filled with beans, squash, melons, peas, tomatoes, and corn to take to market. Surrounding the garden were narrow rows of flowers, each chosen for its ability to keep down insects and discourage weeds. When asked the difference between a flower and a weed, he smiled. "They are all flowers in God's eyes. He made them. All beautiful. A weed is just a flower that grows where someone doesn't want it to."

Queen Anne's lace, for instance, is often considered a weed, but its intricate and delicate wildflower beauty turns many pastures into glorious white-capped seas. Likewise, abandoned land reverts into a riot of wild daisies, violets, and primroses, all of which would be plowed under if someone desired a smooth lawn or garden plot.

God has filled our world with beauty through the creativity He gives us to cultivate it, or through His own "wild" creativity. His touch can be seen in the tiniest of flowers growing just where He wanted it to, reminding us that He is Lord of all creation.

. . . .

Lord, thank You for the bounty and glory of Your creation. You are present in it all and I am grateful for Your provision and love. Amen.

Lessons Learned

⸰°⸰°⸰°⸰°⸰°⸰°⸰°⸰°⸰

Finally, brothers and sisters, whatever is true, whatever is noble, whatever is right, whatever is pure, whatever is lovely, whatever is admirable—if anything is excellent or praiseworthy—think about such things.

PHILIPPIANS 4:8 NIV

As Hurricane Sandy approached the mid-Atlantic coast in October 2012, headlines screamed: "Frankenstorm! One of the largest storms to ever hit the United States!" As my name is Sandy, I considered the destruction my namesake hurricane created, asking myself questions I may not have otherwise asked: Do I churn up the waters in my relationships with discontent, jealousy, or envy? Do my "Category 5" gusts knock people around with unkind words, criticism, or negativity? Is there a trail of destructive debris left behind for others to clean up in my wake?

Hurricane Sandy would not have been so menacing had she not joined forces with an early winter storm from the west and a blast of arctic air from the north. Joining forces with damaging outside influences can make the results even more overwhelming.

Conversely, one of the most important things experts say to remember during a hurricane is to come together to make sure everyone makes it through the storm. Instead of being a force of destruction and ruin through my words or actions, I hope to be the one that reaches out with the love of Christ, especially during the storms of life.

. . . .

Lord, keep me mindful of the impact my life has on others. Amen.

Metamorphosis

Therefore, if anyone is in Christ, the new creation has come: The old has gone, the new is here!

2 CORINTHIANS 5:17 NIV

Imagine if you transformed in the middle of your life into a far more beautiful creature, almost unrecognizable from how you looked before. That's what happens to the caterpillar. After a caterpillar hatches, its task is to eat and grow. Once it is big enough, it is ready to transform, creating a cocoon covered in a protective silk coating. Special cells, once dormant, spring into action to give the creature wings, legs, and antennae. What emerges is stunning. Ready for the reproduction stage of its life, the butterfly is unveiled, its wings bearing a tapestry of colors and intricate designs.

God also transforms us. When Saul of Tarsus was killing early Christians, Jesus appeared to him on the road to Damascus and gave him a new mandate. In a short period of time, Saul went from persecuting God's people to bringing many to faith—a complete metamorphosis of his heart and life's mission.

God is willing to help us shed our old, sinful ways as well. When we fall, He gives us more chances, continually pursuing us. We become a new creation, like the vibrant butterfly, indistinguishable from our former selves, and equipped with spiritual wings to answer God's mission.

. . . .

Father, change me from the inside out, so I can grow more beautiful—more like You. Amen.

Renegade in the Garden

We are God's workmanship, created in Christ Jesus to do good works, which God prepared in advance for us to do.

EPHESIANS 2:10 NIV

Walking past my vegetable bed, I notice a renegade tomato plant in the middle of my zucchini. Crazy! Every year, we have the healthiest tomatoes grow where we don't plant them. I leave the intruder, but it appears lonely hanging out with squash, beets, and zucchini. Does a bird drop the tomato seed there? Or is it sprouting from the compost I add to my garden? Who knows. But against all odds, it's thriving in that spot.

In the same way, God sets us up to be the renegades—blooming wherever He plants us, especially when we are considered the counterculture. It may be lonely, awkward, or even nerve-wracking at times, but the Creator has gifted and equipped us for the work He prepared in advance for us to do.

Another interesting observation from my rogue tomato plant: It remains true to its calling. Never does it consider producing zucchini. Even while all the other vines are growing long green veggies, the tomato's fruit stays red and round. Similarly, the way we live, the actions we take, and the words we speak are the fruit of His Spirit. We bear His fruit when we abide in Him.

* * * * * * * * * * *

Father, thank You for my renegade tomato and the reminder to thrive wherever I am planted, and may I always abide in You—producing fruit that brings You glory. Amen.

The Patient Bird

Therefore I tell you, do not be anxious about your life.

MATTHEW 6:25 ESV

Do you have a patient nature? Most of us are susceptible to our instant gratification society, much to our handicap. But patience is nature's greatest attribute. Every growing and living thing in creation understands it. Everything has a season and a purpose, and God makes everything beautiful in its time (Ecclesiastes 3:1, 11). If only we could be that wise on a regular basis. What does anxiousness add to our life, anyway? Not one single thing (Matthew 6:27).

One day, as my eighty-eight-year-old mother watched the birds at her feeder, she noticed one had a broken wing. Still, the little bird sang away in spite of its plight. As she pondered her own life's circumstances (her husband of nearly seventy years was suffering through dementia), she wrote down her thoughts. It became a lovely poem. In it she expressed how remarkable it was that the bird still sings, even with a broken wing. When pushed aside, the bird waits and tolerates the neglect. The bird doesn't fret, but has patience and accepts. Knowing that God made them both, and cares for them both, Mom added a prayer at the end asking to be as trusting as the little bird. I often pray that line as well.

. . . .

Lord, please forgive my impatience and relieve my anxiety. Help me to trust that You make everything beautiful in Your perfect time for Your greater purpose. Amen.

The Sunflower

The LORD *make his face to shine upon you and be gracious to you.*

NUMBERS 6:25 ESV

We began planting sunflowers each year because we wanted our children to discover the rewards of gardening. This common flower has never failed us, and it exemplifies how God rewards even a small effort.

Have you ever watched a sunflower develop? After we sow the seeds, it only takes a few days for the first green shoots to peek out from the soil. The leaves turn and follow the light through the long summer day. When the buds burst open, the bright golden petals bring a smile to my face. Then the heads grow heavy with seeds, the stems stiffen, and the flowers remain facing east.

Look closely at the center disc and you'll see the seeds form two spirals that curve in different directions. Their symmetry is a perfect example of God's perfect plan and design. Always remember that He took even more care in your design and creation. After all, you were made in His image, and He knows everything about you, even the number of hairs on your head.

As I watch the sunflower follow the light, I'm reminded to keep my eyes on Jesus and that God created me for His pleasure as I grow the sunflowers for mine.

* * * * * * * * * *

Father, help me to grow in Your likeness by keeping my face turned toward You, and may my every thought, action, and deed bring You pleasure. Amen.

Keep Your Eyes on God

I keep my eyes always on the LORD.

PSALM 16:8 NIV

My best friend, Angie, and I spent a whole day hiking in the woods behind my southern Indiana home—a wonderful day for a pair of nine-year-olds. As we climbed back up the hill to my house, I felt a sharp prick on the back of my left calf. "Ouch!" I hollered. "I think something bit me!" I inspected my leg to find two bloody marks. I was positive they were from the fangs of a poisonous snake.

While there were copperheads in those woods, I never saw a snake. Still, I was sure I was going to die. By the time I made it to my back door, I was hysterical. I convinced Daddy that it really was a snakebite, which prompted him to suck "the venom" from leg. However, after further inspection he concluded it was just a laceration from a stick that had popped up and slightly punctured my leg.

You might say I had overreacted a tiny bit. Angie and I still laugh about it, but you know what's not funny? Sometimes I still have that same overreaction when I get my focus off the Lord and onto my problems. By the time I've thought about all the worst-case scenarios, I'm hysterical. Eventually, I hear my heavenly Father reassure me and it's not nearly as bad as I have made it out to be.

. . . .

Father, help me as I learn to keep my eyes on You in all situations. Amen.

A Painted Promise

When I see the rainbow in the clouds, I will remember the eternal covenant between God and every living creature on earth.

GENESIS 9:16 NLT

Seeing the complete arch of a rainbow is something special. Seeing a double arch is rare and photo prompting. I saw a double rainbow recently. I took pictures and, as I've made it a habit of doing, thanked God for being faithful to His promises.

When God placed His rainbow in the sky as a visual reminder for all of us on earth, He then told Noah and his sons: "When I see the rainbow in the clouds, I will remember . . ." (Genesis 9:16 NLT). God sees the rainbow in the clouds. Seeing it means something to *Him* too.

To me, this is a remarkable expression of how we are created in His image. God understands us completely because we are like Him . . . and the fact that this promise painted across the sky is a reminder to Him says that He is like us. The rainbow is a gift to our human senses, but seeing it is special to our Father too.

The next time you see a rainbow, know that you *and* God are both seeing the arch of color in the clouds. For us, it is a beautiful affirmation of a promise kept—for Him, a beautiful reminder of a promise made.

. . . .

Dear Father, thank You for being true to Your promises, and for revealing Your faithfulness in beautiful ways. Amen.

Dancing in the Dark

Then you will shine among them like stars in the sky as you hold firmly to the word of life.

PHILIPPIANS 2:15–16 NIV

We sat in the circle of lantern light as the sun slipped below the horizon. Across the campground fireflies began to glimmer in the deepening dusk. First one, then two, then a symphony of lights dancing through the night. The children caught the fireflies, watched the tiny lights wink in their hands, and let them go. It seemed like the fireflies shone brighter the darker it grew. Fireflies don't mind the dark. They do what they were created to do—shine.

We were also created to shine. Fireflies shine because they produce an enzyme that triggers a light-producing chemical reaction. We shine because the Spirit of God dwells inside us. God intends our light to be visible in a darkened world, shining like stars in the sky as we cling to God's Word, the word of life.

We shine by letting God's power be evident within us. We hold fast to the Word of God, obeying in heart, mind, and deed. We love well and serve others. We proclaim the glory of Christ, who gave everything for us. And like the fireflies, we dance in defiance of the dark. No need to get caught up in trying to chase away the darkness. Darkness is defeated when we shine.

* * * * * * * * * * *

Lord, help me hold fast to Your word of life so the life-giving light is evident within me. Amen.

Breathtaking Beauty

The heavens declare the glory of God, and the sky proclaims the work of His hands.

PSALM 19:1 HCSB

I watched the shadows of the clouds dance across the nearby mountainside. They were performing a delightful ballet. Sitting in the comfortable rocking chair on the porch of a charming mountain inn where I was staying, I was enjoying the view. Earlier in the day the clouds had rested on the mountain, but gradually the mist had lifted to reveal breathtaking beauty.

The flowers smelled heavenly, with bees buzzing all around, drinking their fill of nectar. Several butterflies were fluttering around a nearby flower bush. A couple of squirrels were chasing each other up a tree, and a nearby mockingbird provided the beautiful background music of this secluded paradise. The atmosphere breathed of God's incredible creation. What a blessing to experience this moment, where peace and joy were overwhelming. His glory was everywhere, revealed by the works of His hands.

Even though that experience was in a special place, I know I can encounter the glory of creation wherever I am. I don't have to go any farther than my own backyard to see the wonders of God—wildflowers, squirrels, chipmunks, a variety of birds, and an occasionally a deer. And I haven't even mentioned all the colorful sunrises and sunsets.

* * * * * * * * * * *

Loving God, help me be always aware of the wonders of Your creation. Amen.

Watermelon in the Wild

꧁ ༄ ꧂

They sowed fields and planted vineyards that yielded a fruitful harvest.

PSALM 107:37 NIV

The Georgia sun beat down on our heads as we sat cross-legged in the field with our grandfather. "Daddydee" pulled out his pocket knife and began cutting into the fruit. Instantly our mouths started watering. Watermelon! Red, ripe, and juicy with lots of black seeds. And the best part? Out here, we kids were allowed to slurp and spit to our heart's content! We were reaping all the benefits of a summer harvest of fruit, but Daddydee had done all the farmer's work.

What seeds are you sowing in your life today? Seeds of wisdom, virtue, and faith are just what young lives around us need. Nurturing, watering, and pruning are also essential to growth—both in gardens and in people.

My grandparents lived the motto "We should all plant a few trees that we will never sit under." If we don't plant, how will future generations know of God's wisdom, faithfulness, and power? And there will be a harvest if we do not give up. "The fruit of that righteousness will be peace; its effect will be quietness and confidence forever" (Isaiah 32:17 NIV).

Pray for a legacy of eternal proportions, and spend as much time as possible with children . . . preferably in a watermelon patch.

• • • • • • • • • •

Lord, as I am grateful for all who have gone before, help me also to leave a legacy that will last for generations. Amen.

Grandeur and Vertigo

Since the creation of the world His invisible attributes, His eternal power and divine nature, have been clearly seen, being understood through what has been made, so that they are without excuse.

ROMANS 1:20 NASB

It had sounded like a great way to spend a morning with friends—a slow excursion up into the mountains to some of the most scenic vistas in the country. The tight curves, however, and the bright sunlight flashing through the overhanging trees soon triggered my vertigo. Within an hour, nausea set in and I had to pull over.

I was annoyed at my weakness, feeling like I had let down my friends as well as myself. Yet, as soon as I saw the view from where we ended up, aggravation vanished and was replaced by awe. We were only four thousand feet up, but we were left speechless by the dark green peaks, shadowed gaps, and a glistening river below. A cool breeze helped push away the nausea and I leaned against a post, marveling at the grandeur of God's creation.

The same power that formed these mountains had, in love, brought us here. God's love encompasses us and spreads before us the glory of His creation. In every sunset, every mountaintop, every new day, we are blessed by Him, and we have no excuse to overlook His presence around us.

. . . .

Father, may we always see You in the beauty of the world around us. Let us acknowledge Your power in creation and Your love in us. Amen.

It's All About the Dirt

The seeds that fell on the good soil represent honest, good-hearted people who hear God's word, cling to it, and patiently produce a huge harvest.

LUKE 8:15 NLT

What makes good soil? Each region of the United States has different varieties of soil. Rich, fertile soil found in the Delta or red Georgia clay are two such examples just in the South. If we start to explore the rest of the country, not even mentioning the rest of the world, soil composition differs widely from coast to coast. According to one state's extension service, which conducts soil testing for homeowners, the following items must be in good balance: pH, lime, phosphorus, potassium, magnesium, zinc, and calcium.

Jesus told the parable of the sower in the Gospel of Luke, sharing not only the different kinds of soil but the various outcomes of the seeds planted there. Jesus explained that the soil type represented people's hearts, and the people who would bring forth much fruit for the kingdom were the ones ready to accept the seed of the gospel in their "good dirt." They would "hear God's word, cling to it, and patiently produce a huge harvest."

Perhaps the greatest point of the whole parable was when Jesus said that soil would bear fruit a hundredfold. What a winning combination: the greatest news given to the human race planted in a ready and willing heart.

* * * * * * * * * * *

Father, may the seed You planted in my heart produce a bountiful harvest of souls, all to Your glory. Amen.

Grapes of Great Risk

*They came to the valley of Eshcol and from there cut down a
branch with a single cluster of grapes; and they carried it on
a pole between two men.*

NUMBERS 13:23 NASB

My earliest memories of gardening go back to my grandparents' farm. Since Grandpa Joe was a double amputee
in a wheelchair, I'd stand on his shoulders to pick grapes off
an arbor. Grasping the woody vines for security, I'd toss the
golden globes to Grandpa as he tightly held my ankles.

For the spies entering Canaan, the bravery of Joshua and
Caleb was impressive in that land of giants. But it's the large
grapes carried on poles that cultivate my fascination. I'd loved
to have seen—and tasted—the gargantuan grapes carried on
the shoulders of soldiers that spur childhood memories.

However, like the cowardly spies who shied away from
the conquest of the Promised Land, I've been tempted to retreat into the comfort of the familiar, forgetting a big God has
great blessings after a significant skirmish. The enjoyment of
the mammoth clusters would have been missed if the Hebrew
wanderers had not persevered.

When faced with the difficult or hopeless, I'm strengthened as I remember Grandpa's vine and the security of his
grasp. As I abide in the Lord, I'm held safe whenever I do
battle with giants. I take the risk, pursue the big fruit, and rest
on His shoulders till the harvest is accomplished.

* * * * * * * * * * *

*Lord, teach me to grow sweet fruit in my life as I remain in You.
Amen.*

Deadly Blight

As in Adam all die, so in Christ all will be made alive.

1 CORINTHIANS 15:22 NIV

The impressive American chestnut once dominated the early eastern woodlands, comprising one of every four hardwoods. Some of these stately trees grew to two hundred feet in height with trunk diameters over four yards. Chestnut trees blessed the early settlers, providing logs for their barns, rails for their fences, and heat for their cabins. Abundant nuts not only fed many people but were also a popular fast food for wildlife as well.

Around 1900, a microscopic Asian enemy arrived, and within forty years virtually all of these majestic trees died from the chestnut blight. Today only a handful of mature trees survives while scientists work to bring back this icon. There is hope, but time will tell if this magnificent tree will ever return.

This blight is reminiscent of sin's impact upon us. Once introduced by Adam, sin has brought death to all of his offspring. Evil thoughts and wicked ways now reside within all of us, and we cannot reach our full potential nor bear the good fruit God created us for. Ultimately, our sin blight is 100 percent fatal.

Thankfully, Jesus offers resistance and victory over this destructive force. His death paid the price for our sins and made it possible for us to live forever in His glorious presence.

. . . .

Dear God, I invite You to cure my sin-virus and empower me to become all that You've made me for. Amen.

Spoiled Fruit

The Holy Spirit produces this kind of fruit in our lives: love, joy, peace, patience, kindness, goodness, faithfulness, gentleness, and self-control.

GALATIANS 5:22–23 NLT

We have watched our loquat tree grow in our backyard, anticipating the day fruit would appear. This was the year. For weeks my husband inspected the tree and waited for the moment he could harvest his fruit. Finally he was confident the loquats would be ripe by evening. Around lunchtime, however, I noticed teeth marks on the fruit. Our marauding squirrels had attacked. We work so hard to grow, nurture, and bear fruit only to have something come along and destroy it.

As I looked at the spoiled loquats, I thought about the Fruit of the Spirit. Love—snatched when my feelings are hurt. Joy—snatched when fear attacks. Peace—snatched by that annoying person. Kindness—snatched by unkind words. Goodness—snatched when I feel undervalued. Faithfulness—snatched when I'm lured away by something that catches my attention. Gentleness—snatched when my last nerve is struck. Self-control—snatched when that car cuts me off.

One by one the fruits of faith can be spoiled on any given day. But one by one I can bring them to my heavenly Father, who can restore them. Nature may not give loquats a second chance, but our God is the God of second chances.

* * * * * * * * * * *

Father, help me to keep the Fruit of the Spirit within my grasp, and thank You for Your grace when they slip out of my hand. Amen.

Powerful Niagara Falls

I am not ashamed of the gospel, because it is the power of God that brings salvation to everyone who believes.

ROMANS 1:16 NIV

Have you ever been amazed by a majestic waterfall? As I stood on the American side of Niagara Falls, the kaleidoscope of wondrous sights and sounds astonished me. My eyes darted continuously from the beautiful blue-green water to the myriad of rainbows dancing in the sunlight. The roar of the water muffled both the chatter of excited voices and the hum of hovering helicopters transporting tourists. The rushing power of the water was mesmerizing and incomparable to other wonders of nature I had observed.

Our Canadian neighbors share this scenic spectacle. Each day, thousands of visitors on both sides of the river marvel at the volume of water constantly cascading over the edges. About three thousand tons of water per second plummet downward and generate electricity in nearby hydroelectric plants for both countries. That's incredible power!

Only God could create this marvel of force and beauty. In the same way, only He could devise a salvation plan powerful enough to provide forgiveness for sinful humans *and* an eternal relationship with a holy God. His divine offer is available to anyone who invites Jesus into their lives as Savior and Lord. What a powerful God He is!

. . . .

Heavenly Father, creator of amazing natural wonders, thank You for the power of the gospel that provides eternal life and a relationship with You for all who accept Jesus as Savior. Amen.

God's Ballet

Let the rivers clap their hands; let the hills sing for joy together.

PSALM 98:8 ESV

The sight was so beautiful that I pulled my car to the side of the road so I could watch. Near our home there's a large field with gently rolling hills. The farmer who owns the land grows hay on it, and when summer arrives, I wait impatiently for one of my favorite moments. You see, when the grass gets tall enough and the wind blows at just the right angle, I get to watch the grass dance.

The tall blades swing back and forth in graceful perfection, a silent ballet choreographed by a nail-scarred hand. It's as if the hills are dancing in praise to Him. It moves me to tears each year as I observe the majestic awesomeness of my Creator. Such grace. Such beauty. And such a wonderful reminder that His fingerprints are on every aspect of my life if I just look for them.

God is worthy of praise. Sometimes I ask Him, *When was the last time I stopped to thank You for the ordinary moments I take for granted each day?* For a vivid blue sky dotted with puffy white clouds. For the sweet aroma of honeysuckle and roses. For the bright hues of flowers growing in my yard. And for velvet-green blades of grass that dance before Him as if they can't contain themselves. *Thank You, Lord.*

. . . .

Father, thank You for the sheer beauty of Your creation. You're an amazing God! Amen.

Deer Feet

He makes my feet like the feet of deer, and sets me on my high places.

PSALM 18:33 NKJV

The first hundred times we spotted deer on our property, we gawked and snapped pictures faster than a New Yorker can order a latte. But after the thousandth sighting, it lost its luster. Not to mention they ate most of our okra. To combat their taste for our vegetables, we put up scary milk jugs and tin pie pans that moved with the breeze. We even put life-sized plastic owls along our field to keep them at bay. At first, it worked. But within a few days they meandered past the lifeless owls like . . . well, like they were lifeless.

Tom even tried putting orange twine around our newly plowed rows. On the twine, he attached milk jugs and pie tins and neon tape. Incidentally, we had covered the raised garden beds in white plastic to keep out weeds. The next morning, there were deer hoof prints all over the plastic. They can run full speed through a small fence and glide over tall ones. Their feet are sort of magical.

David's prayer in Psalm 18 speaks of the sure-footedness of the deer to reach safe places on high mountains. Our Creator does the same for us when we call out to Him. He lifts us out of the pit and sets our feet securely on solid rock. Magical!

• • • • • • • • • • •

Lord, thank You for helping me with all of my steps. Amen.

Waves or Ripples

Therefore, with minds that are alert and fully sober, set your hope on the grace to be brought to you when Jesus Christ is revealed at his coming.

1 PETER 1:13 NIV

When we finally had the chance to spend some much-needed time at the seaside, we spent hours watching the waves. We also visited some local gardens where the waterways were calmer, and I was struck by the different ways water reacted when obstacles intruded.

At the shore, the waves were relentless. They crashed into anything in their path—including the beach—hitting again and again, conquering through sheer overwhelming numbers and brute force. However, in the quiet pools at the garden, the water's behavior was quite different. The obstacles that intruded left ripples, and instead of fighting back, the water absorbed what came into its calm environment.

I'm like that—sometimes crashing into obstacles, letting brute strength carry me through. Other times I absorb the changes, letting the stress flow outward until I'm peaceful once more. I think both ways have value. The key is making a conscious decision about which is right for the current circumstance. Although I used to be more of a crashing waves sort of girl, the years have mellowed me and given me a little bit of wisdom. Now I'm just as likely to sit and absorb what has intruded, measuring my response as I consider the effects.

* * * * * * * * * * *

Lord, grant me the wherewithal to react to my circumstances with Your wisdom. Amen.

Orphans No More

A father to the fatherless, a defender of widows, is God in his holy dwelling.

PSALM 68:5 NIV

God gave many mammals the instinct to nurture babies that are left orphaned. Toola, a female sea otter at the Monterey Bay Aquarium, proved how far this motherly impulse can go. After giving birth to a stillborn pup, Toola started raising as her own an orphaned pup someone brought to the aquarium. Never losing this instinct, Toola adopted at least a dozen other pups over more than a decade. Because she mothered these babies, they didn't rely on humans and could be released into the ocean.

Sometimes mammals even care for the young of other species. A pig at an animal sanctuary in Australia acted as a surrogate parent to a lamb. Video evidence has shown sperm whales caring for young dolphins. In Thailand, photographs show a mother tiger allowing piglets to suckle milk.

God considers you part of His family and longs to adopt you as His child. He loves you more than you can grasp. The apostle Paul said it powerfully: "For I am convinced that neither death nor life, neither angels nor demons, neither the present nor the future, nor any powers, neither height nor depth, nor anything else in all creation, will be able to separate us from the love of God that is in Christ Jesus our Lord" (Romans 8:38–39 NIV).

. . . .

Father, thank You for making me one of Your own, for loving me more than I can fathom. Amen.

A Moment in Time

People are like grass; their beauty is like a flower in the field. The grass withers and the flower fades.

1 PETER 1:24 NLT

As a child, I loved to stroll knee-deep through our pasture, threading my fingers through the long wavy strands of prairie grass. It was my playground. I rolled through it, played hide-and-seek, and watched lightning bugs pirouette over its long filaments.

Then one horrible afternoon, the field caught fire. Helplessly I watched as the fire flew through my beloved grass, catching fire faster than sparklers on the Fourth of July. My mom and dad filled buckets and wet towels to stamp out the flames. The next day, funeral black shrouded the field, and I mourned over the burned tufts.

The Bible compares our lives to grass—here today and gone tomorrow. We live for a fleeting moment on this earth before eternity envelops us forever. It's up to each of us to decide how we're going to live our moment in time.

Today, I choose to live with joy, to enjoy the good gifts God gives. To live open-handed and give thanks for the fires I may be walking through, for even they are temporary. The spring after the field burned, my grass grew back, completely swallowing the black ground. In the end, God makes all things new (Revelations 21:5).

* * * * * * * * * * *

Lord, help me to endure the temporary fires and to remember how short life really is so I can live my life for You to the fullest. Amen.

Names Carved
on Fungus

࿏ ⃝⚬⚬⃝ ⃝ ࿏ ⃝⚬⚬⃝ ⃝

Your very lives are a letter that anyone can read by just looking at you. Christ himself wrote it—not with ink, but with God's living Spirit; not chiseled into stone, but carved into human lives.

2 CORINTHIANS 3:3 MSG

My kids say this old picture of my friends looks like a group of mountain-climbing hippies. I guess we were. Some people called us "Jesus freaks" back then. But we loved the outdoors. On this particular camping trip, my college buddies gave me a very special birthday present—a signed piece of fungus. This natural fungus was soft enough to carve their names before it hardened. I loved that unusual gift for what it represented—friendship.

These were the people who knew me when I was young and faltering, so unsure of myself and yet so determined to find my part in God's story—to help change the world. Forty years later, I'm back in the Blue Ridge Mountains with some of those same friends. The carved fungus is long gone but our relationships remain. We often share our hardest life lessons amidst laughter and tears. We are amazed at how we have collectively helped shaped the world for our daughters, and even our granddaughters.

On whose lives have you carved your name? What a blessing it is to develop eternal friendships through Christ.

. . . .

Lord, thank You for friends and family who continue to be there for me, and show me ways to encourage and support them as well. Amen.

Stop, Wait, and Listen

I waited patiently for the LORD; he turned to me and heard my cry.

PSALM 40:1 NIV

Getting lost is never fun, but I've done it enough now that I no longer panic. This was not the case when I broke my ankle on a hiking trip and eventually became separated from my group. I was in pain, off the trail, and frantic with fear. Because of my ankle, my group leader had my pack so I had no way to protect myself or signal for help.

Exhausted, with my brain scrambled from the pain, I sat down under a tree and tried to get a grip on the situation. As I sat there, I began to notice how the smallest things of nature were intricate and beautiful: calling birds, rustling leaves, a grazing deer, and a munching squirrel. The sun warmed me, and even though I was lost, God's active creation surrounded me like a security blanket. Before long, I heard the voices of two hikers who had decided to take a different route.

When we are wounded or lost, panic settles in. The pain and the panic distract us from God's ability to lead us through anything. If we stop, listen, and wait on Him, He will bring us the comfort we need.

* * * * * * * * * * *

Lord, help us remember that You are present in all Your creation. Show us how to wait on Your guiding hand. Amen.

Under the Sea

❝ ◦ ❝◦◦❝◦❝❝◦❝ ◦❝◦◦❝◦❝

Then God said, "Let the water swarm with living creatures."

GENESIS 1:20 HCSB

When you jump into eighty feet of water, your first in-clination is to peer through your diving mask to see what might eat you. At least that is what I always do. When my husband and I used to scuba dive off the Florida coast, we'd travel about twenty miles offshore, get our dive gear organized, fall off the edge of our boat, and look around. After that, we'd swim to the anchor line and travel slowly to the ocean's floor. Every thirty-three feet equals one atmosphere so descending and ascending slowly are not only important, but also tricky. Frankly, it was kind of scary traveling into the abyss. But once we reached the ocean floor, it seemed as if we were transported into a different world. Neon fish swam around us and colorful rocks lay below.

After we landed on the bottom, we'd swim along the edge of the reef and tour God's underwater creation. Many times as we swam along rocky bottoms, I'd glance back. Hoards of curious fish followed at a safe distance. They watched us while we watched them. And every time I viewed living shells, tropical fish, or sea urchins, I would hear myself take a sharp intake of breath—because God's creation under the sea is breathtaking.

God made everything in this world. Just imagine the other worlds in the universe He's created.

• • • • • • • • • • •

Lord, thank You for the beautiful, extravagant underwater world. Amen.

Tuning In

Jesus said, "Whoever has ears to hear, let them hear."

MARK 4:9 NIV

Remember ET, the extraterrestrial? With enormous eyes and tiny ears, the shy tarsier—a tree-dwelling, nocturnal primate of Southeast Asia—might pass as his next of kin. Long slender fingers with large knuckles and fingertips improve the odds of these miniature mammals being mistaken for interstellar visitors. Although they are the smallest primates—six ounces packed into a five-inch body—they can jump twice their length to catch insects for dinner.

Researchers have recently discovered the tarsiers' ability to communicate in super-high vocalizations. For years, scientists believed they were yawning or performing some odd behavior as they opened their mouths widely. We now know they speak at ultrasound levels of seventy kilohertz or higher, which our ears cannot detect. These little guys have been chatting with each other right in front of us and we never knew it!

We wonder sometimes why God seems silent when perhaps the problem is on our end. As we tune our hearts to His frequency, we eliminate the background noise that drowns Him out. Let us pause without our electronics and distractions and use our ears of faith to listen. As we read His Word and invite Him to speak, we hear His voice and enjoy His sweet presence.

. . . .

At every level, Lord, You are communicating with us. Help us tune in to You. Amen.

Don't Take the Bait

If you think you are standing firm, be careful that you don't fall!

I CORINTHIANS 10:12 NIV

After a week away from home, I returned to find intruders in the kitchen. Tiny black sugar ants scurried across the countertop. When a trap was in place, several ants took the bait. More ants followed, bringing their friends and family members to taste the poison. Unwittingly, they carried death, destruction, and doom back to their homes.

While pondering the ants' fate, I considered how we humans take poisonous bait too. We may listen to harmful words, follow harmful people, consume harmful things through what we eat, drink, inhale, watch, listen to, or read. It's bad enough we may take the bait ourselves, but oftentimes we intentionally or unintentionally invite our friends and family to join in, poisoning them as well. Like the ants, poison is brought into our home and before we know it, we're utterly impaired and have damaged those around us. Tragically, if left unchecked, the poison can kill emotionally, physically, or spiritually. In any of those cases, Satan set a trap and someone took the bait.

The ant trap was designed to entice and kill. Satan's traps are designed to do the same. Fortunately, God gives us wisdom and strength to resist temptations. And if by chance we do succumb and take the bait, Jesus is there to rescue us. Just reach out your hand to Him.

. . . .

Jesus, thank You for rescuing me and giving me strength to stand. Amen.

God Enlarges the Harvest

He who supplies seed to the sower and bread for food will supply and multiply your seed for sowing and increase the harvest of your righteousness.

2 CORINTHIANS 9:10 ESV

The Arizona desert bursts into bloom as the giant saguaro cacti sprout their springtime blossoms. The white flowers open at night and close the next day, leaving a short window for insects, birds, and bats to pollinate them. When pollinated, the flowers develop into clusters of red fruit, each filled with over two thousand seeds. An individual cactus may produce forty million seeds in its lifetime, but very few of these seeds ever sprout. Of the few seedlings that do sprout, most perish from drought, freezing conditions, or being eaten by animals. Only a fraction of those forty million seeds ever produce a mature cactus that can reach up to fifty feet in height and weigh up to sixteen thousand pounds.

Thankfully, we are not like the saguaro cactus. God both supplies us with seed and enlarges the harvest. Generosity, compassion, patience, and grace toward others are proof of our righteousness. When you wonder if what you are doing really makes a difference, trust in the God who enlarges the harvest. God supplies us with the courage and ability to live righteously and empowers us to make a difference in our world.

* * * * * * * * * * *

Lord, thank You for supplying me with what I need to live righteously and for empowering me to bear fruit. Amen.

Winter's White Sweater

Above all, love each other deeply, because love covers over a multitude of sins.

1 PETER 4:8 NIV

In spite of the work it creates, snow provides many benefits, including the addition of nitrogen and moisture into the earth. The meltwater percolates through the soil, recharging aquifers for drier summertime days ahead.

One of snow's major benefits is its simple beauty. Few landscapes exceed the glory created by a fresh snowfall. Snow's ability to pile up flake by flake on everything produces a frozen blanket that glistens when the sunlight peeks out after God finishes His winter masterpiece. Everything disappears beneath the pristine purity of winter's white sweater.

Snow's ability to cover imperfections mirrors the incredible power of love. Love's capacity to overlook offenses and forgive hurts is not unlike the blanketing effect of a January snowfall. Even though we have defects and shortcomings, the love of family members and friends covers these, leaving beautiful relationships behind. Likewise, our love for others minimizes their faults and causes them to be more beautiful to us as well.

Ultimately, the overwhelming love of Jesus not only covers our multitude of sins but completely removes them. What He leaves behind is more pure than snow and more beautiful than any winter landscape.

. . . .

God, thank You for Your love that covers my sins, and help me to extend Your love to others. Amen.

Checking Out the Coop

Know well the condition of your flocks, and pay attention to your herds.

PROVERBS 27:23 NASB

G ood morning, ladies!" I shouted to my one-hundred-plus chickens. "And good morning to you too, girl!" I chanted to my eighty-pound livestock guardian dog, Molly. Then I sang a medley of songs to them while I threw feed, filled water containers, and cleaned up. I checked to see if any chickens were hurt or sick. "Hello, lady. Thank you for all your hard work," I said as I petted a chicken's head tucked into the nesting box while I slid my hand under her to retrieve eggs. The eggs make me smile.

Often my chickens make me smile. Like last year on New Year's Eve. I didn't watch the ball drop, but I did watch an egg drop—and I don't mean in soup. It's not every day you see a chicken lay an egg. I much prefer the natural ball drop to Times Square any day. Who knew I'd be tending to my own flock of birds back in the days I thought olives grew with the red pimentos already in them. God did! He led me here; He keeps me here tending the flock.

We all have flocks, don't we? Parents and grandparents do; employers and employees do; pastors do for sure. Everyone does, really. It's whomever you spend your time with. It's who you care about and care for. Who is your flock?

* * * * * * * * * * *

Lord, thank You for all of my beautiful, and sometimes unique, flocks. Amen.

Love Your Enemies

I say to you, love your enemies, bless those who curse you, do good to those who hate you, and pray for those who spitefully use you and persecute you.

MATTHEW 5:44 NKJV

When our daughter decided to move out of her apartment and back home for her final year of college in order to save money for her upcoming wedding, we were thrilled. However, we were not so thrilled to have her cat, Marnie Moo Moo, under our roof. And, our miniature dachshund, Mollie Mae, was even less thrilled than we were. From the very beginning, Marnie and Mollie were bitter enemies. Our days were filled with lots of hissing and growling and swatting and yelping.

So, imagine my surprise when I walked past the living room one afternoon and caught Marnie and Mollie huddled together while napping, snuggling in the stream of sunlight coming through the large bay window. It seems they had found a common love—the warm sunbeam—and for a moment, they had called a truce and decided to get along in order to share the warmth.

Marnie and Mollie set a good example—look for common ground with your enemies. Of course we aren't going to agree on everything with the people in our lives, enemies or otherwise, but we can probably find one common denominator and use that as a starting place for unity.

. . . .

Father, help me to find common ground with my enemies and love them as You do. Amen.

Best Friends

Two are better than one, because they have a good return for their labor: If either of them falls down, one can help the other up. But pity anyone who falls and has no one to help them up.

ECCLESIASTES 4:9–10 NIV

Dear friends of mine have a sweet dog, Finn, that is blind. To keep him from hurting himself by running into sharp edges, they rearranged the furniture in their house. They also placed his food and water bowls in an open area, so nothing could hinder his ability to go straight to the bowls.

When Finn became older, my friends added a puppy to the family. Finn loved the new puppy, Jasper, and Jasper adored his older pal.

Jasper accompanies Finn everywhere he goes. He walks alongside Finn to help him avoid obstacles such as trees and lawn furniture. He guides Finn as they explore the backyard. At the dog park, Finn leads his friend around the park's perimeter to keep him far from danger. The devotion between the two dogs is a beautiful example of the blessings of friendship.

The Lord encourages friendships between His children. From friendships, we gather understanding, advice, and companionship. Friends pick us up when we stumble. If you are struggling with loneliness, why not reach out your hand to someone in friendship.

* * * * * * * * * * *

Father, thank You for placing the need and the joy of friendships in our hearts, and thank You for the help they bestow in times of need. Amen.

The Winding Roads

These things I have spoken to you, that in Me you may have peace. In the world you will have tribulation; but be of good cheer, I have overcome the world.

JOHN 16:33 NKJV

I love living in the eastern Kentucky mountains, and, as an amateur photographer, I enjoy taking pictures of twisty mountain roads. A good photographer will try to find interesting lines that lead the viewer into the photo. Considering that technique, the roads around here are certainly good subjects.

Whether it's a snowy shot of the road winding through the hollow or a colorful picture of a path covered with fall leaves, there's something about a curvy road. You know that path or road is leading somewhere, but there are twists and turns to make the journey interesting.

Jesus warned us the road to heaven would feature bumps and curves—many of them unexpected. The reality of this life is that we will have trouble. When my life path begins to twist and turn like a mountain road, I remember another thing Jesus said: He has overcome the world.

In this part of the country, there is often a feeling of "you can't get there from here" with the mountains that you have to cross to get anywhere. Those winding roads remind me that Jesus knows we're on a journey, but He holds the map and He will take care of us no matter which way the road curves.

. . . .

Father, when my path takes an unexpected turn, lead me to the right way home. Amen.

Squirrel Highway 101

"For I know the plans I have for you," declares the LORD, "plans to prosper you and not to harm you, plans to give you hope and a future."

JEREMIAH 29:11 NIV

The black walnut tree had outdone itself in providing the main ingredient for our Christmas cake. Because of the large crop of nuts, I had plenty to use for my holiday baking and to share with the squirrels.

Every day, I enjoyed watching two bushy-tailed squirrels jump from one tree to the next as they made their way from our front yard to our backyard. Like tightrope walkers, they sometimes seemed in danger of falling, but they always recovered and made it to the stash of nuts I had raked and mounded under the tree. I named the path they traveled Squirrel Highway 101.

The squirrels had marked out a plan for their lives: find food for the winter and locate places to store their hoard of nuts.

Our Father has good plans—plans filled with hope—for His children's lives. Problems arise when we choose to follow a different route than the one He designed for us. Glittering lights, shrill whistles, or melodic bells entice us to strike out on our own paths. How blessed we are to have God's road map, the Bible, at our fingertips to reroute us when we veer off course.

* * * * * * * * * * *

Father, help me to choose the path You have marked out for me, assured that Your plan is always best. Amen.

The Tree Growing
Out of the Rock

*There is no one holy like the LORD; there is no one besides you;
there is no Rock like our God.*

1 SAMUEL 2:2 NIV

The mountain terrain looked as if a giant had shuffled the
layers of the earth and stacked them like a deck of cards
at odd angles. At the crest of the highest peak, a lone tree
stood, gnarled and twisted, its trunk divided into two arms
tightly hugging the boulder from which it sprang. Knobby
roots disappeared in the crevice of the ancient stone, and the
tree reached high into the blue sky.

The ridge plummeted downward on either side of the narrow pinnacle. The wind blew fierce across this apex, and ice
hung heavy during winter storms. How had this tree thrived?
Its branches were strong and they had grown around every
obstacle. The roots, bigger than a man's arm, were burrowed
beyond view beneath the solid surface. This tree was magnifi-
cently anchored in the rock, immovable.

We can be like that tree. Our God is a Rock, and there
is no one holy like Him, no one besides Him who anchors
us against the storms that would break us. Reaching toward
heaven, we will grow tall as the pressures of life bend and twist
around us. Rooted in our God, we will not be moved.

* * * * * * * * * * *

*Dear Lord, anchor me in the Rock, my roots growing deep in You,
that I may be immovable in every storm of life. Amen.*

Skiing on Thin Ice

❀ ❀ ❀ ❀ ❀ ❀ ❀ ❀ ❀ ❀

The breath of God produces ice.

JOB 37:10 NIV

I was determined to learn to snow ski. After all, my new husband was fond of skiing and wanted me to join him. But first I had to learn how to put on the long skinny skis. I was scared to death. Even if I could manage to stand up, where would I find the courage to push down the mountain?

After trying and falling many times I was ready to give up. And so I turned in my skis. I told my disappointed husband that I had tried the sport, but it simply wasn't for me. The truth? I wasn't as frightened of skiing as I was afraid of losing control. To ski, one must jump off a chairlift and then fly down the mountain with only two poles for leverage. Total freedom.

I wasn't ready to be that free. I held too tightly to my need to orchestrate not only my movements on the slopes, but all the changes going on with my marriage and recent adoptions. More than thirty years later, the thin ice on which I was standing was about to crack and it forced me to turn to God for true freedom through His grace.

Do you ever feel your life is careening out of control? Turn to the Creator of ice and snow, and allow Him to set you free.

. . . .

Lord, when I fear being out of control, remind me that in trusting You I enjoy true freedom. Amen.

Through the Storm

Fear not, for I am with you; be not dismayed, for I am your God; I will strengthen you, I will help you, I will uphold you with my righteous right hand.

ISAIAH 41:10 ESV

Fear crept into my heart as I watched the winter storm unfold outside my window—first rain, then sleet, and now more snow on top of the foot already on the ground. People were reporting on social media about their roofs caving in from the weight of the ice and snow. With the road in front of the house unplowed, my family and I were stranded. The lights flickered and then went out.

As I felt the anxiety growing, I retreated to the bedroom and got real with God. "Lord, I'm scared and helpless."

Then the words of my favorite Bible verse, Isaiah 41:10, came to me. I didn't need to fear, for God was with me and would help. "Thanks, Lord. I needed that."

I apologized for my lack of trust and returned to my family. My son and I bundled up and headed out to remove snow and ice from the top of our storage shed.

It was a nasty snowstorm that persisted for days, but God was with me all the way. Life, in general, has some rough storms as well, but I don't have to fear those, either. God is there, strengthening and upholding me.

* * * * * * * * * * *

Lord, help me to trust You when life's storms hit hard. Amen.

Salt Can Heal

*Elisha went out to the spring of water, threw salt in it, and said,
"This is what the LORD says: 'I have healed this water. No longer
will death or unfruitfulness result from it.'"*

2 KINGS 2:21 HCSB

Salt has been a valuable commodity for centuries. It is essential not only to the human diet but to animal and plant diets too. Known mainly for its seasoning and preserving properties, this versatile natural mineral is a hidden gem. It can clean multiple surface types, deodorize, kill poison ivy, deice roadways, and enhance beauty in a myriad of ways. But even more amazing is its power to heal.

The Bible mentions salt and its diversity quite often. This particular passage reveals how God used it to bring healing. The prophet Elijah had just been taken up to heaven in a whirlwind, his earthly ministry ended. Elisha had just picked up Elijah's mantle and taken over his ministry, and was immediately asked to perform a miracle. Jericho needed relief from the bitter water around them. Their survival depended on it. God gave Elisha the command to use a bowl full of salt to "heal" or purify the water, miraculously extending the cure for years to come—verse 22 says "the water remains healthy to this very day."

How comforting to know that we serve a God who cares and always provides a way to meet our basic needs.

· · · · · · · · · · ·

Lord, thank You for taking care of my most essential needs; for listening to and answering my deepest prayers. Amen.

Refining Fire

This third I will put into the fire; I will refine them like silver and test them like gold. They will call on my name and I will answer them; I will say, "They are my people," and they will say, "The Lord is our God."

ZECHARIAH 13:9 NIV

The caverns of Sonora, Texas, are known for their plethora of helictites. While stalagmites grow up and stalactites grow down, helictites grow whichever way they choose—up, down, sideways, or in a corkscrew. Helictites defy gravity because they are subjected to intense pressure—water and minerals forced out of the stone leave behind crystalline deposits in unique formations. The pressure creates beauty.

God has used pressure and pain to create beauty throughout history. Zechariah first wrote his book to the Jews who had returned to Israel after the Babylonian exile. Though the Israelites expected a glorious restoration, they were met with financial hardship, outside opposition, and social conflicts. Zechariah wrote to encourage the people, and God would use their struggles to refine them into a people worthy of being called by His name.

God uses struggles in our lives to refine us as well. Our problems and pressures are an opportunity for us to prove ourselves faithful and for God to demonstrate His power in and through us. Don't lose heart in the hard times. Let God use the pressures of life to create beauty in you.

. . . .

Lord, show me how You are using the pressures and struggles of my life to create beauty in me. Amen.

The Arctic Fox

There is a time for everything, and a season for every activity under the heavens.

ECCLESIASTES 3:1 NIV

The Arctic fox is known for its stunning white coat. When the snow melts, the fox's fur turns to brown, making it less noticeable to predators or while approaching prey. When winter comes again, it changes back to white to blend in with the snow.

God gave this chameleonic animal the ability to blend in because He knew what it would need. He knows what we need too for every season of our lives. While experiencing positive events like a new home, graduations, newborns, or career success, He is there. And when tragedies come like losing a friend or loved one, sickness, or job loss, He is there.

In his old age, King Solomon wrote of the many seasons we face in this life. There is a time for many things—among them weeping and laughter, mourning and dancing, tearing down and building, planting and uprooting (Ecclesiastes 3:2–8). God is there through it all, by our side to navigate the storms. He wants to walk with us through all of life's ups and downs and curves no matter what season we're in now. He's standing by to guide and guard with His armies of angels, and to celebrate or comfort with His unfathomably loving heart.

Father, thank You for preparing me for every season, and help me to make the most of this one with You by my side. Amen.

Masada

The LORD is my rock, my fortress, and my savior; my God is my rock, in whom I find protection.

PSALM 18:2 NLT

The brisk breeze chased the clouds across an ever-changing sky. One moment the sky was blue with white clouds; the next it had changed to gray. The color of the sky was reflected in the body of water below, the Dead Sea, or Salt Sea as some call it. As the sky changed, so the sea appeared to change. I saw shades of aqua, lavender, silver, green, blue, gray, and even a shade of taupe.

I was standing on top of the ancient desert fortress, Masada, in southern Israel. I had not been prepared for the beauty of it and I was totally captivated by what lay before me. The delightful scene was spread out before me like a painting that the artist was constantly changing, as if just one more brushstroke would make it complete. I was amazed—God showing off His spectacular creation!

Isn't it just like God to create such an incredible display of beauty in a place largely uninhabited? His magnificent creation—no matter if it is witnessed by us or not—points to His great love for us, and we can take delight in knowing His touch is everywhere. We can truly appreciate what He has so lovingly created for our enjoyment as well as for nature's own pleasure.

· · · · · · · · · · ·

Creator God, thank You for Your beauty that is consistently there even beyond what my eyes can see. Amen.

The Solitude of Winter

*As long as the earth endures, seedtime and harvest, cold and heat,
summer and winter, day and night will never cease.*

GENESIS 8:22 NIV

The flood and drying of the land had finally ended. Noah
and his family vacated the ark, built an altar, and gave
thanks with offerings to the Lord. Then God made a promise
to maintain the seasons as long as the earth endures. Noah
survived the flood journey because God remained faithful
from the beginning to the end, just as He has remained faithful with all of us on our journeys.

This year we've enjoyed the restoration of spring, the
abundance of summer, and the preparation of autumn. And
we have His promise to bring forth the seasons again next
year. Winter, then, is a great time to prepare spiritually for
next year's journey. The solitude of this season gives us the
opportunity to remember His past faithfulness and to trust
Him in the future.

When pondering your growth this year, ask yourself:
How have these lessons from nature encouraged my spiritual
roots to grow down deeper? Have I had fresh and genuine
encounters with the Creator? As I contemplate how He will
soon bring about the restoration of spring again, how can I
begin to prepare?

God's promise to Noah is for us too. Seasons will progress
as long as the earth endures. We have His word!

• • • • • • • • • •

*Father, open my eyes to see Your faithfulness during the seasons
of life, and prepare my heart for the upcoming new year. Amen.*

There Is Hope

God has given both his promise and his oath. These two things are unchangeable because it is impossible for God to lie. Therefore, we . . . can have great confidence as we hold to the hope that lies before us.

HEBREWS 6:18 NLT

We don't have to go far from our own door to see the cycle of life that God has created around us. While in some areas of the planet the physical changes are slighter than others, nature changes across the seasons—and always does, without fail.

Spring brings an awakening, a rebirth filled with expectation. Summer delivers the full measure of things, with plants and young animals coming to full growth. Autumn slows things down, allowing for the harvest of what's been sown, a time of gathering. Winter brings reflection, a bit of dormancy as the world closes around us, waiting, a promise of things to come.

In God's creation, we thus see a reflection of His promises to us. No matter how many trials we face, the very changes we witness in the seasons tells us that nothing lasts forever. And He will never forsake us. He has promised to be "our refuge and strength, always ready to help in times of trouble" (Psalm 46:1 NLT). On top of all this, God cannot lie. In His presence there is always hope for the future.

. . . .

Father, help me remember that no matter how much the world changes, You are always and forever my strength and my refuge. Amen.

White as Snow

❃ ⚬°⚬°°⚬❃⚬°⚬°°⚬

Though your sins are like scarlet, they shall be as white as snow.

ISAIAH 1:18 ESV

Did you know snow isn't really white? It's actually transparent. Snow appears white because the flakes are crystals and act as prisms that break up the light of the sun into the whole spectrum of color. The human eye is unable to see such overload of color; therefore, we see only white.

It's interesting that God compared our forgiven sin to snow. Transparent snow means it's clear or translucent—something *unseen*. It's like He's saying He sees through our sin or doesn't see it at all anymore.

This gives further meaning beyond the idea that white symbolizes purity. Some of us struggle with comprehending God's complete forgiveness and continue to have guilt over past sins. We also may have a hard time forgiving ourselves. But if we sincerely ask forgiveness, God doesn't see our sins anymore. They are unseen to Him.

Micah 7:19 says, "You will cast all our sins into the depths of the sea" (ESV). The fact is, there are areas of the sea so deep it can't be measured. How's that for unseen? Our sins couldn't be retrieved if we tried.

• • • • • • • • • • •

Dear Lord, thank You for Your forgiveness. Help me to trust in its completeness so I can live the abundant life You have promised me. Amen.

The God Who Sings

The LORD your God is with you, the Mighty Warrior who saves. He will take great delight in you; in his love he will no longer rebuke you, but will rejoice over you with singing.

ZEPHANIAH 3:17 NIV

T he words of Zephaniah are rich with promises: The Lord your God is with you. He saves you. He takes great delight in you. He loves you. He no longer rebukes you. But the final words of the verse are perhaps the most intriguing: He will rejoice over you with singing.

Did you know that the Lord sings? You've surely heard the songs of His creation—the whistle of the wind in the trees, the melody of the sparrows, the rhythmic roar of the ocean's waves. But did you know that God Himself sings? And not only sings, but sings with joy? What could inspire the Lord of all creation to burst into song?

You.

When you turn to Him, when you lean upon His strength, when you surrender your heart and your will to Him, following in His ways, you are delightful to the Lord, and you make Him sing!

. . . .

Lord, may my life be a beautiful melody, and may it make You sing. Amen.

Keeping in Step

Since we live by the Spirit, let us keep in step with the Spirit.

GALATIANS 5:25 NIV

It can be great fun to tromp through the snow. Walking through a winter wonderland full of snow-covered mounds of who-knows-what offers an adventure in beauty and awe. But it can also be quite a challenge. After a while, punching boots through crusted snowbanks of any depth can wear out the most dedicated winter enthusiast. An easy trick to ease the strain—walk in someone else's bootprints. If you can catch the stride right, each step becomes a bit easier as your feet fall on compacted snow.

Anytime we walk in someone else's footprints it makes for a steadier stroll. Just like our walk with the Lord. To keep stride with the Spirit we need to know His voice and be near enough to hear it. Learning to step where He steps is the essence of following Jesus.

Keeping in step with Him means we no longer follow our own whims. Instead, we yield to His path and His directions, knowing that He has an amazing plan and purpose for each one of our lives. If we veer off course, He is faithful to steer us back; and if we become so weary we can no longer walk, He promises to carry us.

* * * * * * * * * * *

Father, teach me to follow You and keep in step with You, and thank You for guiding me through any depth of snow and carrying me when I need it. Amen.